The European Renaissance in American Life

THE EUROPEAN
RENAISSANCE
IN AMERICAN LIFE

Paul F. Grendler

Westport, Connecticut
London

Library of Congress Cataloging-in-Publication Data

Grendler, Paul F.
  The European Renaissance in American life / Paul F. Grendler.
    p. cm.
  Includes bibliographical references and index.
  ISBN 0–275–98486–9 (alk. paper)
1. United States—Civilization—European influences. 2. Renaissance.
  3. Arts, American—European influences. 4. Renaissance—United
  States.   I. Title.
  E169.1.G7556   2006
  303.48'27304—dc22   2006001239

British Library Cataloguing in Publication Data is available.

Library of Congress Catalog Card Number: 2006001239
ISBN: 0–275–98486–9

First published in 2006

Praeger Publishers, 88 Post Road West, Westport, CT 06881
An imprint of Greenwood Publishing Group, Inc.
www.praeger.com

Printed in the United States of America

The paper used in this book complies with the
Permanent Paper Standard issued by the National
Information Standards Organization (Z39.48–1984).

10 9 8 7 6 5 4 3 2 1

For Erika

CONTENTS ✦

ILLUSTRATIONS

Tables

Photographs

PREFACE

This book began as a default assignment. From 1996 through 1999, I was the editor in chief of *Encyclopedia of the Renaissance*, a scholarly reference work, published by Charles Scribner's Sons of New York in December 1999. We wanted to include an article entitled "The Renaissance in the Popular Imagination" in order to describe briefly its influence in modern life. But we could not find anyone to write it. So, Stephen Wagley, the multitalented managing editor of *Encyclopedia of the Renaissance*, and I did it. I thoroughly enjoyed doing it but realized that we had only scratched the surface of a large subject and decided to pursue the topic further.

For the past five years, I have been searching newspapers, films, novels, comic strips, political commentary, "in search of" personal ads, Web sites, product names, advertising references, business uses of Renaissance icons, music, scholarly studies on urban renewal, and anything else that came my way for references to the European Renaissance. The amount of material astonished me. Some of it is comic, some very serious. The Renaissance has penetrated into many areas of American life and culture.

The author's credentials need to be placed on the table. I am an academic historian of Renaissance Italy, the "real Renaissance," the period between 1400 and 1620. I taught the Renaissance to university students for thirty-five years. I have written several scholarly books on the subject and served as editor in chief of *Encyclopedia of the Renaissance,* intended for a learned readership, and *Renaissance: An Encyclopedia for Students*, intended for high school students. Thus, I am very interested with how the Renaissance is seen by people outside the academy.

The European Renaissance in American Life is the result of my search. It examines how the Renaissance resonates in American life and shows the uses that Americans make of it. The historian in me sometimes leads to comments on how accurately a novel, film, or political commentator portrays the real Renaissance. This is necessary, because people do get their history from novels and films. But the main purpose of the book is to uncover and describe the many manifestations of America's love of the Renaissance. It is a survey, often lighthearted, sometimes serious, of the evidence of the influence of the Renaissance in American life. Occasionally, the book reaches back more than a century for the origins of certain developments. But the emphasis is on how Americans look at the Renaissance today.

A number of people have helped me. My thanks go to Stephen Wagley for being a very knowledgeable and professional comrade-in-arms in encyclopedia publishing. I thank Professor Kenneth Gouwens, who shared with me his enthusiasm for the Renaissance in its historical reality and in American life and provided illustrative material. Peter Grendler introduced me to books on the link between the computer revolution and the Renaissance. I am grateful to those who took the time to answer questions: Kim Guarnaccia, founder and editor of *Renaissance*; Agnes Chan of the Renaissance Entrepreneurship Center in San Francisco; Daniel Reed of the Renaissance Computer Institute at the University of

North Carolina; Geraldine Reid of Renaissance Vineyard and Winery; and Professor Norman Jones. Dr. Sherie Mershon and Professor Joel Tarr helped me on the Pittsburgh Renaissance. Professor Marcia Hall brought a novel to my attention. Above all, I am grateful to my wife, Marcella, who pointed out a number of Renaissance examples and read the entire manuscript.

This book is dedicated to Erika Rummel, a distinguished historian of the real Renaissance, in thanks for her friendship over many years.

INTRODUCTION ⤺

Every year, nearly 6 million Americans, many of them dressed in Renaissance costumes, pretend to live in English villages in 1584. Millions more watch films about the Renaissance, such as *Shakespeare in Love*, or read novels that transport them back to the Italian Renaissance. Talented men and women place ads "in search of" a Renaissance man or woman to love. Thousands of businesses across the country insert "Renaissance" into their names, such as Renaissance Auto Care. Travelers lodge at Renaissance Hotels and eat Botticelli chocolates and Michael Angelo's pizza. Massive urban renewal projects are called "the Pittsburgh Renaissance" and "Detroit Renaissance." Neoconservatives cite Niccolò Machiavelli in support of aggressive policies in the Middle East, whereas opponents denounce "Mayberry Machiavellis" in the White House of George W. Bush. Books offer to teach readers how to become a genius like Leonardo da Vinci. Visionaries refer to the computer revolution as a "new Renaissance." Renaissance icons provide abundant material for comic parodies. *The New Yorker* featured a cover entitled "Mona Lewinsky," which inserted Monica Lewinsky's face into the *Mona Lisa* painting. The Renaissance did not end in 1620. It is alive and well today.

Although the Renaissance is enormously popular in American life, no one seems to have noticed. Even though nearly 6 million people attended 157 Renaissance faires in 2004, there is no study of these combination costume parties and outdoor festivals. Although political operatives, management consultants, and social scientists follow the ideas of Niccolò Machiavelli as if he were a highly paid consultant at the other end of a cell phone, this has escaped critical attention. Americans admire the Renaissance for many reasons but especially because they see it as an age of great individuals and a confirmation of their belief in individualism, which is such a fundamental part of American ideology. This book describes America's love affair with the Renaissance. It begins with a summary of the "real" Renaissance—that extraordinary period of European history between 1400 and 1620. It then examines the role of the Renaissance in contemporary life and culture.

Chapter 1

THE REAL RENAISSANCE, 1400–1620

The European Renaissance was a remarkable period of history. It transformed Europe and had a permanent impact on the world, which continues today. It was a period of new ideas and great achievement. No other period of history from the distant past produced so many individuals who are instantly recognized today and remain part of our own culture.

Chronology and New Ideas

The Renaissance was two-sided. It was a period of history lasting a certain number of years, and it was a cultural era in which Europeans developed new views about themselves and the world.

It began in Italy in the late fourteenth century and spread to the rest of Europe over the next century. The Italian scholar and poet Francesco Petrarch (1304–1374) looked at the world around him with fresh eyes and found it wanting. He strongly criticized medieval patterns of thought, in particular the way that universities taught literature, philosophy, science, and theology. He had no use for law, which he had been forced to study in his youth. He rejected medieval Scholasticism, a program of methodical reasoning used in all branches of learning and discussion. Petrarch concluded that men of learning relied too much on the works of Aristotle (384–322 BC), the most important scholar of the ancient world. Aristotle was too dry and scientific, and medieval learning generally was abstract and disembodied. As Petrarch put it, whereas Aristotle and Scholasticism might teach us what is good, they could not move us to do good. Real learning was personal. It must be integrated into the self. But medieval culture, including its greatest religious writers such as St. Thomas Aquinas (1224–1274), failed this test, in his judgment.

In place of the scholastic learning and medieval values of his day, Petrarch looked back to the literature and philosophy of the pagan and Christian ancient world for inspiration and advice on how to live. He greatly admired Cicero (106–43 BC), the golden orator of Rome, and St. Augustine (354–430), the equally eloquent early Christian bishop who abandoned paganism for Christianity without relinquishing his love for the writers of pagan Greece and Rome. Petrarch decided that the ancients offered a program of wisdom allied with eloquence. He believed that Cicero and Augustine could inspire men and women to do good through their example and words.

At first, Petrarch was a lone voice. But because he was an inspiring writer and the person with the greatest knowledge and love of the ancient world of his time, he attracted attention. He criticized medieval learning and praised ancient culture in warm, eloquent, and personal terms, always in Latin, the universal language of the learned. He also wrote the best Italian poetry of his time, in which he sang of his love for Laura in lyrical tones often imitated but seldom matched. Petrarch became something like a cult figure who was wined and dined, honored and heard, in the courts of the influential.

2

By the time of his death in 1374, Petrarch had acquired followers who shared his vision. By 1400, a group of Italian scholars and men from various walks of life had created an intellectual movement called humanism that was simultaneously ethical, philosophical, pedagogical, and eloquent. They began to transform Italian and European civilization. In the next two centuries, the intellectual, artistic, and political initiatives that Petrarch began in Italy spread to the rest of Europe and to the wider world that Europeans discovered.

Naming the Renaissance

From the earliest days of the Renaissance in Italy, some learned men realized that they were at the beginning of a new age. They called it a "renaissance," which means "rebirth." Such self-awareness is not common in history. Most of the time people only realize the character of their own age when they are in the middle or nearing its end.

Again, Petrarch showed the way by offering a new way of looking at the past. He divided history into periods on the basis of culture. He drew a line between the Roman era and the Christian and barbarian period that began in the fourth century when the Roman Empire adopted Christianity and northern tribes moved into the Roman Empire. In the Roman era, men wrote "good" Latin, that is, the classical Latin of Cicero and Augustine and, hence, were highly cultured. In the Christian era they wrote "bad" Latin, that is, the Latin of Scholasticism, and were culturally deficient. Of course, modern scholars do not see classical Latin as good and medieval Latin as bad, so long as each is grammatically correct and follows the usage of its times. They are simply different. Indeed, medieval Latin contains some enduring religious poetry and prose.

Following Petrarch's lead, fifteenth-century Italian historians made the new periodization sharp and definite. They decided that the ancient world lasted until about AD 400. Next came a middle period of a thousand years, which they called the "Middle Ages." And they believed that their own times, beginning about 1400, marked the beginning of a new age.

Italians in the early fifteenth century began to call their own age "Renaissance." They saw it as one of rebirth (*rinascità* in Italian) after a dark Middle Ages. The translation of *rinascità* is "renaissance" in both English and French. Their own age was a Renaissance because it featured the rebirth of learning, literature, and the arts after the dark Middle Ages.

Matteo Palmieri (1406–1475), a Florentine public office holder and humanist scholar, offers a typical expression of this point of view. Writing in the 1430s, Palmieri lamented the cultural barrenness of the Middle Ages, then praised the new age of his own time. "Of [medieval] letters and liberal studies at large it were best to be silent altogether. For these . . . had been lost to mankind for 800 years and more. It is only in our own day that men dare to boast that they see the dawn of better things. . . . Now, indeed, may every thoughtful spirit thank God that it has been permitted to him to be born in this new age, so full of hope and promise."[1] Although the self-congratulatory tone may put readers off, there is no mistaking Palmieri's conviction that he lived in a renaissance.

The name caught on. And because people believed that their age was a renaissance, they made it one. If people look at their own age with the expectation that much will be achieved, it is likely that they will accomplish much. If they see their own age as troubled, it is not likely that they will surmount the difficulties. Men and women of the fifteenth and sixteenth centuries took action to make the new era full of ideas and accomplishments. Calling their own era "Renaissance" became a self-fulfilling prophecy.

Humanism

Humanism was the intellectual movement that came from the enthusiasm for ancient culture of Petrarch and his followers. Humanism was based on the belief that the literary, ethical, historical, political, and philosophical works of ancient Greece and Rome offered the best guides for learning and living. Humanism was the defining intellectual movement of the Renaissance.

The foundation of humanism was an education based on the classics. The Renaissance called it *studia humanitatis,* or humanistic studies. It meant the study of grammar, rhetoric, poetry, history, and moral philosophy based on the reading of the standard ancient authors of ancient Rome and, to a lesser extent, Greece. This is the famous and widely followed definition of humanistic studies articulated by Paul Oskar Kristeller, the dean of Renaissance scholars of the twentieth century.[2] It meant that school children acquired a working knowledge of Latin, then read the works of Vergil for poetry and Cicero for prose. They learned to write eloquently in Latin. And they also learned from the classics the principles of living a moral, responsible, and successful life, or so teachers and parents hoped. Across Europe, humanistic studies became the preferred curriculum in schools for children intended for leadership and professional roles in society. A curriculum based on the classics, later expanded to include science and vernacular literature, lasted well into the twentieth century. And proficiency in Latin and Greek was a requirement for admittance into many programs of university studies in Europe until the educational reforms of the 1960s.

But humanism did more than give students knowledge of the ancient classics and proficiency in Latin and Greek. The Renaissance also invented the term "humanist," which meant a scholar, teacher, or student of the humanities. Studying the ancient world gave humanists the needed perspective to be able to look at their own times with objective, often critical eyes. The world of ancient Greece and Rome presented a standard against which to measure their own and others' efforts. This developed the habit of criticism, of challenging received wisdom. Eventually, men and women of the Renaissance even subjected the wisdom of the ancient world to careful examination. They then set out in new directions. Humanism prepared mankind to look for and welcome novelty, a key trait of the modern world.

But Renaissance humanism had nothing to do with today's so-called secular humanism. Renaissance humanism was neither anti-Christian nor antireligious. Instead, Renaissance humanists believed that the moral wisdom found in the great authors of Greece and Rome was the same moral wisdom as found in the New Testament. This belief was embodied in the phrase, "St. Socrates, pray for us," which Desiderius Erasmus ("Erasmus of Rotterdam"; c. 1466–1536), the famous Dutch humanist, wrote in 1522.[3] He meant that the learned Greek philosopher Socrates (469–c. 399 BC), who lived several centuries before Christ, was a holy and upright man as worthy of respect and veneration as a Christian saint, even though he was a pagan. Renaissance humanists also differed from medieval men because they looked to the New Testament and early Christian authors, such as St. Augustine, rather than to medieval theologians, for the best spiritual advice.

Humanism encouraged men and women to develop their full potential. It helped to develop the many-sided and accomplished men and women of the Renaissance. This is the origin of the term "Renaissance man" and "Renaissance woman," meaning individuals who are accomplished in many fields. Contemporary America has taken the concept of Renaissance man and Renaissance woman to heart (see chapter 4).

Italy was the leader of the European Renaissance. Italian scholars showed the way in the development of humanism and in other scholarly fields. Italian art styles influenced much of Europe. Italian businessmen dominated European commerce and banking. But Italians were not always first. One of the most important innovations of the Renaissance came from Germany.

The Invention of Printing

Of all the scientific and technological breakthroughs of the Renaissance, printing with movable type had the most impact on the Renaissance and posterity. One day in or about 1450 in Mainz, Germany, Johann Gutenberg (c. 1398–1468) pulled the first printed page from the first printing press. He was probably too busy and too harried by his creditors to pause to record that memorable event. Before movable type, imprinting words or an illustration on a piece of paper required great skill, was labor intensive, and extremely slow. One had to carve letters on a wooden board, then put ink on the board, and press paper on the board in order to create a page of words. Then a new board had to be carved for the next page. For more than 1,000 years, the only realistic way of producing multiple copies was to copy the page by hand, which was laborious, slow, and expensive if one hired a scribe to do it.

Gutenberg's invention was movable type. He had been experimenting with casting metal letters, finding the ingredients for an ink that would not leak on paper when subjected to heavy pressure, and solving other problems for several years. He succeeded in carving and casting individual metal letters made of lead and zinc. These were placed in a metal rack (called a forme) with slots ready to receive and hold the letters. Ink was smeared on the letters in the forme. Pressure from an adapted screw press used for crushing grapes forced the ink and paper together. Once the paper received the imprint, the press was released and the printed page was removed. Most important, the letters could be rearranged into a new page of words, and the process repeated. This was printing with movable type. Although the individual steps were relatively straightforward, the sum of the parts made the invention of printing with movable type a remarkable invention for which Gutenberg and his associates deserve every bit of credit that they have received. Moreover, others could easily duplicate his invention or carry the most important part, the type (individual letters), from place to place. By the end of the fifteenth century, some 255 towns across Europe had printing establishments. Many towns had several, some with several presses operating simultaneously.

Gutenberg's first printed book of any size was the beautiful 42-line Bible, given this name because each page has 42 lines of words. It is usually just called "the Gutenberg Bible." Estimates of the press run (a single edition or printing) of the Gutenberg Bible range from 70 to 270; about 50 survive. But the size of an individual press run for ordinary books quickly rose to 1,000 copies and more. And reprints were easy to produce. Although the technology was reasonably complex for the times, printed books could be produced far more quickly than handwritten copies. Consequently, they were much cheaper.

Printing made possible the communication and diffusion of knowledge at a much faster pace than before. One way to make this point is to compare the size of individual libraries before and after the invention of printing. Petrarch had about 200 books, all handwritten, when he died in 1374. It was an immense collection for the times. But Fernando Columbus, the natural son of the explorer, had 15,000 titles when he died in 1539. Printing made it possible for scholars, novelists, poets, and anyone else with something to say to "get into print" and for readers to "get the message." It has been suggested that printing and the invention of the computer 500 years later have been the two most important inventions for the communication of knowledge in human history. There is no underestimating the importance of printing with movable type.

Politics

Renaissance politics were immensely complicated, and that is an understatement. Although the division of Europe into many states produced considerable strife, it also had beneficial effects in other areas of life.

The Renaissance had three different kinds of states: princedoms, monarchies, and oligarchies, which were called republics. In each category there were large and small, strong and weak, states. They were constantly rising and falling in strength and evolving in structure. Naturally, they competed with and fought each other.

A prince ruled a princedom, whether he—and it was a man most of the time—was called prince, duke, count, marquis, or *signore* ("lord"). The source of the prince's power and the nature of his rule varied greatly. He often had displaced another ruler or city council by war, assassination, bribery, diplomacy, or marriage. Once in control, he promulgated rules of succession so that his son or another family member might, with a little luck, succeed him. Whatever the road to office, what mattered most was that the prince possessed effective power to promulgate and enforce laws, to collect taxes, to defeat foreign invaders, and to quell rebellion. He made the key decisions with little restraint from representative body, constitution, or courts. To be sure, wise princes sought to act in accord with the wishes of their subjects whenever possible. And the prince usually came to an accommodation with the strongest groups, the nobility and the merchant community. If the prince commanded the affection and loyalty of his subjects, his task was easier. Many were genuinely loved by most, but never all, of their subjects. Nevertheless, the prince's power was always precarious, and many were assassinated or overthrown, often for good reasons.

Italy and central Europe had an abundance of princedoms, including the small states of Ferrara, Mantua, Milan, Parma,

Piedmont-Savoy, and Urbino in northern Italy, and Bavaria, Brandenburg, Burgundy, Luxembourg, the Palatinate (the territory around the city of Heidelberg), and Saxony in central Europe. Many of these small princedoms consisted of the capital town or city and whatever additional territory of villages and farms the ruler could control. In subsequent centuries, almost all Renaissance princedoms were absorbed into large territorial monarchies, such as the modern Italy, Germany, and France. A handful of Renaissance princedoms, such as the Grand Duchy of Luxembourg and the Principality of Monaco, survive.

A monarchy was a princedom sanctioned by tradition, stronger institutions, and greater claims of legitimacy by its ruler. The majority of monarchies (England, France, Portugal, Scotland, and Spain, for example) were hereditary, whereas Poland, Hungary, Bohemia, and the Holy Roman Empire were elective. Monarchies typically were larger than princedoms; kings normally ruled a larger number of subjects, not all of whom might speak the same language. Monarchies developed laws and rules to determine in advance the succession, with the eldest son almost always the designated heir to the throne. However, when the succession was broken or disputed, or the ruling family deposed by force or external threat, civil war broke out. Monarchies had their share of civil wars, and the constant threat of a new one generated political unrest.

The smallest and most unusual political unit was the republican city-state. It consisted of a city and its surrounding territory of towns, villages, estates, and farms. A republic was an oligarchy—rule by the few. Borrowing terminology and legal principles from ancient Rome and local traditions, the men who formed oligarchies described their governments as "republican" and called their states "republics." They believed that their rule was based on the consent of the people who mattered, those who paid the highest taxes, provided employment, and had the most influence. This usually meant that 5 to 20 percent of the adult males of the city could vote and hold office. Members of government almost always came from leading merchants, manufacturers, bankers, and lawyers. But those with little or no property—workers, clergymen, and most members of the middle and lower classes—were excluded. City-states usually controlled some territory beyond the city's walls, but the people who lived in the outlying villages, towns, and farms had no role in government. They were subjects. Venice, Genoa, Lucca, Florence, Pisa, and Siena in Italy; Augsburg and Nuremberg in Germany; Strasbourg in what is now France; and the Swiss cantons were republics. Most city-state republics were small and weak in comparison with monarchies. But the Republic of Venice commanded an overseas empire of considerable size and commercial importance, and Florence's merchants and bankers played a large role in international trade.

Italy was divided into six republics (Venice, Genoa, Florence, Siena, Pisa, and Lucca), ten major princedoms (Milan, the papal state around Rome, Naples, Mantua, Ferrara, Savoy, and others), and smaller territories ruled by noble families. Germany was even more divided. It had a hundred and more independent cities, princedoms, bishoprics (i.e., small territories in which an archbishop or bishop was both spiritual and temporal ruler), and independent noble estates, some very tiny. Other parts of Europe mostly had monarchies, but these were not so unified politically and territorially as they would be in later centuries.

The division of Europe into so many political units had a strong positive effect on learning and culture. Every state, whether monarchy, princedom, or republic, had a capital that served as the seat of government. The state needed trained personnel, including advisers, secretaries, civil servants, and lawyers, plus judges to operate the judicial system. The humanists were these trained people, and they were in demand. Hence, they moved from court to city to court throughout Italy to serve

11

princes, city councils, and the papacy with their elegant, learned, and flattering pens. The same thing happened in northern Europe, as rulers there also needed trained officials fluent in classical Latin.

The proliferation of capital cities and courts was an even greater boon for artists. Princes, kings, and city councils, plus wealthy nobles, cardinals, and merchants, employed artists. Republics and princedoms sometimes had unique styles in art and architecture, which are recognizable today. For example, Florence and Venice are remarkably different from each other, as are Nuremberg, Salzburg, and Prague. Naturally, all these rulers and republics competed for the talents of the most famous artists of the day. The city of Florence, the duke of Milan, the king of France, church organizations, and wealthy private patrons offered commissions to Leonardo da Vinci. Popes and Medici princes in Florence hired Michelangelo at very high fees and gave him the artistic freedom to create original masterpieces, which he did not always finish. The abundance of independent states permitted a thousand cultural flowers to bloom.

The existence of independent states each with its own cultural policies had profound consequences on history. For example, Frederick III "the Wise" of Saxony (b. 1463; ruled 1486–1525) was the ruler of the small duchy of Saxony-Wittenberg created in 1486 and located in the eastern part of what is now Germany. He needed trained manpower to run his state and wanted to help his subjects obtain university educations without having to travel outside the state, both common motives for founding universities in the Renaissance. So Frederick created the University of Wittenberg in 1502. A young monk named Martin Luther (1483–1546) came to teach there in the winter of 1513–1514 and soon became a popular professor. After Luther broke with Rome, Frederick sheltered and supported Luther. The papacy could not touch Luther without Frederick's permission, which he did not grant.

Why did Frederick protect Luther? Probably for several reasons. One was that Luther was the star professor in Frederick's university. Luther returned the favor by continuing to teach at the University of Wittenberg for the rest of his life. And because Luther and his ideas attracted students, the University of Wittenberg had more students than any other German university in the 1520s.

One Renaissance monarchy deserves special mention because of its prominence in American enthusiasm for the Renaissance. England was small, out of the way, and not very important in European politics in the fifteenth century. It had only 5 million people in 1500. Vicious strife between English families seeking the crown demoralized the country. Henry Tudor finally defeated his chief rival in the Battle of Bosworth in 1485 and became Henry VII (reigned 1485–1509). He did not have a particularly noteworthy reign, nor was he a significant patron of artists and scholars. But he set the stage for the English Renaissance by leaving a unified country to his son Henry VIII (b. 1491, reigned 1509–1547). Henry VIII was very much a Renaissance monarch, for good and for ill. He was handsome and dashing in his youth, well educated for a king, and a patron of humanists and artists. But his headstrong behavior changed England's history forever.

During Henry VIII's reign, continental humanist ideas came to England. Erasmus of Rotterdam, the leading humanist scholar of the continent, visited England several times. Sir Thomas More (1478–1535), Henry's leading government minister from 1529 to 1532 and a distinguished humanist scholar who wrote *Utopia* (1516), led English humanists. A number of them championed Renaissance ideas on conduct, education, history, and politics. Continental artists, including the great German painter Hans Holbein the Younger (1497–1543), came to paint the king and other members of the court. Soon English artists adopted Italian and continental styles in painting, the decorative arts, and architecture.

However, Henry VIII, like a typical Renaissance monarch, became worried about the future of his kingdom because his wife, Catherine of Aragon, a Spanish princess, failed to produce a son. At the same time, he fell in love with the younger Anne Boleyn, who became his mistress. Henry wished to marry her in the expectation that she would produce the desired male heir. He asked the pope to annul his marriage to Catherine of Aragon, on the grounds that it had never been a lawful marriage, because Catherine had previously been betrothed to Henry's older brother, Arthur, who died before the marriage could be consummated. The legal grounds for an annulment were weak. Moreover, Catherine and her nephew, Charles Habsburg, king of Spain and Holy Roman Emperor, the most powerful ruler in Europe, strongly objected. Caught between two powerful forces, the pope stalled. The headstrong Henry took matters in his own hands. He declared that the pope had no jurisdiction in English church matters, obtained permission from the cowed English church to divorce Catherine, and married Anne Boleyn in January 1533. For good measure, he also declared himself Supreme Head of the English Church and seized the property of monasteries and convents in England. He enforced his decision with strong measures, including sham trials and executions of those who did not accept his religious policies, including Thomas More. Although Henry had little sympathy for continental Protestantism, the English Church gradually became Protestant over the rest of the century.

Henry's three surviving legitimate children ruled England for the rest of the Renaissance. The first was Edward VI (ruled 1547–1553), whose advisers were strongly Protestant. But Mary (ruled 1553–1558) returned England to Catholicism during her short reign. Elizabeth I (ruled 1558–1603), the daughter of Anne Boleyn, solidified both the power of the monarchy and the Protestant character of the English church. The military and political highpoint of Elizabeth's regime came when the English fleet, aided by good winds, defeated the Spanish Armada sent by King Philip II of Spain to invade England in 1588. By the early seventeenth century, England was a stronger nation than in 1485.

During these turbulent times and especially during Elizabeth's long reign, literature, art, and architecture so flourished that scholars sometimes refer to the "Elizabethan Renaissance." William Shakespeare (1564–1616) wrote plays, and poets Philip Sidney (1554–1586) and Edmund Spenser (1552/53–1599) created poetic masterpieces. Several English Protestant translations of the Bible culminated in the King James Bible of 1611, even though James I (ruled 1603–1625), the king for which it is named, had little to do with it. These great writers and the new translations of the Bible shaped the English language for the next several centuries and had a permanent impact on English and American culture.

In general, princedoms and republics were strong in the fifteenth century but weakened in the sixteenth. By contrast, monarchies, notably England, France, and Spain, were rudderless in the fifteenth century but became much stronger in the sixteenth. Over the course of the Renaissance, more powerful states, especially monarchies, absorbed smaller states. And one-man or one-family rule became more common.

Renaissance Europe presented a constantly shifting political scene, because political power was never stable. No government escaped external threats, and very few avoided internal strife. The small and weak states tempted powerful states, which usually yielded to the temptation to try to conquer them. Monarchies in particular were always on the watch for another princedom, republic, or independent noble estate to absorb. Many attempts to conquer neighboring states or to overthrow a ruler succeeded, which led to further conflict, as those defeated sought to regain power. It was the same within a state. Powerful individuals, families, and groups attempted through force or stealth to overthrow the king, prince, or city council and seize power. The maneuvering for advantage, the shifting diplomatic alliances, plots, threats of war, and military actions made Renaissance politics unstable. It was a politics of ceaseless movement and intrigue.

Politics was quite personal in the Renaissance. Much depended on the actions of a single ruler or conspirators. The Renaissance had more than its share of unscrupulous princes, warriors, assassins, plotters, and ambitious wives and mistresses. There were also some remarkably able and sympathetic rulers, men and women alike, who navigated difficult waters as best they could. The complexity is the despair of historians trying to understand Renaissance politics, then teach it to students, who have difficulty grasping it. But it has been a boon to novelists and filmmakers, who are drawn to the ruthless individuals, complex plots, and colorful settings of Renaissance politics.

Political Thought

Political instability, changes in forms of government, wars, and the fluidity of international politics stimulated an enormous amount of discussion about politics. Political writers developed a highly sophisticated understanding of statecraft from which posterity has learned. Many talented individuals wrote books of advice for kings and princes, who almost never read them. But these works of political analysis include several masterpieces that are still read and pondered by political philosophers, government officials, advisers to presidents, syndicated columnists, business management experts, and scholars in fields far from history and politics.

The most important political analyst of the Renaissance and probably of all time was the cashiered Florentine civil servant Niccolò Machiavelli (1469–1527), whose life and political thought are briefly described in chapter 7. His writings have become so essential to the understanding of the Western political tradition that it is likely that every high school and/or university student in America, Canada, and Europe is required to read at least one of his works, most often *The Prince*. European politics in the Renaissance, with its quick changes of government, competition for power, diplomacy, and wars, offered practically every possible political scenario for Machiavelli to analyze. His brilliant intellect, nourished on the study of ancient history, did the rest. Although the names have changed, Machiavelli's analysis is still useful because the fundamental nature of the quest for power does not seem to have changed much.

Several other Renaissance figures also wrote insightful analyses of politics and history. Machiavelli's fellow Florentine Francesco Guicciardini (1483–1540) wrote his own treatises on statecraft, plus a comprehensive political history of his own times that is full of acute psychological portraits of the major rulers of his age. Guicciardini was an aloof conservative aristocrat; Machiavelli a warm-hearted man of the people. Despite their differences, the two appreciated each other's intellect and exchanged political commentary. The Frenchman Jean Bodin (1529–1596) supported absolute monarchy. He argued that only if political sovereignty was absolute and undivided could civil strife be avoided. Peace under an absolute monarch was preferable to civil war in a more democratic state. Another Italian, Giovanni Botero (1544–1617), wrote a book entitled *On Reason of State* (1589), which for the first time emphasized the importance of demography, economic planning, clear taxation policies, and the development of a professional state administration as important factors in the health of the state. These men and others wrote pioneering works in political science, even though the term had not yet been coined. One of the reasons for the greatness of the Renaissance is the number of individuals who studied and carefully analyzed what was happening in terms that posterity understands.

Art

Art is the most loved and recognized aspect of the Renaissance. Anyone with the slightest knowledge of art knows that Renaissance artists produced some of the most important masterpieces of Western art. Everyone realizes that Renaissance art is different from medieval art. But what made Renaissance art unique? Why does Renaissance art attract us today, even though it was created 500 years ago?

The early fifteenth century was an age of artistic experimentation in Italy, as painters, sculptors, and architects sought to create a new artistic language. Their examination of surviving ancient art and buildings and the study of ancient treatises helped. Between 1425 and 1427, the precocious Masaccio (1401–c. 1428) painted in the Brancacci Chapel in the church of Santo Spirito in Florence a series of frescoes depicting events in the life of Christ and St. Peter. It was a new kind of dramatic painting that artists from all over Italy came to study. By the later fifteenth century, artists such as Sandro Botticelli (1444/45–1510), Giovanni Bellini (c. 1431/38–1516), and many others had mastered the new language and adapted it to their visions.

The first thing that the casual observer notices about mature Renaissance painting and sculpture is that the human figures appear to be more natural than those in medieval art.[4] The break with the more stylized and didactic paintings of the late Middle Ages in Italy is sharp and clear. Moreover, the best Renaissance art has a dramatic quality that draws in the viewer.

Renaissance artists usually attempted to imitate nature, especially in the depiction of human beings. They did not simply try to copy nature, but studied all the factors involved. Leonardo da Vinci filled thousands of pages of his notebooks with drawings of people and observations about nature. He and Michelangelo dissected bodies in order to be able to depict muscles and bones accurately. Renaissance painters also studied mathematics in order to present perspectival relationships correctly. The painter Piero della Francesca (c. 1412–1492), a masterful user of perspective, was also one of the best mathematicians of his century. Architects studied architectural treatises from the ancient world. Once they acquired the necessary information, master artists, sculptors, and architects passed it on to the junior members of their workshops.

Hence, male and female figures in Renaissance paintings look like human beings. But they are also more than human. They are usually idealized; they are more attractive and more gracefully proportioned than most people are today or were in the Renaissance, which probably had its share of physically unattractive people. Even a suffering Christ and martyred saints often appear as well-proportioned and serene human figures. Perhaps it is the idealized human dimension that enables Renaissance art to transcend centuries and cultures. The combination of a desire to paint and sculpt from nature, considerable study, a focus on human beings, and individual genius produced great art.

Because Renaissance art imitated nature (although not photographically), focused on idealized human beings, is dramatic, and often conveys an emotional message, it is immediately accessible to us today in ways that medieval art is not or that some twentieth-century abstract art is not. The viewer lacking specialized knowledge can love and appreciate Renaissance painting more easily than he can love and appreciate stylized medieval art. Of course, the knowledgeable viewer realizes that medieval art is just as technically sophisticated and can be as moving as Renaissance art.

Another reason for the popularity of Renaissance art is that there is so much of it. The Renaissance had a passion for art. Kings, popes, princes, cardinals, nobles, monasteries, merchants, mercenary captains, and many others commissioned works of art. Rulers commissioned portraits of themselves, as well as their significant acts, illustrious ancestors, consorts, and mistresses. Cities decorated their council halls with huge murals, frescoes, and tapestries depicting great civic moments. Monasteries commissioned artists to paint frescoes in cells and refectories in order to inspire monks and nuns to greater devotion. Members of the middle and working classes wanted small devotional paintings. Civic, dynastic, and religious leaders hired architects to erect enormously expensive buildings to beautify the city or for use as semipublic residences. Such art was designed to celebrate and impress. The Renaissance also produced an abundance of works in the minor arts, including furniture, silver and gold objects, small metal works, table decorations, household objects, colorful ceramics, candlesticks, chalices, and priestly vestments.

Italy had more art than the rest of Europe because it was rich. Italian merchants and bankers led the multinational companies of the time. The profits flowed back to Italy, enabling princes, nobles, and merchants to build palaces and commission art. A great deal of this art is still there *in situ* to be admired by American tourists. But a great deal was also exported, with the result that every museum of any size in America has one or several Renaissance paintings and sculptures. The great quantity of Renaissance art has raised its visibility and cultural importance in contemporary eyes. By contrast, there is not nearly so much medieval art available. And while artists of the seventeenth and eighteenth centuries also produced a great deal of art, especially in Italy, it is not so highly valued or noticed as Renaissance art.

Renaissance artists negotiated for high fees with kings and popes and had an international clientele of patrons. Successful artists became wealthy and enjoyed worldly honors. For example, in 1533 Emperor Charles V conferred a knighthood on the Venetian artist Titian (c. 1488–1576), who executed a stunning equestrian portrait of the emperor. Not surprisingly, some Renaissance artists were intensively competitive with each other, another tràit that makes them kindred spirits to many Americans.

Because they were highly valued producers of a great deal of art, the social and intellectual position of artists changed in the Renaissance. At the beginning of the age, the artist was an anonymous craftsman who occupied a modest social position. He was tied to his guild, which dictated conditions of work. He followed local artistic traditions and produced paintings for local patrons, probably for low fees. In the course of the Renaissance, artists became self-conscious creators of complex, original works of art. They conversed with humanists and argued with patrons over the schemes of their works. Renaissance artists were the first to write extensively about their art. The Renaissance produced the first modern art historian, Giorgio Vasari (1511–1574), who was also a practicing artist. His *The Lives of the Artists* (1550, revised edition 1568) is a storehouse of information. In much of this, Renaissance artists were like today's artists.

Vernacular Literature

The Renaissance saw a spectacular development of vernacular languages. In 1400, English, French, German, Portuguese, Spanish and other vernacular languages did not exist in standard forms. People spoke and wrote a variety of regional dialects with multiple vocabularies and haphazard spelling. By the end of the Renaissance, most European languages had made significant progress toward the standard eloquent vernaculars used today. A combination of literary masterpieces by great authors, the printing press, and government actions produced these results.

Italian was the first to develop. Three great authors, Dante Alighieri (1265–1321) of Florence, Francesco Petrarch (1304–1374) of Arezzo, and Giovanni Boccaccio (1313–1375) of Florence, started the process. Dante wrote the *Commedia*, usually called *The Divine Comedy* in recognition of its stature. Petrarch wrote love sonnets to his beloved Laura and *canzoni* ("songs," i.e., extended lyrical poems) celebrating Italy and nature. He perfected and popularized the Petrarchan sonnet (14 hendecasyllable lines with the rhyme scheme ababab cdecde) that others imitated in many languages for centuries. And Boccaccio wrote the *Decameron,* his famous collection of one hundred often funny and scabrous tales. Because all three authors were geniuses, and all wrote in the Tuscan dialect, they started Tuscan on the road to becoming modern Italian. A number of other fine writers followed their example. They included Baldessare Castiglione (1478–1529), who wrote *The Courtier* (published 1528), the consummate book on how to be an honorable and accomplished gentleman that influenced European manners and morals for centuries, and the epic poet Ludovico Ariosto (1474–1533). Even though Castiglione came from Mantua and Ariosto from Ferrara, each wrote in Tuscan. The printing press encouraged standardization, which reinforced the dominance of Tuscan.

The development of modern High German in the sixteenth century illustrates the process even better. German-speaking lands inherited many varieties of German from the Middle Ages. In the fifteenth century, some state governments began to use German instead of Latin for their documents and pronouncements. Hence, versions of German used by the governments of the most important states, including the East Middle Saxon dialect used by the government of Saxony, became more influential. Next, printing encouraged writers and editors to standardize spelling and usage in order to reach a wider readership and to sell more books. Most important, Martin Luther published his German translation of the Bible (New Testament in 1522, complete Bible in 1534). Luther's translation may have had 300 editions and more than 500,000 printed copies by 1600, enormous figures in an age of limited literacy and small population, as Germany had only 9 million people in 1500 and 12 million in 1600. Many Germans began to imitate Luther's style, usage, and vocabulary. Because he wrote in East Middle Saxon, the same language used by the government of Saxony, and because of his influence, this version of German eventually became modern High German.

One reason for the popularity of Renaissance literature is that modern readers and speakers can understand and savor it. Today's English speaker can understand and appreciate Shakespeare's English. This cannot be said about medieval English literature. Certainly, medieval English has masterpieces, such as *The Canterbury Tales* (written 1390–1400) of Geoffrey Chaucer (c. 1345–1400). But Chaucer wrote such a different variety of English that modern English speakers cannot easily read him. It must be modernized, that is, practically translated into modern English, to be understood easily, and then it loses much of its flavor, humor, and rhythm.

Social Structure and Minorities

The Renaissance had a mixed record on social issues and attitudes toward minorities and women, topics that matter a great deal to contemporary Americans. Observers of the twenty-first century, including some scholars and many novelists, judge the Renaissance harshly for its social stratification and lack of sympathy for the rights of women and minorities. The Renaissance certainly did not measure up to today's standards and sensibilities. But compared with the preceding medieval centuries, and the two centuries that followed, the Renaissance looks better.

It was not an age of social and economic equality. Far from it. The social position of parents largely determined a child's future position in society. Nevertheless, the fluidity of politics and the large number of competing capitals and courts offered some opportunity for the lowborn to rise through their talents. There are some spectacular examples of those who succeeded. Francesco Sforza (1401–1466), a mercenary soldier of obscure origins, rose to become duke of Milan. Michele Ghislieri, a pious shepherd boy, became Pope Pius V (1566–1572). More common were merchants and bankers who rose to become aristocrats and rulers through acumen and money. The Medici family rose from obscure origins to make themselves the uncrowned rulers of Florence by the middle of the fifteenth century and princes in the sixteenth. The Renaissance was less socially rigid than the late Middle Ages that preceded it and the period 1620 to 1789 that followed.

It was an age of great extremes of power and wealth. The powerful and the wealthy practiced unproductive conspicuous consumption of luxury goods, such as works of art. They kept the lower classes in their places. It was not easy to be poor, homeless, or to suffer from an illness considered to be the result of sinful behavior. On the other hand, ecclesiastical, lay, and civic charitable institutions provided for orphans, the sick, the hungry, and the syphilitic ill. They gave poor girls dowries enabling them to marry. Various organizations, most of them religiously motivated, provided shelter to the unfortunate members of society, including elderly prostitutes.

From the viewpoint of the twenty-first century, the Renaissance attitude toward women was mixed. Cultural and legal barriers, whose strength varied across Europe, limited the roles that most women could play in society. But many women overcame the barriers. No century before or since had as many queens who actually ruled as the sixteenth century: Isabella of Castile, Mary Tudor, Elizabeth I, and the luckless Mary Stuart of Scotland. Margaret of Parma (1522–1586), the illegitimate issue of a union between Emperor Charles V and a Dutch servant woman, ruled The Netherlands from 1559 to 1567 and again from 1580 to 1583 as regent for her half-brother, King Philip II of Spain. Catherine de' Medici (1519–1589) was the powerful queen mother behind three French kings.

The sixteenth century had more prominent female writers than any century before the nineteenth. Vittoria Colonna (1492–1547), Veronica Gambara (1485–1550), Gaspara Stampa (1523?–1554), Tullia d'Aragona (c. 1510–1556), Laura Terracina (1519–c. 1577), and Veronica Franco (1546–1591) were esteemed and published writers of poetry and prose. Margaret of Navarre (1492–1549) wrote poems, a dialogue, and a collection of stories, the *Heptaméron*, which is viewed as one of the great prose works of the French Renaissance. These women came from different ranks of society. Colonna, Gambara, and Margaret of Navarre were noble-women, whereas Franco, Stampa, and Tullia d'Aragona were cour-tesans (i.e., high-class prostitutes). At the end of the Renaissance a few women, including Moderata Fonte (1555–1592) and Lucrezia Marinella (1571–1653), wrote treatises protesting the dominion of men and arguing for the superiority of women. The Renaissance also had a number of female artists, such as Sofonisba Anguissola (c. 1535–1625), Lavinia Fontana (1552–1614), and Artemisia Gen-tileschi (1593–1652/3). The last has attracted considerable attention from both art historians and novelists (see chapter 9). Overall, women had as strong or stronger position in Renaissance society as they did in the Middle Ages that preceded it and the period from 1620 to 1789 that followed. Today's feminist scholars have been quick to study Renaissance women in order to understand how they managed to do so well despite society's restrictions.

The heaviest charge of intolerance levied against the Renais-sance is persecution of Jews. The early Renaissance (roughly the fifteenth century) tolerated limited roles for Jews in the larger Christian society, chiefly money lending and some forms of com-merce. Some learned Jews became honored physicians to the pow-erful and wealthy. A few humanists, notably Giovanni Pico della

Mirandola (1463–1494), had considerable interest in and sympathy for Jewish learning. But most of the time Christian society left Jews alone. The atmosphere changed at the end of the fifteenth century and intolerance grew under the pressure of war and religious conflict in the sixteenth century. The Spanish Inquisition persecuted Jews accused of being insincere converts to Christianity and executed some by burning. The Republic of Venice instituted the first ghetto in 1516. Copies of the Talmud were destroyed at mid-century, and the printing of Hebrew books was prohibited or subjected to censorship for alleged anti-Christian sentiments. But persecution was always spotty and began to ease in the late sixteenth century. Eventually the French Revolution, which began in 1789, led to the granting of full civil rights to Jews.

The overall record of the Renaissance on social equality and the rights of women and minorities was that of a rigid, old-fashioned society in which rights taken for granted today in the Western world were lacking. But a lot of loopholes existed in Renaissance society through which many talented individuals slipped and achieved great success.

Studying the Renaissance

Despite the importance of the Renaissance and its profound influence on the modern world, few American scholars studied it before 1945. Extensive academic study of the Renaissance, especially the Italian Renaissance, came only after World War II.

In the first half of the twentieth century, American scholars preferred to study the Protestant Reformation. The reason is obvious: America was culturally and academically very Protestant and much influenced by England.[5] English Protestants, such as the Puritans who came to Massachusetts, played key roles in the founding of the new country and were rightly studied for their impact on the new nation. By contrast, the Renaissance was seen as Italian and Catholic, neither of which were very popular in America, especially in elite universities where most historical research was done.

Felix Gilbert (1905–1991), a Jewish historian of the Italian Renaissance who fled Hitler's Germany, noticed this when he arrived in England in October 1933. He saw a lack of interest in the Renaissance and a hostile attitude toward Machiavelli. "I was surprised and somewhat shocked that in England in the 1930s study of the Renaissance was left almost exclusively to art and literary historians. Machiavelli seemed a somewhat questionable subject . . . he was not in the line of (Hugo) Grotius, (John) Locke, or Adam Smith, which made human freedom a cornerstone of political life. The suspicion . . . that Machiavelli was really an advocate of the devil lingered on."[6] Gilbert's description of the English attitude was just as true for America and Canada at the time.

The neglect of the Renaissance changed because of the efforts of several individuals. The person who unintentionally did the most to develop the study of the Renaissance in America was Adolf Hitler. When he came to power in 1933, he barred Jews from teaching in universities. The same thing happened in Italy, when Benito Mussolini, influenced by Hitler, promulgated laws against Jews in 1938. As war approached in Europe, many scholars, Jewish and non-Jewish alike, fled Germany and Italy. The majority of these emigré scholars of the Renaissance moved to the United States, while a smaller number settled in England and Canada. They brought with them an unequaled knowledge of the Renaissance, a passionate commitment to the subject, innovative scholarly approaches, and indefatigable industry. Although struggling to find university teaching positions in America, these scholars stimulated research on the Renaissance through their writing and teaching.

Felix Gilbert, mentioned above, went on to America in 1936, taught for years at Bryn Mawr College and elsewhere before moving to the Institute of Advanced Study in Princeton, New Jersey. He wrote many books, including *Machiavelli and Guicciardini: Politics and History in Sixteenth-Century Florence* (Princeton, NJ: Princeton University Press, 1965), which demonstrated that Machiavelli was not an advocate of the devil but a brilliant and perceptive observer of his times. Paul Oskar Kristeller (1905–1999) left Germany in 1934, spent more than four years teaching in Italy, then went to the United States in 1939. He taught Renaissance philosophy at Columbia University for many years. Generations of graduate students in philosophy, history, and literature profited from his teaching and research on Renaissance intellectual history. Hans Baron (1900–1988) left Germany in 1937 for England and went on to America in 1938. He was a member of the Institute for Advanced Study in Princeton from 1944 to 1948, then was a research fellow at the Newberry Library in Chicago until retirement in 1970, as well as serving as a visiting professor in various universities. His publications on Renaissance Florence stimulated much new research. The above were all young scholars when they left Germany. Erwin Panofksy (1892–1968) was an established scholar who lost his professorship in 1933 because he was Jewish and went to the United States in 1934. His scholarship and teaching drew attention to the links between Renaissance art and its cultural and historical context and has been immensely stimulating to art historians.

These scholars did not create a rebirth of American study of the Renaissance, because there was nothing to be reborn. Instead, they created American scholarly study of the Renaissance. The young American scholars whom they attracted to the study of the Renaissance seldom had a personal reason, such as Italian ancestry, to lead them to the Renaissance. Rather, they were attracted to the period by its intrinsic interest and importance, which the books and teaching of the distinguished emigré scholars had revealed to them.

The second political figure who did a great deal to support Renaissance studies was Senator J. William Fulbright of Arkansas, whose goal was to support American scholarship on all parts of Europe and, later, the rest of the world. He conceived an international exchange scholarship program, which Congress enacted as the Fulbright Act of 1946. Beginning in the early to mid-1950s , it enabled young scholars, mostly graduate students, to study abroad. The Fulbright-Hays Act (also called the Mutual Educational and Cultural Act) of 1961 consolidated and expanded this international study program. A graduate student typically did all of his or her course work, language study, and comprehensive examinations for the Ph.D. on a topic involving Renaissance Europe, then applied for a Fulbright scholarship. The fortunate winners received funding enabling them to research their doctoral dissertations in the archives and libraries of Europe for a year and occasionally two years.

The two Fulbright Acts made it possible for young American scholars to do advanced research on the Renaissance in European archives and libraries. This was very important before the advent of inexpensive air travel to Europe. They also had the opportunity to meet foreign scholars, to learn about the host country, and to mix with other young American scholars with similar interests. The graduate student returned to America with a trunkful of handwritten notes (no computers or photocopy machines in those days), a wealth of experience, and a beginning of the dissertation. The student typically completed the dissertation the following year, either back in graduate school or in a temporary teaching position, and then began an academic career teaching others about the Renaissance.

Of course, the two Fulbright Acts enabled scholars to study other eras besides the Renaissance and parts of the world beyond Europe. And it enabled foreign scholars to come to America. But it was fundamental for American study of the Renaissance. The combination of great emigré scholars, the majority Jewish, who inspired and taught American students, and the Fulbright Acts produced hundreds of well-prepared scholars of the Renaissance in history, literature, art history, music, philosophy, and so on.

The author's experience was typical. I did my graduate study and examinations in Renaissance history between 1959 and 1962 at the University of Wisconsin, Madison, under the direction of George L. Mosse (1918–1999). Younger than the emigré scholars mentioned above, Mosse was a member of a prominent Jewish family in Berlin that left Germany in 1933. He obtained a Ph.D. at Harvard, then embarked on a long and distinguished career of teaching and research in European history at the universities of Iowa and Wisconsin. His autobiography, *Confronting History: A Memoir* (Madison, WI: University of Wisconsin Press, 2000) is a fascinating account of his youth in Germany and his becoming an American. I received a Fulbright fellowship for study and research in Italy for the academic year 1962–1963 and sailed for Italy on the USS Constitution in September 1962. The Fulbright stipend provided just enough money for one person to live modestly in Italy. Because I married in summer 1962, my wife and I had to borrow money for the year in Italy. Returning to America in summer 1963, I spent one year in a temporary teaching position while completing my dissertation, then began a tenure-track position at another university in the fall of 1964. Many other Renaissance scholars had similar experiences.

By the 1960s and 1970s, American universities became major centers outside of Europe for the study of the Renaissance. Of course, Italy has many fine scholars who study the Italian

Renaissance, France has many excellent scholars who study the French Renaissance, and so on. But most European scholars study the history and culture of their own country. American universities, by contrast, offer training and scholarship for those wishing to study all the geographical areas of the European Renaissance.

Today many American universities also offer undergraduate instruction about the European Renaissance where it happened. Several hundred American universities have junior-year abroad programs for their undergraduates. In a typical program, some thirty to fifty students drawn from one or several universities collaborating in a joint program spend a year in Rome, Madrid, Paris, or elsewhere. Having acquired some language training in advance, the students receive further instruction in the history, culture, and language of the host country from a mix of instructors from their home universities and local scholars. They usually do considerable traveling as part of the program and on their own. Italy, because of the Renaissance, is a favorite destination for junior-year-abroad programs. American universities have programs in Rome, Florence, Venice, and many other Italian cities.

Mass tourism made possible by inexpensive air flights to Europe has completed the American conversion to the Renaissance. It is impossible to estimate how many millions of Americans have taken advantage of the opportunity to walk the streets of Florence, Rome, Venice, Paris, Strasbourg, and other cities that bear the stamp of the Renaissance. They look at the monuments and admire the works of art. They get a feel, however incomplete, of the era of the Renaissance. They return with snapshots, souvenirs, and some familiarity with the period. The combination of academic study of the Renaissance and mass tourism has stimulated the American love affair with the Renaissance in the past fifty to sixty years.

This was the "real Renaissance," a remarkable period of history between 1400 and 1620 that was important in itself and was determining for the modern world. Contemporary America finds it to be intensely interesting and worth reliving.

Part I

RELIVING THE RENAISSANCE

T he best way to celebrate the Renaissance is to relive it. And that is what millions of Americans do in a variety of ways. They dress, act, and speak like English men and women in the sixteenth century. They think of themselves as Renaissance men and women, that is, as multitalented human beings. If they are not as talented as Leonardo da Vinci, they study Leonardo's methods in order to be like him. Fortunately, they receive a lot of help in reliving the Renaissance from businesses that sell Renaissance products, food, and lodging. Renaissance images and icons remind Americans of the great figures of the European Renaissance. Computer experts explain that the invention of the computer is like the invention of printing in the Renaissance with even more potential to expand learning. Religious paintings from the Renaissance help Americans to get closer to God. In all these ways, Americans try to relive a period of history that occurred 500 years ago.

Chapter 2

RENAISSANCE FAIRES

Will Shakespeare, on vacation from London, walks along the Queen's Way in the village of Wixonshire. He spies a servant girl in a rough brown dress and dirty apron coming out of a thatched cottage. He sees her pretty face and fetching eye, and nudges his companion: "Yon wench is most marvelous comely. Perchance we may greete her over a pottle of ale at the Boare and the Beare." Then they hear shouts. They come upon two men in plumed hats, full-sleeved red shirts, black tights, and high leather boots, the garb of nobles. One accuses the other of making a slighting remark about Good Queen Bess and draws his sword. They fight with verbal insults and swinging swords, while the crowd eggs them on. Will pauses to watch with a bemused expression on his face. So goes life in Renaissance England in 1594.

But this is not 1594, rather 2004. And the place is Plantersville, Texas, not Wixonshire, England. For seven weekends in October and November 2004, thousands dressed themselves in period clothing, put on swords, and descended on Plantersville for the Texas Renaissance Festival. They came in order to relive the Renaissance. Nearly 6 million Americans relived the Renaissance by participating in Renaissance faires in 2004.

Come to the Faire

Renaissance faires are a combination of outdoor costume party, interactive entertainment, and commercial enterprise. (Everyone associated with them writes "faires" instead of "fairs" and "garb" instead of "costume.") Even though they often refer to England and Shakespeare, Renaissance faires are completely different from serious Shakespeare festivals, which produce performances of Shakespeare's plays and other dramatic works and train theater professionals. By contrast, the goal of Renaissance faires is to provide fun and light entertainment. Operators of faires and the merchants who sell Renaissance artifacts and garb try to make a profit. And the fairegoers only want to relive the Renaissance for a day. Although this phenomenal expression of enthusiasm for a part of the distant past attracts little attention from students of American culture, faires mean a great deal to the participants, merchants, and local communities.

Renaissance faires may have begun in California in 1963. One group asserts that Phyllis and Ronald Patterson created and opened to the public the first Renaissance faire in Laurel Canyon in the Hollywood Hills on May 11 and 12, 1963.[1] So far, no one has disputed this claim of priority. Others followed. The Northern California Renaissance Faire, which now meets in Hollister, southwest of San Jose, states that it began in 1967.[2] The Pattersons founded a fall Renaissance faire in Marin County, directly north of San Francisco, in 1968. It continues today in Novato, also in Marin County. These seem to be the oldest continuously running Renaissance faires. It is possible that others, begun in the 1960s, have since disappeared.

Several other faires, including some of the largest, began in the 1970s.[3] The huge Minnesota Renaissance Festival at Shakopee, just south of Minneapolis, began in 1971, and the Bristol Renaissance Faire at Kenosha, Wisconsin, began in 1973. The very large

Texas Renaissance Festival at Plantersville (near Houston) followed in 1975, the Colorado Renaissance Festival now at Larkspur (near Denver) in 1976, the Norman, Oklahoma, Medieval Faire in 1976, and the Maryland Renaissance Festival at Crownsville (near Annapolis) in 1977.

Renaissance faires have experienced steady growth in new foundations over the past forty years.

Table 2.1 - Active Renaissance Faires in 2004 with Known Foundation Dates	
Founded in the 1960s:	3 faires
Founded in the 1970s:	12 faires
Founded in the 1980s:	21 faires
Founded in the 1990s:	38 faires
Founded 2000–2004:	c. 20 faires

The figures apply only to living faires for which foundation dates are known.

One hundred and fifty-seven faires in forty states opened their gates to the public in the United States in 2004, plus six more in Canada. There may be additional small faires that attract only local attention. As there were 115 known Renaissance faires in America and Canada in 1999, the number is growing.[4]

California, with thirty, had the most in 2004, followed by Florida with eleven, Michigan with nine, and Ohio and Washington with seven each. Some faires are open only for a two-day weekend in spring or fall and attract a thousand or fewer visitors. Others are open for up to six or seven consecutive weekends and attract 200,000 to more than 300,000 visitors. The majority are in between, with 30,000 to 50,000 visitors. All the large Renaissance faires and most smaller ones have permanent sites. A few of the smaller faires rotate from place to place within a state. Some faires have campgrounds, whereas others direct visitors to nearby campgrounds.

The two largest faires are located in very different parts of the country. The Texas Renaissance Festival at Plantersville was open on Saturdays and Sundays, from 9 a.m. until dusk, October 2 through November 14, 2004, a total of fourteen days, and attracted 320,000 visitors. The Minnesota Renaissance Festival is located at Shakopee, thirty minutes south of Minneapolis on a major highway. Its 22-acre site was open from 9 a.m. to 7 p.m. for seven weekends from August 14 through September 26, 2004, with attendance of about 315,0000. The Maryland Renaissance Festival is located on a permanent 26-acre site at Crownsville, just outside of Annapolis. It ran for nine weekends from August 28 through October 24, with attendance of 290,000. Other large Renaissance faires include the Arizona Renaissance Festival, near Phoenix, with about 265,000 visitors, the Georgia Renaissance Festival at Fairburn, Georgia, with 250,000 visitors, and the Michigan Renaissance Festival near Detroit had about 230,000 visitors. Seven other Renaissance faires in California (two), Colorado, Massachusetts, Oklahoma, Pennsylvania, and Texas had estimated attendance of 200,000 in 2004.

The 157 known American faires attracted a grand total of about 5,900,000 paying visitors in 2004, an average of about 38,000 each.[5] This does not mean that 5,900,000 different individuals each attended a faire for a single day. Some patrons paid admission for more than one day or attended more than one faire. On the other hand, the figures do not include entertainers, the merchants selling goods in their booths, and the employees of food courts.

The largest faires are multimillion-dollar operations. Admission ranges from $15 to $21 for adults, and some do not offer lower priced tickets for children and seniors. For example, when the 320,000 visitors at the Texas Renaissance Festival pay the admission price of $21 (no discounts for seniors and children), this produces admissions income of $6,720,000. The Minnesota Renaissance Festival charges adults $17.95, seniors aged 60 and older $15.95, children six to twelve years $8.95, with children under five free. Although the mix of adults, seniors, and children is unknown, it is likely that entrance fees generated more than $5,000,000. The Maryland Renaissance Festival charges $14.95 for admission, with no discounts for children or seniors. With attendance of 290,000, this produced admissions income of $4,335,000. In earlier decades, faires often offered free or reduced admission prices to those who came in costume. This has almost completely disappeared. A handful of faires are run to raise money for charity, and a few small faires are free. But the vast majority of faires, especially the large ones, are significant commercial ventures.

Faire managements also derive income in other ways. Most forbid attendees to bring in food or drink. Thus, visitors must buy food, beer, mead, ale, wine, or soft drinks at the faire, plus all kinds of merchandise. Management sells or rents small frame buildings that serve as commercial booths and rents space for tents for those wishing to sell merchandise, food, and drink. In 2004, the sale price of a small-frame non-winterized building with frontage of 16 feet or more was $25,000 to $50,000 at large faires, plus rent for the frontage on the paths that visitors trod.[6] The advantage to the purchaser is that he or she has possession of the building and may use it year after year. Rent for a building costs $1,000 to $3,000 per season and for a tent a few hundred dollars. A vetting process ensures that the building or space will be used for activities consistent with the faire's activities. As always, the three most important considerations are location, location, and location. A booth or tent space in a main thoroughfare, or near the entrance, or adjacent to a stage or arena, costs more than one in a remote part of the faire. Liability insurance, legal fees, and sometimes license fees to operate rides, sell food, or to perform certain activities such as glassblowing or hair dressing add to the cost for the merchants.

Dedicated fairegoers tend to be young, middle-class, and better educated than the population at large. According to a 1998 survey, slightly more women than men (53 percent to 46 percent) attended faires. They were young: 35 percent were aged 35 or younger, 28 percent were 36 to 45 years of age, 24 percent were 46 to 55 years of age, and only 5 percent older than 56.[7] Only 44 percent were married, the consequence of relative youth. Sixty percent had annual incomes between $21,000 and $60,000, and 24 percent had incomes of more than $60,000. Fifty-two percent were homeowners. They need a certain level of income, because a day at a Renaissance faire can be expensive. One veteran fairegoer estimated in 2003 that a day at the Texas Renaissance Festival could cost a family of four $200 to $250 for admission, food, and purchases.[8] Sixty-four percent had college degrees, making them considerably better educated than the population at large. Ninety-three percent purchase at least one book about the Renaissance or Middle Ages annually. Although there is no precise information, it is very likely that dedicated fairegoers hold white-collar positions and are overwhelmingly white rather than members of minority groups. Eighty-one percent of committed fairegoers own one or more Renaissance costumes (garb). About half of them, probably almost all men, possess one or more of sword, dagger, and knife. Many attend two Renaissance faires annually. Although these are dedicated faire patrons, it is likely that more casual patrons fit the same demographic, income, and education profiles.

The first California Renaissance Faire took the English Renaissance as its historical theme, and the majority of faires have emphasized sixteenth-century England ever since.[9] If they are more precise, they focus on the reign of Queen Elizabeth I (1558–1603), or the lifetime of William Shakespeare (1564–1616) or, less often, the reign of Henry VIII (1509–1547). Most Renaissance faires also announce that they are re-creating a precise place (often fictitious) and year. In 2004, the places and years included Scarborough in 1533, New Market in 1540, Lamont in 1562, Coventry Live Oak in 1565, Kingston upon Hull in the 1570s, Wixonshire in 1575, West-minster in 1593, Larkspur in 1598, and Hollygrove in 1600. Revel Grove and the Kingdom of Avondale without dates were also the sites of faires. A handful of faires announce themselves as medieval faires, and choose accordingly, such as the Camlann Medieval Faire in Carnation (near Redmond), Washington, whose theme was Cam-lann Village. It announced that it was bringing to life "the com-plete, colorful world of Chaucer in the year 1376." Geoffrey Chaucer, the great English poet and author of *The Canterbury Tales*, lived from about 1340 until 1400.

An exception to the English emphasis is the Italian Renais-sance Festival at the former Hialeah Race Track in Hialeah, Florida. It advertises itself as "the only Italian Renaissance Festival in the Western Hemisphere." It claims to re-create or evoke the real city of Lucca, Italy, in Tuscany, in 1502, a year of no particular signif-icance in Italy. The Italian Renaissance Festival promises that Michelangelo and Leonardo da Vinci will come. So will "over 225 authentically costumed characters in our daily Grand Parade." The festival emphasizes Italian acts, including a man who announces himself as "Guido Libido, the Hopeless Romantic! Friend to all women. Alllllll women! Sometimes twice! I tell love stories throughout the ages, the way they REALLY happened! Because in the books they got it all wrong."[10] Elegantly gowned courtesans also appear at the fair. The Italian Renaissance Festival explains that "during the Renaissance, a Courtesan was chosen for her Beauty, Charm, Wit and Intelligence in order to serve as compan-ion to the Gentlemen of the Court. It was expected that a Courte-san was educated in classical subjects as Art, Music, Poetry and Politics."[11] (This was sometimes true but not the whole story. However graceful and learned she might be, a courtesan's primary role was to provide sex outside of marriage. And her life was not always glamorous.)

Of course, the purpose of Renaissance faires is to enable the paying customers to have a good time. Hence, all the unpleasant aspects of the Renaissance, such as war, disease, and poverty, are ignored. Faires want visitors to enjoy themselves and to come again.

Advertisements for Renaissance faires emphasize reliving the past, colorful activities and characters, entertainment, playacting, and nostalgia. For example, the Northern California Renaissance Faire of September and October 2004 announced a return to "our lovely English Village" for a harvest time marketplace faire. "We'll step back once more to the romantic and bawdy days of the Renaissance." "We will welcome back with pride our beloved Queen Elizabeth I and her noble court." "Visitors will find a colorful reception in our witty Washer Women, our tireless Mongers, . . . our colorful Fools, our crooked Constables, and our beloved peasants." "Ales will be cold, Belles will be beautiful and bawdy, swashbuckling swordfighters will be dashing and daring. Heroic Knights in armor will awaken the arena with full contact jousting, while jugglers and jesters bring mirth to the stages." "Our aim is to provide our audience with the highest quality entertainment and standard of illusion in order to escape the modern world, if only for a day."[12]

The Minnesota Renaissance Festival invites visitors to "live the legend." "The legend of the 16th century comes to life at the Minnesota Renaissance Festival. Become part of the fantasy and magic, when kings reigned supreme and the arts flourished."[13] Note that the Renaissance is seen as an era when the arts flourished, a correct view of the European Renaissance. The Colorado Renaissance Festival is "where pleasures reign and merrymaking is the rule." At the Arizona Renaissance Festival, visitors may "mingle and interact with nearly 2,000 costumed characters and their endless merriment and mayhem. The festivities include twelve stages of music and comedy show, demonstrations of the ancient art of falconry, and a 5,000-seat arena for tournaments of armored jousting."[14] Faires stress their uniqueness. As the Pittsburgh Renaissance Festival put it, "each and every faire has its very own developed personality. No two festivals are alike as no two shires are ever alike. Going to one festival is definitely not going to all of them."[15] The point is to encourage people to visit multiple faires.

Faires want visitors to have a good time. "Ten stages of continuous entertainment, Full Combat Jousting, . . . Artisan Demonstrations, over 200 unique shoppes featuring handmade wares; music, games of skill & chance," "five food courts and seven open air taverns." Areas of the faire grounds are given period names. Pathways between booths are called Queen's Way, Old Highland Highway, and Reveler's Way. Entertainment areas become The Grande Tournament Arena, Field of Honor, the Dancing Dragon, the Unicorn Stage, and the Red Lion Stage.

The Anatomy of Faires

Every faire has four elements. First, there is live entertainment, often including jousting. There are games and activities for adults and children. Second, faires sell merchandise. Large faires have 100 to 200 booths and tents offering for sale merchandise with some connection to the Renaissance or the Middle Ages. Third, faires are places for eating and drinking. Fourth, and most important, faires are costume parties. Both the professional entertainers and a large number of visitors walk around, often in groups, in colorful Renaissance garb. They exchange verbal banter with each other in an Elizabethan patois. They create a world of make-believe.

Much of the free live entertainment is interactive historical comedy. The largest faires have ten to twenty stages or arenas offering free entertainment throughout the day, sometimes with acts changing every thirty minutes. For example, two men in English Renaissance costume engage in a mock duel in which they threaten each other and fumble and stumble as they swing their swords wildly. They exchange comic insults, with asides to members of the audience, who are just beyond an improvised fence. Another act features a solo performer who calls himself "The Renaissance Man." He boasts that he takes the audience on "hysterically historical journeys" about life in medieval and Renaissance times in which "the atrocious is made amusing, the rotten made risible, the horrible made humorous and the terrible made to tickle your ribs." The historical journeys include "A visit to the physic (leeching)," "Queen Elizabeth's wrathful side," "A London couple attacked by a fearsome brigand," "the proper use of a chamberpot," and a comic version of bear-baiting.[16] Then there is Bob Da Vinci, "Leonardo's younger brother," who does an act called "the da Vinci Bros." His comic acts include "the real story behind the Mona Lisa," "Galileo's finger," and "Michelangelo and the Sistine Chapel." He invites members of the audience to take a 1519 personality test.[17]

Juggling acts are popular. Comics do takeoffs from scenes or monologues from Shakespeare and Christopher Marlowe (1564–1593), another great Renaissance playwright. Storytellers are common. So are groups of dancers performing English, Scottish, Scandinavian, and other national dances. And when a group of singers performs English madrigals (intricate vocal music set to love poetry, with or without accompanying instruments; singing madrigals well requires skill), the entertainment reaches a higher artistic level. For example, the North Carolina Renaissance Faire Madrigal Singers issued a call for auditions in which the singers were required to sing a song, do a Shakespearean reading in "your best Elizabethan accent," have Renaissance garb, and attend regular rehearsals.[18] Sometimes the entertainment is mildly educational.

Inside the rustic olde taverne, speakers explain the history of beer, ale, and mead. And sometimes the gruesome past is transformed into the comic present. At one Renaissance faire, I saw a costumed man walking through the grounds carrying a sign reading "Witch Trial at 4:30. Fun for the whole family."

Most faires also have some large-scale entertainment events. Jousting tournaments with knights in armor on horseback are common and popular. Grand parades led by Queen Elizabeth and her court sweep through the grounds. Visitors in Renaissance garb are encouraged to join the parade.

After watching actors duel, visitors may try it themselves. In one arena, participants are given swords (i.e., sticks covered in foam rubber). They flail away at each other. If a duelist is hit in the arm, he may no longer use the arm. If hit in the leg, he must hop around on the other foot until "killed" with a thrust to the body. Other games include tests of strength and throwing of the ax, knife, or darts. Rides are available, but not the mechanized rides of the twenty-first century. Faires usually include activities for children. For the more serious minded, the Pittsburgh Renaissance Festival offers a nondenominational church service at 11 a.m. on Sunday mornings.

Although Renaissance faires are a little like county and state fairs, they differ in ways besides the Renaissance theme. There is less distance or separation between the paid entertainers and the audience. In county and state fairs, the musical entertainment and horse or auto racing take place on a pavillon or racetrack at some distance from the grandstand full of spectators. Renaissance faires are more intimate. They have no large-scale pop music acts with amplifiers. Above all, visitors are encouraged to interact with the entertainers and, to some extent, become part of the entertainment through wearing garb (costumes).

The second part, selling merchandise, is important. The largest Renaissance faires have 200 to 300 booths, many of them tents, but also buildings holding several booths, selling all kinds of wares. In this sense, Renaissance faires are the distant descendants of medieval and Renaissance trade fairs in which merchants came from near and far to buy and sell goods. However, the merchants at today's Renaissance faires sell wares more or less connected to the Renaissance.

Clothing, especially Renaissance clothing, is the most important merchandise.[19] For $100, $200, or more, one may buy the entire costume (garb) of an archer, a brewmaster, or an "apprentice wench." Booths offer elegant gowns for would-be noblewomen and ladies-in-waiting. There are numerous individual pieces of clothing for sale, such as a yeoman's jerkin (a short, close-fitting jacket), a lady's bodice made of suede leather, a man's studded doublet, Elizabethan corsets for women, tights for a man or woman, a Elizabethan surcoat, and much else. Much footware is available. One may buy pointed-toe shoes, thigh-high boots of many styles, black-beaded shoes, and all kinds of women's shoes. Musketeer boots are available, even though they are a little anachronistic, because musketeers were seventeenth-century French soldiers, rather than Renaissance men-at-arms. "Medieval moccasins" are popular, even though medieval Europeans could not possibly have known about the footware of North American Indians until after 1492. On the other hand, one- and two-handed swords and their scabbards certainly were worn in the Renaissance and are widely available at faires. Indeed, one can find a considerable variety of weaponry at many price levels.

Renaissance period dress or garb is an essential component. Hence, it can be purchased outside faires. Costume houses sell costumes labeled Lady Juliet, Romeo, Renaissance peasant, village wench, Renaissance knight, bar maiden from Burgundy, Queen

Isabella (queen of Castile and Spain from 1474 to 1504), tavern lady, Renaissance sorceress, merchant's wife, faire (sic) maiden, sexy Gwenhyfar, Renaissance countess, swashbuckler, and even executioner (an all-black and hooded male costume, with the advertisement showing a picture of the executioner brandishing an ax).

For those who prefer to do their own sewing, the catalogues of major pattern houses, such as Simplicity and McCall's, sell for $12 to $15 patterns for Renaissance costumes to be made and worn to the faire.[20] Some pattern names refer to Renaissance faires. For example, there is Simplicity's "Fair Maiden of the Renaissance Faire" pattern, advertised as "perfect for the joust matches." It is a pattern for the dress of a noble or upper-class Renaissance woman of uncertain nationality. Another group of patterns is called "Dress thyself for the Faire," and features bodices and skirts. There are court jester costumes and patterns "for the Romeo in your life." There are also patterns for "Renaissance Peasants," described as "beggars, serfs, & knaves of the Renaissance." There is a "Young Renaissance Maiden" pattern for teen sizes 7 to 14, and "Young Renaissance Attendant" patterns for boys and girls sizes 3 to 8. For little girls, a pattern called "Shakespearean Sprite" pictures a dress with soft-hued flowing gauze something like a ballet tutu.

Merchants at faires sell other items as well. Mugs and leather goods are available. Much jewelry evoking the Renaissance or done in period style is offered, including brooches, earrings, necklaces, pins, and poison rings. Renaissance faires are to a limited extent craft faires, because swords, jewelry, and the like are handmade by craftspersons. Items available in lesser profusion include books about the Renaissance and compact discs of performances of more or less authentic Renaissance music. For a price, artists will paint one's portrait against a background of castle and forest. For those who do not bring enough cash, signs assure them that "We doth honor Lady Visa and the Master of the Card."

The third part is eating and drinking, an important source of revenue for merchants. The food courts sell wine, beer, and ale, which were widely drunk and often brewed at home in the Renaissance. They also sell mead, an alcoholic drink made of fermented honey and water, sometimes with some malt added, and flavored with spices. In the Middle Ages and Renaissance, mead was popular in regions of northern and eastern Europe where grapes could not be grown. And familiar twenty-first-century fast food is available, sometimes under a changed name that links it to the Renaissance.

The fourth and most important part of Renaissance faires is that visitors try to relive the Renaissance through their costumes and participation in faire activities. Faire managements encourage participation. The Colorado Renaissance Festival tells visitors to bring imagination, good humor, and a sense of participation. Visitors participate by dressing in period costumes and interacting with the strolling actors and sometimes with the comedy acts.

Men, women, and children, young adults and the middle-aged, come dressed as Renaissance queens and kings, ladies and knights, courtesans and courtiers, shopkeepers, wenches, peasants, pages, and jesters. ("Wench" is a name that faire enthusiasts like to use to describe a young woman of the lower classes who is looking for a good time and might have loose morals.) Some faires encourage patrons to come in costume by offering prizes for the best ones. Patrons lacking their own Renaissance garb may rent costumes for the day. Although more women than men dress in Renaissance garb, there are always a significant number of men in costume, often with swords at the belt. Although it varies from faire to faire and day to day, it is likely that one-third or more paying customers wear Renaissance clothing. The visitors in Renaissance garb are a significant part of the act and make Renaissance faires unique in the world of outdoor festivals. They are large costume parties generated by the same urge that has made Halloween a huge holiday.

The male visitors who come dressed in Renaissance costume including swords present a potential problem to management. On one hand, faires wish to encourage paying customers to wear Renaissance garb, including swords and other weapons. But they do not want patrons to use them. The vast majority of Renaissance faires have hit upon a compromise: they permit visitors to carry weapons so long as they are sheathed and "peace-tied." "Peace-tied" means that the weapons are tied to their carrying piece, such as a scabbard, in such a way that no second party can pull them out and use them.

The Minnesota Renaissance Festival has different rules for different weapons. It permits patrons to wear swords, knives, dirks, and daggers so long as they are completely sheathed and peace-tied. But it bars antique firearms, toy guns, pikes, and halberds (a shaft of wood with a head and crosspiece of steel). It permits claymores (a two-edged broadsword used in Scotland) and maces, so long as they are peace-tied to the body (i.e., strapped to the back or tied to the belt). It permits bows and arrows so long as bows are unstrung and arrows tied to the quiver. And it permits walking sticks or quarterstaffs without restrictions.[21] A small number of faires do not permit visitors to bring in weapons of any kind.

Why They Love the Faire

Renaissance faire enthusiasts, those who attend year after year and dress in garb, invariably offer two reasons for their initial visits to a Renaissance faire: an interest in history and a love of playacting.[22]

"Thanks to my mom and dad, I have always been a history buff and costume junkie," writes one. Many Renaissance faire enthusiasts had parents who loved history and passed on that love to their children, by reading to them, by stopping the car to read historical markers, and other ways. Another person relates that she had two college friends who were "ren faire junkies." At first she resisted their entreaties to come along. But then "being the history buff that I am, I finally made it and had a blast. Nice people, great atmosphere, and so much to see and do! . . . I started wearing garb last year, and love planning my persona (the Renaissance role to be played; see below) for each faire." Another fairegoer was introduced to faires through the medieval and Renaissance club at her Louisiana high school in 1993, became hooked, and in 2002 was married at the Texas Renaissance Festival. And while she did not meet her husband at a Renaissance faire, more than one rennie (Renaissance faire enthusiast) did meet future spouses at faires.

For another enthusiast, a search for his English and Welsh family roots led him to want to know more and to Renaissance faires. Of course, it was not always history that inspired the first visit. One man went to the Southern California Renaissance Pleasure Faire in 1971 because he had heard that "it was a good place to score dope, get stoned . . . and meet like-minded members of the opposite sex." He has been attending faires ever since, probably without the dope and sex, because faires have become more family-oriented over the years. A masculine reason for attending is that men find the swords worn by fairegoers and offered for sale fascinating. One veteran fairegoer confesses that he drools over the weaponry and likes to buy swords.

History's bastard siblings, fantasy and legend, also lead some to Renaissance faires. As one rennie explained, "I've always loved fantasy stories ever since I can remember being able to read: the swords, magic, adventure, big tough heroes, and strong cunning ladies. I loved to read *The Lord of the Rings*, . . . the legends of

King Arthur, and so many other great books and movies. Then when I went to college in Minnesota I heard about this 'ren faire' thing." Another person remembers that his mother read to him tales of King Arthur as a child. He also played with swords, as many boys probably still do. Thus J. R. Tolkien's *Lord of the Rings,* which has no connection with the Renaissance, can lead people to Renaissance faires. The same is true of King Arthur and the Knights of the Round Table, even though Arthur was a medieval king who flourished between about 490 and 540, if he ever existed. But there is some connection between the legendary King Arthur and the Renaissance. Like today's readers, people living in the historical Renaissance of the fifteenth and sixteenth centuries loved chivalric romances, including stories of the battles and loves of Arthur, Guinevere, Lancelot, Gawain, Tristan, Isolde, and other knights.[23]

A handful of small Renaissance faires take advantage of this interest and emphasize legend and fantasy. For example, the Camelot Harvest Faire at Beaver Dam, Wisconsin, near Milwaukee, which met for a weekend in October 2004, had as its theme an "Arthurian England Harvest Fest" in AD 450. The purpose of the faire was to raise money for the "Historic Camelot Project, a non-profit organization that "is seeking to build a recreation of a 5th-century Briton hillfort/village as an open-air experiential museum." It recommended that patrons come in Arthurian costumes, which it called "pre-medieval England." One has to compliment the organizers for placing Arthur in the fifth century, a transition period between late-Roman and early medieval England.

There is also the Journey to Camelot faire, which calls itself "Portland's [Oregon] first annual Renaissance Faire;" King Arthur and the Knights of the Round Table invite all to come. Of course, there is an obvious historical contradiction: legendary early medieval Camelot has nothing to do with the Renaissance. The Four Winds Renaissance Faire in Troup (near Tyler), Texas, holds a special Tolkien festival on Easter weekend, in which patrons are invited "to dress as their favorite Tolkien characters and interact with our cast." And just to complete the historical confusion, its theme is the "17th-century Cavalier Period—the Three Muske-teers," which came after the Renaissance. Finally, there is the Robin Hood Faire at Hammond Castle at Gloucester, Massachu-setts. Again, the stories about Robin Hood are based on a leg-endary medieval outlaw who probably never existed. And if the Robin Hood legend is based on real outlaws, they must have lived before 1250, long before the Renaissance. Finally, even Renaissance faires that emphasize historical accuracy do provide some fantasy entertainment, such as dancing dragons and dragon egg hunts. In general, Renaissance faires, although they may announce thematic dates that are clearly Renaissance, tend to elide or ignore the chronological and other differences between the Middle Ages and the Renaissance, especially in the case of popular entertainment.

Mundanes, Rennies, Playtrons, and Masquers

For the serious Renaissance faire attendee, there are different lev-els of participation, a vocabulary to be learned, and etiquette to be followed.[24] The least committed fairegoer is the "mundane," sometimes called "outlander." This is the person who comes dressed in "regular" or twenty-first-century garb. Mundanes or outlanders come for a good time, but they are very green about the whole experience.

The "Ren faire enthusiast," sometimes also called a "rennie" or "ren-rat," has a greater commitment to the faire. (Rennie also refers to those who follow the faire circuit as workers in the ven-dor booths because they love the gypsy-like life.) Ren faire enthu-siasts wear Renaissance garb even when it is not completely historically accurate. Indeed, they may have a considerable amount of Renaissance garb and wear it outside the faire, which offends faire purists. Because they come to escape the outside world and to enjoy themselves, rennies also spend much time in the pubs and campgrounds. Because of their enthusiasm, they can be a nuisance to members of performing companies. On the other hand, many become playtrons (see the next page).

There is an obvious difference in commitment to reliving the Renaissance between mundanes and Ren faire enthusiasts. It is most apparent in dress, because mundanes often dress inappropriately. Rennies have no problem with those who wear twenty-first-century clothing to the faire. But they object to those who attend in the wrong costumes, such as storm trooper and Star Trek outfits, or as Batman and Elvis Presley. Storm troopers are empire soldiers in the Star Wars films; they wear all-white armored suits, including masks, and carry ray guns. This seriously offends rennies and playtrons.

Nevertheless, at least one faire invites visitors to come wearing anachronistic costumes. The Ingleside (Texas) Renaissance Faire and Christmas Craft Bazaar, which met on December 11 and 12, 2004, encouraged patrons to come in medieval, Renaissance, and Elizabethan costumes, but then added, "The occasional Klingon will only spice things up, as the natives will be scared out of their wits."

Ren faire enthusiasts condemn this attitude and those who come to faires dressed in wildly anachronistic costumes. But they counsel education. They hope to be able to explain politely to storm troopers and trekkies why their costumes are inappropriate. Another approach is to make fun of them. Those in Renaissance garb assume the personae of mystified sixteenth-century knights. They poke fun at the trekkie and ask impertinent questions about his strange outfit.

Veteran Renaissance faire participants are more tolerant of people who come only partly clad in Renaissance garb, whose

Renaissance costume is not very good or who wear sneakers with tights, or are clad in authentic Renaissance garb but walk around with cell phones in their ears. ("Don't kill the illusion with a blatant modern convenience," chides one veteran fairegoer.) Most recognize that these patrons help keep faires going through their admission fees and purchases. They realize that semiaccurate garb still represents an attempt to enter into the spirit of the past. Moreover, well aware that full Renaissance costumes are expensive, they forgive those who cannot afford them or who make their own less-than-perfect outfits. Indeed, they see their earlier selves in the outlanders who come in inadequate costumes. They remember their own first visits in partial or poor garb. But they caught the spirit, developed an understanding of faires, and made many more visits in garb. Hence, veteran fairegoers try to make the neophytes welcome in the hope and expectation that they will have a good time, get bitten by the Renaissance bug, and return.

The playtron "is the die-hard fan of a festival." He or she comes to the faire in excellent and very authentic garb and does more. He has developed a "persona," the character of someone from the Renaissance. The playtron knows well the historical theme of the faire, its place, and the year. He understands faire etiquette. If he encounters a performer, one of the paid entertainers, in the "lanes" (anywhere in the faire site beyond the stage or arena), he knows that the performer must maintain his persona, even though no longer on stage. So he plays along with the performer by pretending to be living in the Renaissance and speaking so. A playtron is so committed and knowledgeable that he might be close to becoming a member of the performing company. Indeed, the heartfelt desire of many playtrons is to become "masquers."

Masquers or stage performers are the members of the acts who travel the Renaissance faire circuit. In the judgment of masquers and playtrons alike, the best are those who have a good historical knowledge of the Renaissance and put it to use in a well-honed interactive historical comedic act. The less-skilled masquers rely too much on making jokes about the obvious differences between the Renaissance and the twenty-first century in order to get laughs. Masquers may also be hired to work the lanes (i.e., to walk around the faire grounds talking to the patrons while maintaining their Renaissance personae).

All masquers are paid performers who do their act several times a day, then go on to the next faire. They work the faire circuit nine or ten months of the year and use January and February to renew their acts. For some of the masquers, the special thrill of performing at a Renaissance faire is that they are both entertainers and educators teaching the audience something about the past. Many also perform for schools, corporate groups, and private parties, and some of them have other acts not involving the Renaissance. These actors earn their living performing. Others are enthusiastic amateurs. They get together as a performing group in order to perform at nearby faires for a few weekends every year.

The most important part for masquers and playtrons alike is building a persona. It should be based on a Renaissance occupation and a name that is reasonably historical. It might be Lady Ellen of the Clan of McShuggenah, a Scottish reference, or a cloth merchant named Robert Whitewoole. Names should not be goofy, cute, or anachronistic, such as Bettsy Bigboobs for a Renaissance wench, or Black N. Decker for a Renaissance carpenter. Nor should the character come from a cult movie or Tolkien. Elves, fairies, and wizards do not belong. The persona must be historical, and the garb should tell viewers the character's occupation and social status. Hence, clothing must be of the appropriate color, such as purple for a king or queen; black, red, and other vivid tones for nobles and the wealthy; and earth tones for commoners. Hats are important for almost all costumes. But jewelry and fur are limited to personae representing the rich and highborn of the Renaissance.

Language is important. The desired language is simplified Elizabethan speech. As one fairegoer put it, if you want to learn from the best, read Shakespeare. A shorter way is to consult Shakespeare lexicons. Several Web sites offer glossaries of terms. But for the average rennie or playtron it is enough to sprinkle Elizabethan or Shakespearean phrases into ordinary speech. Hence, one should use "anon" (until later), "morrow" (day), "aye" and "nay," "verily," "fie" (a curse), "mayhap" and "perchance," and so on. Adding "right," "well," and "most" also achieves the desired effect. And one should try to use several words instead of two: "thou art most beauteous fair," "she doth be most marvelous comely." Although not mentioned as such, this advice demonstrates an awareness that Elizabethan English was more elaborate and rhetorical than twenty-first-century American English.

The fact that the fairegoer, whether mundane, enthusiast, or playtron, is encouraged to, and often does, wear historical costumes, create a persona, and speak Elizabethan English underscores two points. The committed fairegoer really does want to relive the Renaissance, at least for the day. The second is that interactive historical experiences are a key part of Renaissance faires. The patrons want to be able to interact as historical characters with the garbed performers. They wish to behave as men and women from the Renaissance. To the extent that they manage this, fairegoers become part of the faire and the Renaissance.

There is no doubt that the people who attend and/or participate in many Renaissance faires have a strong historical interest in the Renaissance period. But it is likely that for most of them, knowledge of the real Renaissance does not go much beyond surface aspects of the period, notably dress, language (so long as it is English), tournaments, and famous kings, queens, and artists.

Limited evidence in support for this assessment comes in the form of short essays about the Renaissance that faire enthusiasts submit to a contest sponsored by a leading Renaissance faire Web site. The contestants submit short essays of 1,000 to 1,500 words about any aspect of the historical Renaissance. The winning essays are then posted.[25] Despite the effort and enthusiasm of the writers, the winning essays do not demonstrate a great deal of knowledge. They often repeat common misconceptions about the Renaissance and embrace factual errors. The problem is that, like far too many high school and university students, the essayists mostly regurgitate material found in two or three books. Unfortunately, the books used are often out-of-date accounts written for general readers. The essayists avoid reference works, which may be dry but are accurate. Nor do they use university-level textbooks on the Renaissance or Western European history. Such criticism may be a little unfaire, if the reader will pardon the pun, because inexperienced authors usually need guidance from a teacher or librarian in order to locate reliable sources of information. Nevertheless, the authors deserve full praise for trying. The fact that they take the trouble to research and write about the Renaissance testifies to their eagerness to learn.

Renaissance faires and the Society for Creative Anachronism (SCA) are not the same. The SCA usually has a booth at Renaissance faires to explain itself, to solicit members, and to sell merchandise. But it is different in chronology, events, and organization. Although it advertises that it focuses on Europe before 1600, it really is medieval in its focus, that is, it concentrates on the period before 1400.[26] SCA literature and its Web site make this clear. Another difference is that the SCA emphasizes tournaments and chivalry. It lacks the broader range of activities found in Renaissance faires. The SCA's most important annual events are elaborate faux wars involving knights in armor wielding swords and shooting arrows. They do not use firearms because medieval warriors lacked effective firearms. Renaissance men had them, and it made a deadly difference.

There are also organizational differences. The SCA is a non-profit educational organization with about 30,000 dues-paying members organized into chapters and with an elaborate hierarchy spread across the United States and abroad. Renaissance fairegoers lack a formal organization, and there are many more of them. Although Renaissance faires and the SCA offer ways to relive the past, they are different.

Renaissance Faires Online and in Print

The Internet and print journalism enable rennies, playtrons, and others to share their enthusiasm and to learn more about faires and the Renaissance itself. The most important electronic listserv, www.renaissancefestival.com, has more than 2,000 members. Each member participates through his or her persona, that is, an assumed name with some connection with the Renaissance. They discuss all aspects of faires and related topics, such as favorite Renaissance and medieval films.

The magazine *Renaissance* is an integral part of faire culture. It is the creation of Yale graduate Kim Guarnaccia, whose persona is Lady Kimberly of Sherburne Isle.[27] She attended her first Renaissance faire in 1992, at which time she was "awestruck" by the number of people who "lived their characters—dressing in period costume . . . and speaking fluently in faire accents." In 1994, she decided to have a Renaissance wedding. "When I began to organize the music, decorations, costuming, and entertainment, I was amazed by the lack of reference material available to the mainstream." A "comprehensive source for Renaissance information" was needed. Thus, the idea of *Renaissance* was born. After her wedding, she and a few friends worked hard for a year and produced the first issue in January 1996. As of the end of 2004, forty had appeared, and it is now a bimonthly. The magazine tells potential readers "Thou art cordially invited to subscribe." The newsstand price is $5.95 per issue. A year's mail subscription (six issues) costs $29, but the magazine tells Canadian and overseas subscribers to "pr'ythee add $9 per year." Lady Kimberly remains the editor and publisher. She appears at the Web site in a bright red period dress with laced bodice and white blouse with puffed sleeves as "The Most Honourable Creator of this Cherished Gazette." The cherished gazette has a circulation of 35,000.

Each issue contains 96 pages, of which 24 plus the four cover pages are in color.[28] Two thirds of each issue is given to stories, news, columns, features, directories, letters to the editor, and a crossword puzzle. Each issue is structured around a theme. The cover story is a discussion of a large topic in several linked articles and black-and-white illustrations. A recent topic was Richard III and the princes of the tower as part of the War of the Roses in England. This was the conflict between the houses of Lancaster and York in the fifteenth century from which Henry VII (Tudor, reigned 1485–1509) emerged triumphant. The story includes the evidence pro and con about whether King Richard III (reigned 1483–1485) had the boy princes, who had better claims to the throne than he, murdered in the Tower of London. The cover story in another issue is a primer on making armor; it includes interviews with armorers. The debate over the authorship of Shakespeare's plays, a perennial conspiracy theory that intrigues amateurs and irritates Shakespeare scholars, is another cover story. The authors are freelance writers. *Renaissance* encourages unsolicited manuscripts and pays 8 cents per published word.

The regular features of *Renaissance* include news about recent events concerning the historical Renaissance, such as the opening to the public of the restored Ospedale Santa Maria della Scala in Siena, with its superb fifteenth-century frescos. The magazine lists Renaissance art exhibitions in major American, English, French, and Italian museums. There are thoughtful reviews of "nonfiction books, such as histories (for general readers, not professional scholars) of the Renaissance, novels, films, and music recordings. There usually is an article on how to make an item of Renaissance clothing, and a quiz article in which the reader is invited to guess the meanings of unusual English Renaissance words and phrases, some of them bawdy. A list of current Renaissance faires appears in every issue. There is a gallery of color portraits of elegantly costumed faire participants. And each issue concludes with a crossword puzzle on the theme of the cover story.

The Court Jester writes comic articles, such as "A Medieval TV Guide."[29] The television programs include "One Wife to Give: A new soap opera featuring Henry VIII and Anne Boleyn." "Charlie's Anglos: Three beautiful French wenches disguise themselves as English nuns to sabotage the British while working for France's King Charles the Bold." "Saxons and the City" has a season premiere described thus: "After he gives her a pair of Bruno Mali glass slippers to die for, Lady Carrie unlocks her chastity belt for Sir Big and then dishes the dirt over grog Cosmopolitan martinis with her three best wenchfriends." For those who want investigative reporting, there is "Sixtus Minutes: Pope Sixtus IV interviews insincere converts to Christianity and then has them executed." (Sixtus IV was pope from 1471 to 1484, but never acted in this way.) It is an apt parody of the relentless questioning of Mike Wallace and his colleagues.

One third of each issue is devoted to advertising. There are full-page color ads for Renaissance faires and numerous ads for Renaissance clothing, jewelry, armor, hand-painted metal shields, tents ("Makers of authentic period tentage"), footwear, and much else. Several advertisements offer to create a Renaissance wedding in every detail. The nuptial couple may rent a castle in Arizona ("Renaissance weddings in Arizona"), Oklahoma, or Louisiana for the celebration. "A replica of an English Norman keep castle is a spectacular setting for a Renaissance wedding . . . Stay in our Juliet suite."[30] One wonders how a suite named for Juliet, who supposedly lived in Verona, Italy, could be found in a medieval English castle. There are many small classified ads for merchants with names designed to capture the reader's attention, such as "Olde Soles: Handmade Renaissance footwear." *Renaissance* is carefully planned to appeal to fairegoers and merchants. It is a successful niche publication catering to a strong special interest.

Conclusion

In March 1999, the nationally syndicated humorist Dave Barry wrote a column about members of the Renaissance Historical Society of Florida who were rehearsing a sword fight for a future Renaissance faire. "They belong to the Renaissance Historical Society of Florida, a group of people who wear costumes and pretend they're living during the Renaissance. The Renaissance . . . was the historical period that started in the 15th century at approximately 3:30 p.m. when humanity, after centuries of being cooped up in the Dark Ages, finally stumbled out into the light . . . . This was followed by tremendous advances in science, philosophy, literature, and paintings of naked women."[31] He goes on with humorous remarks about codpieces, sword fights, and other topics, as the group prepares for the next Renaissance faire.

Barry's comic piece emphasizes the importance of the Renaissance and Renaissance faires in popular culture—so long as one ignores his negative comments about the Middle Ages. Renaissance faires probably bring more people to some understanding of the Renaissance than any other event, with the possible exception of popular films. But whereas films are fleeting and passive, the faires engage those who attend and endure. For the dedicated faire enthusiast and playtron, participating in Renaissance faires is a culture; that is, a group of people who give themselves to activities centering on a theme. Participants acquire a limited knowledge about the historical Renaissance and put it to use. For all visitors, Renaissance faires offer the opportunity for reliving the Renaissance and having a good time.

Chapter 3

RENAISSANCE
WEEKENDS
AND LIVING
LAST SUPPERS

T alented, well-educated, and affluent men and women engage in spirited and witty conversation in comfortable and elegant surroundings. They enjoy the discussion and each other's company. After a few days, the participants must leave, each to his own court or city. But they vow to return to continue the dialogue. This is what happened in the ducal palace of Urbino, Italy, in the winter of 1506. It also happens four or five times a year in Hilton Head, South Carolina; Santa Fe, New Mexico; Monterey, California; Charleston, South Carolina; and Jackson Hole, Wyoming. These are Renaissance Weekends.

Leonardo da Vinci painted the scene in which Jesus met with all his apostles for the last time. After the supper the apostles disbursed, and Jesus was arrested and crucified. Devout Christians now reenact Leonardo's painting with living persons and call their dramatic presentations "Living Last Suppers." Thus, twenty-first-century Americans re-create two well-known parts of the Renaissance: intelligent dialogue on important issues and its most famous religious painting.

Renaissance Weekends

Learned and witty conversation was a valued part of upper-class life in the Renaissance. Men and women conversed in order to explore complicated issues, to weigh alternatives, and sometimes to display their wit and sophistication. We have no transcriptions of what they said. But Renaissance authors wrote numerous books that claimed to be accounts of conversations that took place. In the books, the interlocutors meet in a palace or villa and discuss current issues as equals in an atmosphere of civility, respect, and good humor. Of course, authors undoubtedly improved the conversations that took place, and they wrote works about conversations that never took place. Nevertheless, there is ample evidence that enlightened, civil, and intelligent conversation was a prized feature of Renaissance life.

The most famous account of a Renaissance conversation is *The Book of the Courtier* (published 1528) of Baldessare Castiglione (1478–1529).[1] The author claimed to report a series of conversations that took place over four long nights in the ducal palace of Urbino in north central Italy in the winter of 1506. One can visit the room in the palace at Urbino where the conversations may have taken place. It has a large fireplace, a good reason for gathering there on winter nights.

According to the book, a group of well-spoken aristocratic men and women from different parts of Italy engaged in long, brilliant, and always civil conversations. The announced theme, chosen by one of the women present, was the physical and moral qualities of the perfect courtier, a man who assists and serves a worthy prince. The speakers discussed this at length. But they also discussed practically every other major issue of interest to the intelligentsia of Italy, including education, whether birth or virtuous accomplishment constituted true nobility, the political woes of Italy, whether painting or sculpture was the greater art, how to get ahead at court, and the proper behavior for different social situations. At times, the conversations rose to great eloquence as they discussed the nature of love, truth, and beauty, and the obligations of an honorable man. At other times, it descended into jokes and puns. Throughout the participants spoke with easy grace, without labored effort or didacticism. They avoided stridency, even when presenting strongly held views. Even though it is very unlikely that any spontaneous conversations were so graceful and well modulated as those reported by Castiglione, the book is based on reality. All the speakers were historical figures known to Castiglione, and the majority, perhaps all, were present in Urbino in 1506. Several are known to have held views attributed to them by Castiglione.

The historical lesson to be learned from books such as Castiglione's *The Book of the Courtier*—and there were many similar works, although none so elegant—is that upper-class Renaissance men and women believed that civil conversation in a congenial atmosphere could stimulate the mind and was part of the good life. Indeed, another Italian, Stefano Guazzo (1530–1593), wrote a book called *The Civil Conversation* (1574), which had many editions in Italian and in English translation.

Renaissance Weekend tries to replicate Renaissance conversation in the twenty-first century. Five times a year, several hundred accomplished and reasonably affluent Americans meet for four days to talk about a wide variety of issues. Renaissance Weekend is the creation of the husband-and-wife team of Philip Lader and Linda LeSourd Lader.[2] Philip Lader (b. 1946) is a lawyer who became president of a company that develops and organizes recreation communities. He was then president of Winthrop University in South Carolina and ran unsuccessfully for the Democratic nomination for governor of South Carolina in 1986. He later served in the Clinton White House as deputy chief of staff and assistant to the president in 1993 and 1994, as administrator of the

Small Business Administration from 1994 to 1997, and as ambassador to the Court of St. James (i.e., ambassador to England) from 1997 until 2001. Linda Le Sourd Lader assisted White House liaison with religious groups in Clinton's first term and currently serves on the boards of several nonprofit organizations including Habitat for Humanity International. She is president of Renaissance Institute, the entity that oversees Renaissance Weekends.

The purpose of Renaissance Weekend is to bring together accomplished people from a wide variety of backgrounds to hold conversations about all sorts of issues on an informal, off-the-record basis in a relaxed atmosphere. They began in 1981. The Laders heard friends lamenting that they rarely had the occasion to learn "in a personal and substantive way" from the fascinating people whom they met.[3] So they organized the first Renaissance Weekend, which was attended by 60 families on the New Year's weekend of January 1981. A year later, some 90 participants plus spouses and children came. Now they meet four or five times a year in various locations in the United States and, occasionally, Canada. Attendance reached 500 for the New Year's weekend of January 1, 1989. This grew to 1,500 on January 1, 1997, and about 1,350 on January 1, 1999.[4] Weekends at other times of the year are smaller.

Each Renaissance Weekend "seeks to build bridges across traditional divides of professions and politics, geography and generations, religions and philosophies."[5] The overall goal of these retreats is "to encourage personal and national renewal." To do this, the weekends bring together "distinguished participants—CEOs, venture capitalists and entrepreneurs, Nobel laureates and Pulitzer Prize-winners, artists and scientists, astronauts and Olympians, judges, diplomats and work-at-home parents, presidents, prime ministers, professors and priests, Republicans, Democrats and Independents. Civility prevails. Partisanship is frowned upon, and commercialism is banned." In order to emphasize the Renaissance theme, the art work on the 2004 invitation included a stylized version of Filippo Brunelleschi's dome of the cathedral of Florence, built between 1420 and 1436, perhaps the greatest architectural and engineering feat of the Italian Renaissance.

Although important to the participants, Renaissance Weekends did not attract much attention until one of its regular attendees from the earliest years, William Jefferson Clinton, was elected president in 1992. Then the media paid attention. Clinton, usually accompanied by Hillary Rodham Clinton and daughter Chelsea, continued to attend and participate throughout his presidency. He usually attended the New Year's weekends held at Hilton Head Island in South Carolina; that of late December 1998 through January 1, 1999, was the fifteenth for Clinton.[6] He normally participated in one or more of the panel discussions and played golf. The weekends encourage recreational activities.

Because the conversations may not be reported, Renaissance Weekends are best known for their participants. They include former president Gerald Ford and several failed presidential candidates: the late Eugene McCarthy, the late Terry Sanford, Wesley Clark, Howard Dean, and Robert Graham.[7] Senators and members of the House of Representatives, cabinet secretaries, and aides to presidents have attended. So have a number of Nobel laureates, MacArthur Prize and Pulitzer Prize winners, plus many other people in business, education, law, medicine, journalism, and religion.

The easiest way to describe a Renaissance Weekend is to describe my participation. First, one must be invited. Former participants are invited to nominate people for future weekends and, if Renaissance Weekend agrees, invitations are mailed to the nominees. I received an invitation in August 1999. I have no idea who nominated me. But because the invitation was sent to the address of the literary agent who represented me when I was editor in chief of *Encyclopedia of the Renaissance* (published 1999), it may be that nominator and organizers were intrigued by the thought of having a historian of the "real" Renaissance in attendance.

The invitation offers one the opportunity to attend one or all of the weekends in a given year. I chose to attend the Renaissance Weekend in Santa Fe, New Mexico, February 17–21, 2000. I was then asked to submit a brief curriculum vitae and statement of interests and topics about which I might like to speak. This enables the organizers to assign participants to appropriate discussion groups. Participants are encouraged to bring spouses and children; indeed, programs, excursions, and games are organized for children.

About 360 adults and 80 children, from toddlers through university students, descended on a Santa Fe hotel on February 17, 2000.[8] Participants were almost evenly divided between men and women. The vast majority were white, a small handful were African Americans and Hispanics. Business, law, medicine, and university administration were best represented. There were many people from the world of high technology in Silicon Valley and elsewhere. CEOs of other kinds of companies, especially small ones, were also there, along with a sprinkling of venture capitalists and people from financial institutions. The academic world was well represented at the senior administrative level: several university and college presidents, deans of university units (business school, medical school, arts and sciences), and two leaders of elite private schools. By contrast, there were very few ordinary humanities professors and only two historians of Europe: myself and one from an Ivy League university. Law was well represented with five judges and a number of attorneys. So was medicine and medical research. Psychologists and psychotherapists, health care managers, as well as a few nurses who were female spouses of other participants, were part of the gathering.

There were several publishers and editors, but only two widely recognized print or television journalists: the syndicated columnist William Raspberry and Nina Totenberg, legal affairs correspondent for PBS and ABC. A few clergymen from mainline churches—Episcopalian, Presbyterian, and Roman Catholic—were present, but none from more fundamentalist Christian churches. One congressman, a former astronaut, and a MacArthur fellow were there. A number of participants straddled professions (e.g., a computer expert who developed medical technology). There were many professional couples present. And women who listed "homemaker" as their occupation almost always were simultaneously involved in a business or profession or had been. Conspicuously absent were people from Hollywood, the television entertainment industry, and the worlds of sports, arts, and music, both classical and popular. Nor were any active or retired military officers in attendance.

The majority, but not all, seemed to be well-educated, reasonably affluent people with high expectations for themselves and their children, the kinds of people who send their children to private schools followed by Harvard, Yale, Princeton, or Stanford. One reason for a relatively comfortable clientele is that participants must pay registration fees, food, and lodging for four days, and transportation to and from the venue. The cost for the four to five days reaches $2,000 to $2,500 per adult and half or more of that for each child.

The program of a Renaissance Weekend is a series of conversations. Each participant is assigned to two or three panels. At Santa Fe there were about 100 panel discussions, with up to eight running simultaneously. Larger Weekends have 300 to 400 panels. They begin in the evening of the first day, resume at 8:00 a.m., and run through the day and early evening for the next three days, and conclude at midmorning of the fifth day. Each panel or group discussion has a moderator and from ten to fifteen, occasionally six to twenty, speakers.

At Santa Fe, the panels were grouped under broadly defined themes, such as Renaissance Policy, Renaissance Academy, Renaissance Advanced Management, Renaissance Education, Renaissance Families, Renaissance Law Forum, Renaissance Quest, and Renaissance Sci/Tech. The individual topics for the panel discussions included "Creating Values," "Money Politics, Managed Care & Other Seemingly Insoluble Problems," "Venture Capital Free-for-all," "The 21st Century American Marriage," "How Will We be Living in 2020?," "The Internet's Consequences & the Digital Divide," and "American Cities in the New Century." There were discussions on what has been learned about early childhood education and on aging, on surviving cancer (all panelists were either survivors or medical experts), and on spiritual life in the new millennium. Lawyers and judges discussed constitutional issues and controversial problems. There was a discussion of world hot spots. Speakers were encouraged to present arresting and stimulating ideas based on their own expertise or experience. There were only a handful of sessions on politics, and these were nonpartisan, such as a panel about the possibilities and limitations of the last year of a presidency, and another on what twentieth-century presidencies might teach twenty-first-century presidents. All discussions are off-the-record, with no recording devices allowed. Nothing anyone says may be quoted.

Some panels were light-hearted, such as the one in which speakers presented humorous wish lists if they became emperors of the world. Lifting steins of beer was the "work" in one Renaissance Workshop. Conversations continued at meals, as table leaders and themes were announced. Anyone who wanted to eat and talk at a particular table was welcome on a first-come basis. A few sessions were planned for children and young adults. For example, a twelve-year-old served as moderator for a group of six-, seven-, and eight-year-olds on the topic "The person I most admire is . . .

because . . . ." Games, sports, and activities were offered to children and young adults and excursions to adults and children.

Because most sessions lasted eighty to eighty-five minutes, speakers were expected to limit their remarks to three to five minutes, in order to allow time for questions and discussion. Hence, speakers could only make one or two points. The benefits were that speakers expressed themselves clearly and concisely, while listeners were stimulated to think and to ask questions. The discussions moved briskly and were not boring. The disadvantages were that there was not enough time to develop an idea, to explain its consequences, or for members of the audience to realize objections and present counterarguments.

Any assessment of the atmosphere and style of a Renaissance Weekend can only be that of one person able to attend a limited number of panels and talk to a minority of the participants. Keeping that caution in mind, two strong themes appeared at the Santa Fe Weekend: speculation about what the twenty-first century might hold and the growing impact of the Internet on all areas of life. The first theme was natural for a meeting in February 2000, and the relatively large number of participants from the high-tech world helped project the second theme. The participants displayed a genuine curiosity to know more about the many swift changes occurring in American life.

Most participants seemed to be moderately liberal and their mood rationally optimistic. They wanted to make the world better through traditional American means: expanding knowledge, better technology, intelligent development, and reasoned small changes in public policy. They were not radicals but people prepared to work through the system. A certain amount of pragmatic do-goodism surfaced in the discussions. If a criticism might be made, it is that there was little discussion about the world beyond the borders of the United States. It is likely that much more discussion about the rest of the world has occurred at weekends after September 2001.

I encountered only a handful of political conservatives at the Santa Fe meeting, which seems to be the pattern. The Web site list of Renaissance Weekend participants from government and politics over the past twenty years includes very few recognizable conservative figures, such as political commentator Norman Ornstein of the American Enterprise Institute, former Republican senator from Wyoming Alan Simpson, and Richard Viguerie, conservative direct mail impresario and editor of *Conservative Digest*.[9] Many more individuals with Democratic links are listed.

The small number of conservative participants has led conservatives to criticize Renaissance Weekend for its alleged liberal and Democratic bias. For example, the managing editor of *National Review*, the very conservative political opinion journal founded by William Buckley Jr., accepted an invitation to attend a Renaissance Weekend in 2004. He then reported on his experience.[10] He complimented the Laders for their kindness, hospitality, and ecumenism. But then he portrayed his fellow participants as ill-mannered liberals who hissed and shook their heads when he spoke and had a visceral hatred for George W. Bush. (I did not see this kind of behavior in February 2000, but that now seems like an earlier historical age.) He then launched his own message, which was to lambaste National Public Radio, PBS, *The New York Times*, and ABC news anchor Peter Jennings as cornerstones of a biased liberal press, and to view Bush as a latter-day Abraham Lincoln. It does not appear that this attempt of the Laders to reach out to conservatives for civil conversation succeeded.

Renaissance Weekends have a broad appeal. Possibly the most important reason for attending is the opportunity to listen to and meet informally accomplished people, some of them newsworthy, from different professions and areas of life. Another reason is to hear new ideas. A third motivation is to gain a little inside knowledge, for example, to hear Nina Totenberg's anecdotes about members of the Supreme Court. Networking opportunities probably attract some participants. And the combination of intellectual stimulation and family vacation that Renaissance Weekends offer persuades some to return year after year. For those with the interest, time, and money, Renaissance Weekends are attractive.

The small group of aristocratic men and women who spent long evenings conversing about the issues that mattered to them in a palace in 1506 and the accomplished, affluent, and articulate Americans who meet in hotels in vacation areas of the United States share some similarities. Although the former did not discuss social problems or the impact of technology, the urge to hold civil conversations transcends time and distance.

Living Last Suppers

Another way to relive the Renaissance is to reenact its most famous religious painting in order to inspire religious devotion. Between 1495 and 1497, Leonardo da Vinci painted the *Last Supper*. The painting, some fifteen by twenty-nine feet, is on the wall of the refectory (the room in which the friars ate their meals) in the Dominican monastery of Santa Maria delle Grazie in Milan. The painting is about the Last Supper, the meal in which Jesus and his disciples celebrated the Passover meal the night before he was crucified. At the Last Supper, Jesus instituted the Eucharist, the commemorative eating of bread and drinking of wine that celebrates the union of Christians with Jesus. The Eucharist is a major part of the theology and liturgy of Christian churches, although each gives it different definition and meaning. This gathering of Jesus and his twelve apostles is remembered throughout the Christian world on Holy or Maundy Thursday, which is the day before the crucifixion and three days before Easter.

But Leonardo did not depict this most solemn theological moment of the Last Supper. Rather, he painted the scene of consternation when Jesus told his disciples that one of them would betray him. The apostles were greatly distressed and immediately began to ask, "Is it I, Lord?" while simultaneously affirming that they could not possibly betray him and wondering whom it could be (Matthew 26:20–25; Mark 14:17–19). Leonardo's painting captures this dramatic moment. The thirteen figures are carefully balanced in a dramatic setting. Jesus sits calmly in the center, while the apostles in four groups of three are agitatedly gesturing and talking. Judas is the fourth figure on the right of Jesus (the viewer's left), the only one not displaying emotion. His face is partly in shadow, perhaps indicating that he was no longer in the light of Christ. With its three-dimensional interior space, table set with dishes, walls and ceiling, and landscape seen through the windows, the painting handles complicated perspective issues brilliantly. Most important, Leonardo pays careful attention to expressions and gestures, which seem to illuminate the inner thoughts of each apostle The painting is a tour de force in composition and expression.

Unfortunately, the painting began deteriorating almost immediately as a result of Leonardo's experimental techniques. The painting is not a fresco, in which paint is applied quickly to wet plaster. This would have required Leonardo to work quickly and without revising, something he never did. Rather, he painted in fits and starts, was constantly retouching, and often left paintings unfinished. In order to avoid making it a fresco, Leonardo applied a base made of various materials on the wall, then painted on this base. Unfortunately, Leonardo's experiment did not work. The paint began to chip and flake almost immediately. Repainting in later centuries made matters worse, although a restoration completed in 1999 has recovered some of its former beauty. Despite physical decay, the *Last Supper* is the best known religious painting of the Renaissance, perhaps of all time, and has been reproduced countless times.

Although the *Last Supper* was painted more than 500 years ago, it is a living work of art, because it is constantly being re-created. Numerous American Protestant churches re-create the *Last Supper* with members of the congregation. A far from exhaustive Internet search reveals that Baptist, Lutheran, Methodist, Presbyterian, and nondenominational Protestant churches in California, Illinois, Minnesota, Nebraska, North Carolina, Texas, Virginia, and the island of Okinawa have created *Last Supper* dramas or tableaus in 2003 and 2004.[11] Some of these churches have been doing so annually for up to twenty years. No doubt many other churches present *Last Supper* reenactments but do not post pictures on their Web sites or have no Web sites.

Members of the Ephesus Baptist Church of Raleigh, NC, present a Living Last Supper. [Photograph in *The News & Observer* of March 25, 2005, page B1. Reprinted by permission of *The News & Observer* of Raleigh, North Carolina]

MEMBERS OF THE CHRIST UNITED METHODIST CHURCH OF CHAPEL HILL, NC, PRESENT A LIVING LAST SUPPER. [PHOTOGRAPH IN *THE NEWS & OBSERVER* OF APRIL 7, 2004, PAGE C1. REPRINTED BY PERMISSION OF *THE NEWS & OBSERVER* OF RALEIGH, NORTH CAROLINA.]

The universal name for the reenactments is Living Last Supper. They are presented on Holy Thursday. A table with tablecloth and dishes is erected in the church. In more elaborate productions, a large painted background with a reproduction of the walls, ceiling, and windows of the original painting is added. The participants, who are members of the congregation, dress in the clothes of Jesus and the apostles. They grow beards and long hair. Exceptions are the closely shaven military men from the Koza Baptist Church in Okinawa, who must don false beards and long hair.[12] The Living Last Supper can be a tableau, with thirteen actors holding their positions while a narrator reads from the New Testament and explains the meaning. More often it becomes a religious drama, as Jesus and the apostles speak. The living apostles ask, is it I? They castigate themselves for their sins. They testify about how they met Jesus, and what Jesus means to them. Living Last

Supper dramas may take an hour or more. Participants usually follow texts written for these presentations. The Rev. Ernest K. Emurian of Las Vegas, author of many religious dramas, wrote one that is often used, but there are others. Overall, Living Last Suppers are part of a centuries-old tradition of dramatizing stories from the New and Old Testaments that began in the Middle Ages. Living Last Suppers continue that tradition with the help of the most famous religious painting of the Renaissance.

It is believed that Leonardo modeled the faces in his painting from living people, a common practice of Renaissance artists. This has led to the creation of a pious legend of uncertain origin that appears in almost identical form at several church Web sites. According to the story, Leonardo sought a model for the face of Jesus before turning to the other faces. After much searching, he found a young man of nineteen whose face radiated the innocence appropriate for the Son of God. Leonardo made the young man's face the face of Jesus. Leonardo then turned to the apostles. After seven years' labor (an exaggeration, because the painting was done in about three years), he was at an impasse. He had not been able to find anyone whose face was so marked by evil as to serve as the face of Judas. Then he heard about a hardened criminal awaiting execution for murder and other crimes in the dungeons of Rome. Leonardo went to Rome to see him and concluded that this vicious, depraved man had a countenance so evil that he could serve as the model for Judas who betrayed Jesus. He had him transported to Milan, where Leonardo copied his face into the painting. When he finished, the prisoner cried out, "Leonardo, don't you recognize me?" Leonardo stared at him intently and shook his head. He had never seen the man before meeting him in a Roman dungeon. The prisoner cried again, "Oh, God, have I fallen so low?" He then told Leonardo, "I am the same man you painted just seven years ago as the figure of Christ." His life of crime had so changed him that not even the amazingly keen eye of the painter recognized him. The story concludes with the moral that a life of sin and crime can change a perfectly innocent man into "the most traitorous character ever known in the history of the world."[13]

By contrast, Giorgio Vasari tells a more light-hearted story about the faces in his *Lives of the Artists* (1550; second edition 1568). The prior of the monastery was exasperated by Leonardo's slow pace, as the painter often spent half a day contemplating the painting without lifting his brush. The prior complained to the duke of Milan, who then called on Leonardo to explain in the presence of the prior why he was so slow. Leonardo answered that his inability to paint the heads of Jesus and Judas held him up. For the former, he was not looking for a human model, because no human could shine forth the divinity of Jesus. As for Judas, he was finding it very difficult to find any human being so depraved that he could betray the creator of the world. He would keep searching. But if he could not find someone, he would use the face of the prior as the model for Judas. The duke roared with laughter, and the prior bothered Leonardo no longer.[14]

The *Last Supper* has only men in it, which has led feminists to use the painting as a way of drawing attention to the slighting of female artists. In 1971, the American artist Mary Beth Edelson created a poster with her version of the *Last Supper* and called it "Some Living American Women Artists/Last Supper." Using Leonardo's room, table, and background, it shows a female "Jesus" seated in the center with twelve female artists in the same poses and gestures of the twelve apostles. The border of the painting adds the faces of many other American female artists.[15] An advertisement selling reproductions of the poster states that "The intention (of the poster) was to identify and commemorate women artists who were receiving little recognition at that time, as well as to tweak the nose of patriarchal religion for cutting women out of positions of power and authority."[16] A book makes a similar argument. *Who Cooked the Last Supper? The Women's History of the*

World by Rosalind Miles (New York: Three Rivers Press, 2001) seeks to overturn "the phallusy of history" and to celebrate the works and lives of women throughout history.

It is likely that the participants in Renaissance Weekends and Living Last Suppers come from different segments of American society. But like those who attend Renaissance Faires, they try to relive aspects of the Renaissance that they admire.

Chapter 4

THE RENAISSANCE MAN AND WOMAN

In 1998, a personal ad read: "Renaissance Man, former art student turned professional engineer/manager turned free-lance artist; very handsome; sensitive, financially secure. In search of white professional female with similar qualities and interests as soulmate for companionship and romance."[1] Why did this man believe that claiming to be a Renaissance man would improve his chances of finding a woman to love? The reason is that calling someone a Renaissance man or woman is very high praise.

Definition of a Renaissance Man

Jacob Burckhardt (1818–1897), in his famous book *The Civilization of the Renaissance in Italy* (1860), announced that the Renaissance produced a new kind of man, the all-sided or universal man. Such a man had a powerful and varied nature and had mastered all the elements of the culture of the age, as Burckhardt put it in grandiloquent language. The universal man of the Renaissance had wide interests, many skills, and did everything well. He was practical as well as learned, like the Florentine merchant who became wealthy through his commercial skills but also could read ancient philosophical texts in their original Latin or Greek.

Burckhardt's chief example of the universal Renaissance man was Leon Battista Alberti (1404–1471). According to contemporaries, as a child Alberti already performed extraordinary gymnastic feats. Although he learned music without a teacher, professional musicians admired his compositions. He painted and sculpted but was also skilled in physics and mathematics. His treatise on painting explained the new technique of creating the illusion of perspective on a flat surface. He wrote brilliantly in Latin and Italian in a variety of genres, including a mock funeral oration for his dog. Alberti was a gifted architect whose churches were admired then and now for the way that he used ancient architectural styles. He had the gift of prophecy, and he was moved by beautiful landscapes. He did everything well and with sympathetic intensity.[2] Burckhardt also allowed that Lorenzo de' Medici, the ruler of Florence who wrote elegant Latin and vernacular poetry and conversed with artists and learned men as an equal, was another. Another universal man was Leonardo da Vinci. From Burckhardt's description and the example of these extraordinary real men came the modern concept of "the Renaissance man," which Americans embrace. The Renaissance man or woman has skills in different fields and does everything well. Americans have added to the concept the expectation that the Renaissance man will enjoy success in whatever he does.

Renaissance Men, Students, and Jocks

Contemporary America certainly has Renaissance men. Sometimes people come to the realization that an individual was a Renaissance man while assessing his accomplishments after death. The writer of the obituary of the legal scholar Charles L. Black

(1915–2001) called him a Renaissance man because he had skills in quite different fields. He was a distinguished legal scholar and teacher who assisted in the famous *Brown v. Board of Education* case of 1954 in which the U.S. Supreme Court struck down segregated education. Black was an expert on civil rights law and on impeachment procedures, and he loved jazz. He published three volumes of poetry, painted landscapes in oil, and played the trumpet and the harmonica.[3] Archie K. Davis (1911–1998) was "North Carolina's Renaissance man, because his interests ranged far and wide, and everything he touched found success." Davis was a very successful banker who became rich. But he also served the greater good. He persuaded others to give large amounts of money to purchase the land for the Research Triangle Park in central North Carolina, which became the home of many high-tech companies and helped the state's economy. He contributed to, and raised money from others in order to establish the National Humanities Center, a research center for scholars from America and abroad located in North Carolina. In his sixties, Davis earned a Ph.D. in history; his dissertation became a book on the American Civil War that went into four printings.[4] Thus, Davis was a Renaissance man because he was skilled and successful in several fields and contributed to the common good.

Sometimes because of adverse social and political circumstances, a person is not hailed as a Renaissance man until long after his death. An example is James Weldon Johnson (1871–1938), an African-American author and activist whose writings were recently added to the Library of America, a canonical collection of the works of major American authors. He was a key figure in the Harlem Renaissance, a flowering of African-American literature, art, and music centered in New York City from about 1920 until the middle years of the 1930s. Johnson was also a lawyer, a teacher, and a diplomat who served in the United States Foreign Service.

And he composed "Lift Every Voice and Sing," an unofficial anthem for African Americans.[5] The actress Lauren Bacall called the English playwright Noël Coward (1899–1973) "a true Renaissance man—author, composer, actor, playwright, cabaret performer."[6] Numerous similar descriptions of Renaissance men and women can be found in newspapers and Web sites, with greater or lesser justification. The concept is well established.

One does not have to be dead to be acknowledged as a Renaissance man nor have quite such a long list of accomplishments. Americans like to see Renaissance men walking among them. Former president Bill Clinton has been hailed as a Renaissance man "because he knows more about more things than many people I've met."[7] The new librarian of the New York Public Library, appointed May 2004, is hailed as a Renaissance man "who combines the life of the mind with a practical and collaborative approach to serving the diverse needs of library clients."[8]

The University of Southern California encourages and rewards undergraduates who become Renaissance students. In 2000, it launched a Renaissance Scholars program in order to honor students who excel in different fields. The program views Leonardo da Vinci as its example. "Like Leonardo da Vinci, who was equally adept in the arts and sciences, Renaissance Scholars are students whose majors and minors are from widely separated fields of study."[9] The objective of the program is "breadth with depth, and the extraordinary release of intellectual energy that often occurs when two widely separate fields of thought are brought together in the same mind." The university believes that its Renaissance Scholars will be well prepared for the opportunities of the twenty-first century. In order to emphasize the point and to establish the link with the Renaissance, the Web site and literature for the program include Leonardo's self-portrait, his Vitruvian Man design, and other drawings of Leonardo.

Students who wish to become Renaissance Scholars must maintain a 3.5 overall grade point average and complete their degrees within five years. In the year 2004, the university recognized 239 graduating seniors as Renaissance Scholars. Some of their double majors, or majors and minors, were chemistry and art history, English and biomedical engineering, and piano performance and public policy. The graduating Renaissance Scholars are entitled to enter the Renaissance Scholar Prize Competition for which they must write an essay discussing how the two fields of study helped the student's development. Ten Renaissance Scholars received prizes of $10,000 to be used for graduate studies.

Athletes can be Renaissance men. The *Sporting News* called professional basketball player Terry Cummings "a genuine Renaissance man," because he was also a minister, a scholar, a writer, and a music producer.[10] When Duke University won the national collegiate championship in men's basketball in 2001, a local newspaper hailed its star player as "a Renaissance Man," who could be president one day. Maybe he will. But at present he is playing professional basketball.[11] The *Sporting News* also called an excellent high school football player "a seventeen-year-old Renaissance man" because he was an honors student who had studied classical piano for eleven years, the violin for five, and expected to study medicine in college.[12]

One of the reasons that sportswriters consider these athletes to be Renaissance men is that athletes are not expected to be competent in such areas as classical music and medicine. Because college athletes often do not do as well in the classroom as nonathletes, the term "Renaissance jocks" has arisen. It describes "athletes who have the discipline, creativity, and intelligence to pursue both excellence in the classroom and victories on the court, field, and track."[13]

In Search of Renaissance Men and Women

Obviously, Renaissance men or women are highly prized. But where are there? How do we find them? Easily. By publishing a personal "in search of" ad for a Renaissance man or woman. And the surprising news is that there are many Renaissance men and women out there. They have quite specific Renaissance skills and personality traits. Best of all, they are looking for love.

Renaissance men describe themselves as professionals who are handsome, well educated, and romantic. They usually call themselves romantic rather than sensual or sexy. Renaissance men are physically well proportioned. They come in all ages, with a preponderance in their mid-forties to the late fifties. They are well traveled and enjoy the arts, typically classical music, opera, and/or jazz. They play tennis and ski.

Here is a typical personal ad from a Renaissance Man:

Renaissance Man—D[ivorced]W[hite]M[ale], former art student turned professional engineer/manager turned free-lance artist; very handsome, looks youthful 50s, 5'10", trim & fit, neatly trimmed beard; honest, sensitive, self-aware, wry sense of humor; financially secure, ethnically Jewish but non-religious, N[on]S[moking]; interests include the arts, classical music, theatre, museums, festivals, fine dining & ethnic food, gourmet cooking, skiing (advanced), & golf (duffer). I[n]S[earch]O[f] very pretty, intelligent, vivacious, S[ingle]/D[ivorced] W[hite]P[rofessional]F[emale] (40s-50s) w/similar qualities & interests (except for the beard) as soulmate for companionship, romance & L[ong]T[erm]R[elationship].

This personal ad appeared in *The Washingtonian*, a monthly magazine published in Washington, DC, in 1998. It generated sixty-two responses, four times the average number.[14] Who wouldn't want to meet this Renaissance man?

Sometimes the men who place the ads offer proof that they are truly Renaissance men by proclaiming their accomplishments in detail: "Renaissance Man, Stanford graduate, PhD, athletic, sensual, sensitive, 5'10", 175 lbs, seeking comely enantiomorph, 45+, LTR. Concerts, opera, jazz."[15] Does a Stanford Ph.D. make him more of a Renaissance man than a doctorate from the University of California at Berkeley or any other school? The use of "enantiomorph" demonstrates that this Renaissance man possesses esoteric technical knowledge and a large vocabulary. An enantiomorph means someone who combines opposites such as can happen in the structures of crystals. In other words, this Renaissance man is looking for a woman who is somewhat different but will blend with him to make a harmonious whole. He is showing off his recondite knowledge. One wonders if this ad intrigued or irritated potential respondents, by causing them to go to the dictionary in order to understand what this Renaissance man was looking for.

About twice as many Renaissance men search for women as Renaissance women search for men, which can only mean that there are more Renaissance men than Renaissance women in America. Although less numerous, Renaissance women are also attractive, accomplished, successful, and have diverse interests. And they are better looking and more youthful than Renaissance men. For example, one Renaissance woman is a 5'6" Ingrid Bergman/ Meryl Streep look-alike. (How can she look like both?) She is in her fabulous fifties, but looks forty. She is a redhead with a peaches & cream complexion, well educated, a great cook, and has a sense of humor. A brunette Renaissance woman has beauty, brains, and balance. She is single, white, professional, 5'6", weighs 125 lb, is in her early forties but looks a decade younger. She has many talents and avocations, loves animals and nature, and "seeks life as a soulful adventurer." A "Renaissance woman of the year" is "a cultural connoisseur, an outdoor adventurer, and a savvy investor." A Renaissance adventuress who loves life, laughter, nature, and music describes herself as "Rubenesque," another Renaissance image. Women of a certain size writing personal ads often call themselves "Rubenesque," a reference to the famous late Renaissance painter Peter Paul Rubens (1577–1640), whose canvasses featured generously proportioned women with lovely rosy complexions.[16] And because they are usually scantily clad, one can see a great deal of their lovely flesh. Once again, making reference to a painter of the Renaissance conveys positive meaning.

Sometimes non-Renaissance women look for a Renaissance man. One such ad searches for a Renaissance man who is fit, thirty-seven to forty-seven years of age, can ride a Harley motorcycle to the theater, glide between rock and jazz, and likes candlelight dinners and picnics. A man who modestly does not call himself a Renaissance man, but searches for a Renaissance woman, mentions his many accomplishments and attractions at greater length than the desired qualities of the Renaissance woman he seeks. Nevertheless, she should be able to match him and be active, attractive, have many interests and talents, be gentle and passionate, and be willing to go camping, followed immediately by a concert of classical music.[17] One hopes that she will be allowed time to change clothes between camping and concert.

In the best of all possible worlds, a Renaissance man deserves a Renaissance woman and vice versa. In one ad, a Renaissance woman describes herself as an "international Town & Country girl executive who is athletic, worldly, bilingual, and enjoys the finer things in life." She is a "Daisy Fuentes/Jackie Onassis" type. (*Town & Country* is a magazine that emphasizes fine clothing, jewelry, dining, travel, and homes. Daisy Fuentes is a beautiful Cuban-born actress who starred in the film of that name.) She searches for a Renaissance man who is comfortable at Maxime's or McDonald's, is able to converse on topics ranging from theology to the new hair color of the model Linda Evangelista, and has a body like that of

Jesse Ventura, the wrestler and former governor of Minnesota.[18] Let us hope that they find each other.

Some Renaissance women seek other women, and some Renaissance men seek other men. The qualities sought of a Renaissance partner of the same sex are intelligence, sensitivity, humor, and the ability to pursue and enjoy diverse interests, just like heterosexual Renaissance persons. But ads in search of homosexual or lesbian Renaissance partners give little information about professional accomplishments and worldly success.[19]

Men and women searching for lovers of the opposite sex like to compare themselves to famous Renaissance lovers. Romeo searches for Juliet and, less often, Juliet searches for Romeo. Other great Renaissance lovers can also be found in contemporary America. One man calls himself Don Quixote in search of Dulcinea.[20] Don Quixote was the idealistic would-be knight who loved the lady Dulcinea from afar in the great novel *Don Quixote* (part one 1605, part two 1615) by the Spanish Renaissance author Miguel de Cervantes (1547–1616).

Although none of the Renaissance men or women appearing in personal ads claims to be as supremely talented as Leon Battista Alberti, Lorenzo de' Medici, or Leonardo da Vinci, they certainly are beautiful, handsome, gifted, successful, affluent, stylish, and have wide interests. The emphasis on highly talented and successful Renaissance men and women produces the occasional rueful inversion. After being called lazy, ugly, and lacking personality, a character in a Dilbert comic strip plaintively asks, "Would you say I'm kind of a Renaissance loser?"[21] And it can lead to protest. The praise for and emphasis on male sensitivity led one woman to protest: "If a woman shows compassion, she's overly sensitive. If a man shows compassion, he's a Renaissance man."[22]

How to Be Like Leonardo Da Vinci

If one is not a Renaissance man or woman, how can one become such a talented and accomplished person? A book with a plan teaches Americans how to become Renaissance men and women. And not just any Renaissance man or woman, but Leonardo da Vinci.

The secret is found in *How to Think like Leonardo da Vinci: Seven Steps to Genius Every Day* (1998) by Michael J. Gelb. The author is a teacher of creative thinking, a motivational speaker, conductor of "Executive Renaissance seminars," and founder of a "High Performance Learning Center." According to the author's Web site, the book has sold more than 300,000 copies and has been translated into eighteen languages.[23]

The book begins with a brief summary of the historical Renaissance, viewing it as a period in which fundamental assumptions, preconceptions, and beliefs were transformed. The book observes that today's world is changing even more dramatically through the expansion of knowledge, capitalism, and interconnection. The modern Renaissance man or woman is a well-rounded person who has a good knowledge of the traditional liberal arts. He or she is computer literate, aware of the potential of the human brain, and globally aware. Modern Renaissance men and women see racism, sexism, religious persecution, homophobia, and nationalism as aspects of an earlier, more primitive stage of man's evolution.[24] But the book does not dwell on the mildly liberal political and cultural values of the Renaissance man. Rather, it offers a program to enable the individual to become more creative intellectually and to live his or her life as a work of art. This is the way that individuals become Renaissance men and women.

Leonardo da Vinci teaches us how. According to Gelb, Leonardo's greatest strength was in his ideas. The book then presents ways to imitate Leonardo's thinking. The book includes many quotes of Leonardo's striking observations about nature, plus many reproductions of his drawings, paintings, and inventions.

At the same time, the book sees Leonardo as a great scientist who pioneered modern comparative anatomy and botanical science. This is not true. Leonardo made many acute observations as a result of his dissections of bodies and observations of nature and had ideas that were centuries ahead of his time. But he did not turn his observations and dreams into science, because, in addition to observing phenomena, the scientist must explain with a theory or law why the phenomena acts as it does. Once an explanatory theory is proposed, he can determine whether the theory accounts for other observations, he can devise experiments to expand the theory, and he can predict future phenomena. Most important, other scientists can test the theory with their own experiments. In other words, science both makes perceptive observations of nature and offers explanations for the observations, which other scientists may test, confirm, deny, modify, or expand. Leonardo never turned his observations into science. Galileo Galilei did and is rightly acclaimed a great Renaissance scientist. Gelb's claim that Leonardo was a great scientist is a common misunderstanding of both Leonardo and the nature of science.

Never mind. Gelb uses Leonardo as the perfect example of the acutely perceptive individual Renaissance man. He derives from Leonardo's life and thought "seven steps to genius every day." If the reader will follow these steps, he or she will think like Leonardo. To emphasize the connection of the method with Leonardo and the Renaissance, Gelb presents the principles in Italian.

Because curiosity was the key to Leonardo's creative problem solving, the first principle is "Curiosità" (capitalized even though Italian does not capitalize common nouns). Gelb gives several examples of Leonardo's splendid curiosity, then offers a method to become curious like Leonardo. Keep a notebook, as Leonardo did, then list 100 questions that are most important to you. Choose the ten most significant. Then select a theme for the day, such as emotions, seeing, listening, or animals. Record your observations on this theme for the entire day. Do not worry about speculations, opinions, or theories. Just observe. Then do contemplation and stream of consciousness exercises. Write down whatever comes into your head even if it is gibberish. This is a sign that you are overriding the superficial aspects of the thought process. Eventually your intuitive intelligence will break through. Gelb criticizes ordinary schooling for not developing curiosity, delight in ambiguity, and question-asking skill. "The authority-pleasing, question-suppressing, rule-following approach to education may have served to provide society with assembly-line workers and bureaucrats, but it does not do much to prepare us for a new Renaissance."[25]

The second principle is "Dimostrazione," or demonstration, which is learning by experience. Demonstration is put into practice through self-assessment, which includes ways to learn from mistakes and to avoid making the same mistake twice. Gelb reports that senior business executives say that failure to heed their own experiences is the prime cause of their worst decisions. Dimostrazione is designed to avoid this. Gelb urges the reader to examine his or her beliefs and opinions from at least three different perspectives. Try to see them from the perspective of a different country or race; interview friends for different perspectives. Practice resisting the onslaughts of advertising. Then create self-affirmations.

Next comes "Sensazione" or sensation, which is the refinement of the senses, especially that of sight. It means learning to see the world more clearly and perceiving what you missed through failure to concentrate. It includes the practice of visualization, which means consciously focusing the mind on imagining a desired process or outcome. One way to achieve greater sensation is to look closely at sunsets; another is to visit art museums with purpose and notebook. Ignore the names of painters and titles of works, but look at the painting and jot down your perceptions. The same method continues through hearing, in which Gelb strongly endorses listening to classical music in order to cultivate appreciation of sound and subtleties of hearing. To improve taste and smell, taste different wines, then describe each stage of the tasting process precisely and poetically. Eventually one should combine the senses. For example, one should listen to music and then express one's impressions by drawing shapes and colors. As an aside, Gelb emphasizes the importance of attractive, well-designed, and colorful workplaces. He notes that companies want their employees to "think out of the box," then confine them to colorless boxes.

Next comes "Sfumato," which means literally "gone up in smoke." Although Gelb does not mention it, sfumato is an art historical term used in both Italian and English to describe a painting style or a picture characterized by vaguely outlined figures and hazy appearance. For Gelb, sfumato means a willingness to embrace ambiguity, paradox, and uncertainty, just as Leonardo did. Today's individual should also learn to make friends with ambiguity. One exercise is to try to smile like Mona Lisa, because she is the ultimate expression of ambiguity. Does this change your thinking? Embrace ambiguity and trust your gut is the argument.

Then come "Arte/Scienza," whose goal is to develop a balance between science and imagination. There is considerable discussion of "mind mapping," which is a method for discovering the maximum number of creative associations for any key word. It includes illustrating relationships by writing words and images on a large sheet of paper, then drawing lines between them, and using colors, highlighting, and other devices to show further links. The goal is to see associations and connections. Mind mapping is presented as a tool for simplifying complex tasks, such as strategic planning and preparation for a presentation. Throughout the book, Gelb promises that his techniques will help in the workplace.

Then comes "Corporalità," corporality, which means the cultivation of grace, ambidexterity, fitness, and poise. According to Gelb, Leònardo was an athletic man with remarkable physical energy, whom one can emulate with a good fitness program. Gelb endorses Leonardo's rules for good health, which are similar to today's rules with one exception: Leonardo tells us to avoid doctors. Gelb adds "the Da Vinci Diet," which is the normal healthy diet recommended by almost every health organization today, but garnished with Leonardo's axioms and some Italian eating practices, such as drinking quantities of mineral water and wine, and eating much fruit. The larger purpose of Corporalità is to learn to release tension and feel good, so that the brain will work better.

The last of the seven principles for learning to think like Leonardo is "Connessione," the interconnectedness of all things and phenomena. It is the ability to see relationships and patterns, to make unusual connections and combinations. Interconnectedness is the core of creativity, and Gelb includes many comments from Leonardo to drive home the point, including his vague musings about how the microcosm (the individual) is part of the macrocosm (the world), a Renaissance commonplace, about which Leonardo had nothing interesting to say. One can practice connessione by making connections in the mind between quite disparate objects, such as an oak leaf and a human hand, mathematics and Leonardo's *Last Supper*, a pig's tail and a bottle of wine. Another way is to imagine dialogues between different people, such as Muhammed Ali and Mona Lisa, Bill Gates and Lorenzo de' Medici. The book concludes with a chapter on "the beginner's Da Vinci drawing course," a primer on how to draw.

How to Think like Leonardo is a self-improvement book that ties twentieth-century self-awareness techniques to Leonardo da Vinci and the Italian Renaissance. The book's format, with its numerous quotes and illustrations from Leonardo's works and references to his accomplishments, helps make the case. The book is not ostensibly about getting ahead, even though it hints that following its principles will lead to worldly success. Rather, it promises to enable the reader to think like Leonardo da Vinci. The promise is appealing because Americans admire individual creativity and long to be self-aware and well rounded. *How to Think Like Leonardo da Vinci* assumes that the reader is interested in higher things and endorses art and classical music. Will following the principles of Curiosità, Dimostrazione, and so on, make one think like Leonardo? It is not likely, but it will do no harm.

Conclusion

The concept of a Renaissance man or woman is a cherished legacy from the Renaissance and a way of demonstrating the admiration that we have for those who are wonderfully accomplished. The particular meaning of Renaissance man or woman is that he or she is accomplished in several areas, especially in skills that are very different from one another. Today, a person must have native ability, years of education, much application, and probably a bit of luck in order to achieve very much in one area of learning, life, or the workplace. Thus, it is no wonder that we honor those with accomplishments in several fields. Praise for a Renaissance man or woman counters what some see as overspecialization in education, career, and research. A Renaissance man or woman is the antithesis of the specialist. The respect accorded to Renaissance men and women also reflects the belief or hope that an individual highly skilled in disparate fields may combine those skills and produce a scientific or technological breakthrough. This is probably part of the rationale behind the Renaissance Scholars program at the University of Southern California and the book that teaches the reader to think like Leonardo. A Renaissance man or woman is a creative person.

The Renaissance man or woman is an individual. There are no Renaissance departments or Renaissances teams. The terms "Renaissance man" and "Renaissance woman" honor the individual for his or her achievement. This is simultaneously the way that Americans see the Renaissance and a fundamental part of American ideology.

American culture has added two particularly American requirements to the traditional definition of a Renaissance man or woman. He or she must be successful in more than one field; it is not enough to be merely competent. A brilliant medical scholar who is a mediocre artist is not a Renaissance man. Second, as "in search of" ads explain, the Renaissance man or woman should be handsome or beautiful, physically fit, youthful in appearance, sensitive, and romantic. A man who is overweight, looks his age, and is an insensitive clod cannot be a Renaissance man, whatever his accomplishments. One wonders if Leonardo da Vinci, who was not handsome and did look his age in his self-portrait, would qualify? Or Lorenzo de' Medici, who was crippled by gout and had a crooked nose? Were Leon Battista Alberti and Michelangelo sensitive and romantic? The standards for today's Renaissance men and women are very high.

Finally, those who praise today's Renaissance men and women never suggest that they had a lot of help in achieving greatness. The descriptions do not mention the advantage of being born into wealth or having the luck to be in the right place at the right time. The Renaissance man concept means that the person accomplished great deeds through his own efforts. This is another example of the connection that American culture makes between the Renaissance and individualism.

Chapter 5

RENAISSANCE BRAND NAMES AND ICONS

E very city and numerous small towns have businesses that include Renaissance in their names: Renaissance Financial Planning, Renaissance Limousine Service, Renaissance Vineyard, and countless others. Product manufacturers evoke famous figures of the Renaissance: Botticelli Chocolates and Michael Angelo's Pizza. The computer world has embraced the Renaissance. The *Mona Lisa* painting has become an icon denoting mystery even for Monica Lewinsky, who was not mysterious at all. Medici, Romeo and Juliet, and Savonarola have instant iconic meaning. What is going on?

Businesses use the names of well-known individuals and images from the Renaissance to sell their products and services because Americans see the Renaissance as a period of great accomplishment, beauty, and creativity. Some individuals and works of art are so recognized that they have become icons; that is, they have a meaning that is instantly understood. Renaissance icons are well-enough integrated into American life and values that they easily lend themselves to comedy and parody.

Eating and Sleeping the Renaissance

A friend gave me a box of Botticelli chocolates. *Botticelli . . . the Art of Chocolate* is a brand name of Dynamic Chocolates, a manufacturer of boxed chocolates, with a head office and production center in Delta, British Columbia, plus additional production facilities in Utah and in Ohio. The chocolate maker's Web site states that "Fine art inspires fine chocolate. Botticelli's miniature masterpieces are meticulously crafted, aspiring to the same classical perfection as those of the famous artist." These are the "chocolatiers' works of art."[1]

The chocolate maker claims that it produces classic, tasteful chocolates, delicately flavored and not too sweet, comparable to the delicate paintings of the great Florentine artist, Sandro Botticelli (1445–1510). His Birth of Venus (known familiarly as "Venus on the Half Shell") and Primavera ("Spring") were inspired by mythological themes; their perfection makes them among the best-loved paintings of the Italian Renaissance. I found Botticelli chocolates to be quite good.

For those who want more than chocolates, famous artists from the Italian Renaissance offer fine dining all over America.[2] There are Botticelli Restaurants in Sioux City, Iowa; Rapid City, South Dakota; and Casper, Wyoming—making the Great Plains a culinary Renaissance. There is also a Botticelli Café in Seattle, Washington, a Café Botticelli in Houston, Texas, and a Botticelli Trattoria in South Miami, Florida.

Not to be outdone by his fellow Florentine, Michelangelo has restaurants, pizzerias, and even coffee houses from coast to coast, including New York City, Houston, Tucson, and Seattle. The Michelangelo restaurant in Suffolk County, Long Island, modestly states that "as Michelangelo was passionate about his art, the staff at Michelangelo restaurant is passionate about its cooking. . . .

Every dish is a masterpiece."[3] Sometimes they offer more than food: Michelangelo's Restaurante in Houston "serves pasta and romance in the same house." It seems that even as a cook and a restauranteur, Michelangelo is a Renaissance man skilled in many things. Some Renaissance restaurants offer political food. During the 2004 presidential campaign, Alessandra Kerry spoke on behalf of her father at the Michelangelo Coffee House in Madison, Wisconsin.

Just as he competed with Michelangelo in painting, so Leonardo da Vinci competes with him in eating. There are Leonardo da Vinci restaurants, lounges, and pizzerias in Jamaica, New York; Chicago, Illinois; Romulus, Michigan; Birmingham, Alabama; Huntington Beach, California; and elsewhere. The diner at Renaissance restaurants may sip from Michelangelo Flute or Michelangelo Masterpiece wine glasses, products of Libbey Inc., a manufacturer of glassware for food service operations.[4] And Leonardo's mysterious Mona Lisa urges the wine drinker to purchase a corkscrew named "the original Rabbit" to open the bottle of wine to pour into Michelangelo Flutes. The advertisement admits that "Mona Lisa . . . can't open wine in three seconds like the Rabbit. Her inscrutable smile, however, may be due to the wine she drank while sitting for her portrait." The person who does not want to go to a Renaissance restaurant, but still wishes to eat the food of a great artist, may buy "Michael Angelo's" pizza, lasagna, or veal parmesan frozen entrées at the supermarket. The package depicts God creating Adam from the Sistine Chapel ceiling and carries the words, "the art of Italian cuisine."[5]

There are not very many restaurants named for William Shakespeare, which may be a negative judgment on English cuisine. But there are restaurants named for Romeo and Juliet, which usually serve Italian food. On the other hand, one Web site named "Shakespeare Restaurant" is not a restaurant at all but the gateway to a service that sells term papers to students, including an

If you can't give Dad the original Mona Lisa, give him the original Rabbit.

Dad may have a broken lever corkscrew in a drawer somewhere. But it's not the original Rabbit Corkscrew. And chances are it has no warranty, while the Rabbit's is good for ten years. Even if you could afford to give Mona Lisa to Dad, she can't open wine in three seconds like the Rabbit. Her inscrutable smile, however, may be due to the wine she drank while sitting for her portrait.

Where To Go Rabbit Hunting:
Crate & Barrel, Sur La Table, Bloomingdale's, Marshall Field's, Total Wine & More, Hecht's/Strawbridge's, Beverages & More, IWAwine.com

THE USE OF MONA LISA IN AN ADVERTISEMENT FOR "THE ORIGINAL RABBIT," A CORKSCREW, IN *THE ATLANTIC*, VOL. 296 NO. 1 (JULY–AUGUST 2005). [REPRODUCED WITH PERMISSION OF METROKANE.]

abundance of papers on Shakespeare and his plays. In other words, Shakespeare Restaurant provides a large menu of research papers for students willing to pay others to do their work. The prices are $8.95/page for previously prepared term papers and $18.95/page for custom-researched papers, in which the service researches and writes a paper on a subject named by the student.[6] At those prices, an honest student willing to do his or her own research and writing could afford a fabulous meal on the money saved. That is food for thought.

If dining at Renaissance restaurants adds undesirable pounds, the Da Vinci diet is prepared to take them off. It is the brainchild of a baker concerned that Americans should not reject bread for having too many carbohydrates. The Da Vinci diet emphasizes foods from areas around the Mediterranean Sea, the lands of Greece and Rome, and the Italian Renaissance, such as fish, cheese, vegetables, meat, nuts, wine, and bread. It believes that the perfect diet consists of 52 percent carbohydrates, 20 percent protein, and 28 percent fat, proportions based on an ancient mathematical formula. The Da Vinci diet adheres to federal eating guidelines pretty closely except for offering fewer carbohydrates and more protein.[7]

The Renaissance was known for its elegant palaces where kings, princes, nobles, and cardinals lived. Americans may also have Renaissance roofs over their heads, if they can afford them. "Renaissance" is the name of a golf course community with some 500 homes on 501 acres in Fort Myers, Florida. A private 18–hole golf course, clubhouse, swimming pool, spa, exercise facilities, tennis courts, and other amenities are part of this Renaissance. The cost of the Mediterranean-style homes ranges from about $450,000 to more than $2,000,000, which suggests that although the residents might not be as rich as Renaissance nobles, they are not poor.[8] But America offers less expensive Renaissance housing as well. For example, there is a planned Renaissance Community of single-family homes in Hendersonville, North Carolina, in the mountains of the western part of the state. Or one can live in the Renaissance III housing development in Longmont, Colorado, where homes named "The Hamlet," "The Hathaway" (for Anne Hathaway, Shakespeare's wife), the MacBeth, and the Othello may be purchased for as little as $225,000. But what woman would want to live in a house named for Shakespeare's Moor, who smothered his wife in their marriage bed?

There are many Renaissance apartment complexes across the nation, such as Renaissance Place Apartments in Buffalo, New York. Senior citizens may wish to live in Renaissance Senior Living, a copyrighted name for an assisted living community in Santa Monica, California. Those who cannot afford to live in the Renaissance all the time may still book a room in a Renaissance Hotel, a chain of upscale hotels owned by Marriott. One advertisement for Renaissance Hotels uses Leonardo da Vinci's *Mona Lisa* painting to boast of the service to guests: "Pleasing guests is an art we take quite seriously at Renaissance Hotels and Resorts." The advertisement finishes by saying that "It's time for a Renaissance." The hotel chain uses Renaissance and mentions art in order to convince potential guests of its excellence.

For many years, Renaissance Cruise offered both Renaissance food and lodging on its cruises in the Mediterranean Sea and elsewhere. Although it declared bankruptcy in late September 2001, its ships have been leased or sold to other companies. Two of them are the Columbus and the Magellan, the latter named for Ferdinand Magellan (c. 1480–1521), the Portuguese explorer whose small fleet sailed around the world between 1519 and 1522, although he died in the Philippines. He is considered the greatest explorer of the Renaissance and, perhaps, of all time. A mail-order house for women's clothing offers a Botticelli dress and a Da Vinci sweater, just the right clothing for a Renaissance cruise.[9] One can also purchase luggage, maps, clothing, and much else in preparation for a Renaissance voyage at Magellan's, a mail-order house for travel supplies, located in Santa Barbara, California. The wistful, stay-at-home traveler who cannot afford a cruise can still enjoy the soft comfort of Renaissance towels, advertised as luxurious towels made in England of Egyptian cotton, from several mail-order houses for linens.

Even today, one may commission a Renaissance artist to create a work of art. Well, not quite. But the business of reproducing and marketing of Renaissance sculptures suitable for garden and lawn is thriving. For $1,500, one may buy a 30-inch-high hard plaster reproduction of the head of Michelangelo's *David* to mount in the garden. The catalogue assures the buyer that "This rare authentic cast of Michelangelo's *David* will add Renaissance grandeur to your grounds." Or for $400, one may buy a 45-inch fiberglass reproduction of the entire statue along with a 28-inch column on which to mount it.[10] Anyone can have a garden of Renaissance art.

Renaissance Businesses and Professions

Large cities and small towns across America have businesses whose names begin with Renaissance. Chicago has Renaissance Adult Day

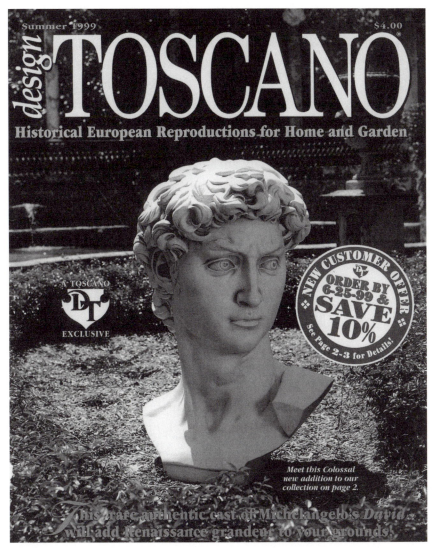

REPRODUCTION OF THE HEAD OF MICHELANGELO'S *DAVID* FROM THE COVER OF THE
1999 CATALOGUE OF *DESIGN TOSCANO*, A FIRM WHICH SELLS REPRODUCTIONS OF
RENAISSANCE SCULPTURES. [REPRODUCED WITH PERMISSION OF DESIGN TOSCANO OF
ELK GROVE, IL.]

Services Inc., Renaissance Financial Planning, Renaissance Mortgage Corporation, and Renaissance Remodeling, among many others. A number of financial advice firms across the country manage to include Renaissance and Capital in their names. It is not likely that they inform their customers that the best-known financial institution of the Italian Renaissance, the Medici Bank, failed in the late fifteenth century, because Lorenzo de' Medici did not manage it well. Perhaps he was too busy being a Renaissance man ruling Florence and writing poetry to pay attention to the family business. Cleveland, Ohio, has a Renaissance Barber Shop, Renaissance Executive Limousine Service, Renaissance Garage, Renaissance Health Plan, Renaissance Janitorial Services, Renaissance Management, Renaissance Painting (to paint houses), and Renaissance Plastics. Madison, Wisconsin, has Renaissance Clocks, Renaissance Kids Inc., Renaissance for Singles, and Renaissance Travel. Buffalo, New York, has Renaissance Refinishing Inc., Renaissance Salon & Day Spa, and Renaissance Studios. San Jose, California, has Renaissance Builders, Renaissance Interior Design, Renaissance Painting and Decorating, Renaissance Roofing Inc., Renaissance Stone Care and Waterproofing, and Renaissance Women Property Management. Small towns also have Renaissance businesses, such as Renaissance Antiques and Reproductions in Kalispell, Montana, a town of 12,000 inhabitants. Bozeman, Montana, a little larger, has Renaissance Precious Metals, which buys and sells gold, silver, and platinum. And in the great outdoors further north, Renaissance Energy Ltd. looks for oil in western Canada.

Renaissance Vineyard and Winery of Oregon House, California, in the foothills of the Sierra Nevada, takes its name from the rebirth of winemaking in the harsh land and climate of northern Yuba County in the 1970s. Renaissance Greenhouses of Seattle, Washington, advertises that you may have "your own Renaissance" by hiring the company to build a greenhouse for you. "A Renaissance greenhouse is the perfect centerpiece for your landscape design . . . ." Here Renaissance means beauty, harmony, and "Old World details and components."[11] Even businesses not named Renaissance sometimes have a Renaissance man on the premises. Newspaper advertisements for Midas in Durham, Raleigh, and Garner, North Carolina, show an auto mechanic who says "Some call me a 'jack-of-all-trades.' I prefer 'renaissance man.' We are experts at brakes, factory scheduled maintenance, oil changes, tire rotations, mufflers, and a lot more."[12] Some cities have Renaissance shopping centers. For example, the Renaissance Center at Southpoint is a shopping center in Durham, North Carolina, consisting of 206,000 square feet of retail, restaurant, and office space. Naturally, the new road from the highway to the Renaissance Center is named "Renaissance Parkway."

It is clear that businesses and marketers use the name and icons of the Renaissance in the belief that they resonate positively. But how so? What affirmative meaning does the label Renaissance convey? The words "art," "classic," "elegant," "rich color," and "sensual" appear repeatedly in advertisements for Renaissance products. When the words Renaissance or

A BOTTLE OF RENAISSANCE WINE. [REPRODUCED WITH PERMISSION OF RENAISSANCE VINEYARD AND WINERY OF OREGON HOUSE, CA.]

Botticelli are attached to clothing and household items, such as dresses and towels, they are described as rich in texture and color, with maroon and gold favored. Thus, Renaissance signifies artistic, classy, elegant, sophisticated, tasteful, decorative, richly colored, and tastefully ornate.

When using a painting of Botticelli or Michelangelo without identification, the advertiser expects that the viewer will recognize the Renaissance image or artifact. Moreover, the business using Renaissance in its name or great images and individuals from the period assumes that potential customers have a positive view of the Renaissance as an age of genius, art, and beauty. Therefore, the person who responds to the advertisement or patronizes the business must be knowledgeable, sophisticated, and have refined taste. The business or marketer pays potential customers the compliment of seeing them as cultured.

Not all commercial evocations of the Renaissance are classy, elegant, and sophisticated. In the late 1980s, four Teenage Mutant Ninja Turtles, which were children's toys and cartoon characters, boasted the names Leonardo, Raphael, Michelangelo, and Donatello. The manufacturer and advertiser could use these names without explanation because these Renaissance artists are instantly recognized and admired. The Ninja Turtles were extraordinarily popular for a brief time, then faded.

Other commercial uses trade on the positive view of the Renaissance for the purposes of marketing kitsch. One may buy pop art reproductions of Renaissance paintings on many everyday objects. For example, coffee mugs, beer steins, mouse pads, sweatshirts, tee shirts, tote bags, and women's thong underwear, all bearing the image of Botticelli's *Birth of Venus*, may be purchased. Men may also proclaim their admiration for Botticelli's painting by wearing ties with reproductions of Botticelli's *Venus*.[13]

Renaissance also means the rebirth of small business. The Renaissance Entrepreneurship Center (REC) in San Francisco was founded in 1985 to offer training to people who want to start their own businesses.[14] In its evening classes, successful entrepreneurs teach such subjects as how to start up, advice for women launching businesses, planning, and e-mail marketing. In 1990, it added the Renaissance Business Incubator to offer support services for fledgling entrepreneurs. Renaissance Incubator provides low-cost office space, reception services, high-speed Internet connections, monthly group forums with guest speakers, and consultations with experts for periods of six months to three years. Over the years, the REC has helped many entrepreneurs get started.

The founders chose the name Renaissance because they wanted to bring about a rebirth of jobs and wealth in San Francisco through the creation of small businesses at a time when people were deserting the city for lack of jobs and opportunity. The Renaissance

A TIE WITH A REPRODUCTION OF *BIRTH OF VENUS* PAINTED CA. 1484 BY SANDRO BOTTICELLI (1446–1510). [SOLD BY NECKTIES.COM, OWNED BY PAUL F. GRENDLER.]

Entrepreneurship Center especially wanted to encourage entrepreneurship in previously disadvantaged segments of the population. Although they did not necessarily have the historical Renaissance as a model, they believe that there are similarities because, like the Renaissance, their organization relies on creative energy, emphasizes renewal, and gives birth to microenterprises.[15]

Lawyers are not far behind. The Renaissance Lawyer Society is a national nonprofit educational organization founded in 2001 in order to address "issues of innovation and transformation in the legal profession, and (to) support lawyers."[16] It promotes "renaissance law," an umbrella term for innovative approaches including visionary law, transformational law, holistic law, and/or collaborative law. All emphasize practicing law in new ways. They mean abandoning the win-at-any-cost approach in favor of collaboration, conciliation, mediation, and taking into account the best interests of clients in ways that go beyond winning the case. The Renaissance lawyer wishes to reintroduce the human and compassionate element into the practice of law, according to the society. For example, in collaborative law, the attorneys work with the parties in order to arrive at a solution in which both may win. The parties share information and agree that they will not litigate during the process. And if litigation is unavoidable, Renaissance lawyers strive to do it with compassion, kindness, and respect. Renaissance lawyers aspire to be peacemakers and healers.

The Renaissance Lawyer Society also wishes to restore the spirits of jaded lawyers who have lost the altruistic goals that inspired them to enter law school. According to its Web site, one third to two thirds of lawyers want to leave the profession, one in five is clinically depressed, one in eleven thinks of suicide on a regular basis, and "too many lawyers are actually killing themselves." The Renaissance Lawyer Society wants lawyers and other legal professionals "to experience satisfaction and joy in the law." A Renaissance lawyer is a balanced human being who has time for family and to practice yoga. He or she is happy with practicing law and with life. Annual dues are $100, for which the member receives a monthly electronic news bulletin, a quarterly electronic newsletter, invitations to workshops and annual conferences, and the opportunity to join with others who share the values of the Renaissance Law Society. It is too bad that there was no such society in the Renaissance itself, because it was a litigious era, and the legal profession had a bad reputation then, as it does now. Maybe lawyers are destined to be unpopular in all ages.

The Renaissance and the Computer

Many computer professionals judge the invention of the computer to be a revolution in the diffusion of knowledge comparable with the invention of printing. They point out that both printing and the computer were technological inventions that produced enormous advances in the availability and diffusion of information. More ambitious computer scholars make larger claims. They compare the invention of the computer with the Renaissance as a whole and see more subtle and more profound changes coming from the computer. Realizing that the Renaissance involved much more than diffusing more knowledge through printing, they see it as an age of great originality and creativity in ideas and believe that the computer can do the same. They believe that the computer is as revolutionary as the Renaissance because it makes possible the generation of new kinds of knowledge. The comparisons are interesting.

The New Renaissance: Computers and the Next Level of Civilization (New York: Oxford University Press, 1998) by Douglas S. Robertson, a British mathematician and computer expert, argues that the abundance of information gathered and diffused through printing helped make possible the great accomplishments of the Renaissance. Although printing at first produced much misinformation, such as reports of dragons and unicorns, he writes, the quantity of misinformation dropped quickly, because printing made it easier to check and correct error. And the amount and availability of accurate information soared. So it is with computers, he believes. Moreover, the invention of printing led to new ways of organizing information. (Although the author does not offer evidence, this is true. A simple example is that printed books had much more comprehensive and sophisticated indices than did manuscripts, and this encouraged more analytical and organizational approaches to knowledge as a whole.) Computers will do the same. Robertson argues that a greater quantity of information produces qualitative changes in thinking, that is, more information encourages new theories. Robertson correctly notes that in the Renaissance one revolutionary development, printing, was followed by other revolutions, such as the Copernican revolution, which saw the universe in a new way, and the discovery of the New World, which changed the view of the whole world. So it is and will be with computers.

Robertson argues that calling the fifteenth and sixteenth centuries "Renaissance" is a misnomer, because what happened was not the rebirth of the ancient world, but something very new and different.[17] He is correct that it was an age of new ideas and discoveries rather than the rebirth of the ancient world. But he is wrong in thinking that the Renaissance was the rebirth of the ancient world. Instead, intense study of ancient learning and literature gave Renaissance men and women the necessary perspective to be able to look at their own times with fresh, critical eyes and to do new things. Study of the past enabled them to think outside of the box in profound and unexpected ways.

Computer professionals feel the same thrill of excitement about the possibilities of discovering new knowledge today as did scholars in the Renaissance. The computer language designer and essayist Paul Graham compares Florence in 1450 with New York in

2004. Why? Because Renaissance Florence had "the kind of turbulent and ambitious people you find now in America." The unruly, gleeful, rule-breaking American iconoclasts found in Silicon Valley (and the author believes that it is no accident that Silicon Valley is in America rather than elsewhere) produce the breakthroughs of today, just as their counterparts did in Florence in the fifteenth century, according to Graham.[18]

The computer world has embraced the Renaissance. In early 2004, the Renaissance Computer Institute (RENCI) was founded at the University of North Carolina at Chapel Hill. It intends to be a place where computer scientists and technicians can work with artists, biologists, engineers, geneticists, historians, statisticians, and scholars in other fields, to produce new and different knowledge. The goal of RENCI is to bring advanced and powerful computer resources, both people and supercomputers, into collaboration with scholars and government agencies, health organizations, and research institutes in order to solve problems. In particular, it wishes to help scholars whose large ideas cross disciplines to realize their projects.[19]

The director, Daniel A. Reed, chose Renaissance as part of the name of Renaissance Computer Institute in order to invoke the historical Renaissance. To reinforce the connection, the logo of RENCI includes an image of Leonardo da Vinci's Vitruvian Man. Reed uses Renaissance because he sees the historical Renaissance as a period of "explosive growth of ideas and inquiry," which he hopes that RENCI will help to bring about in the twenty-first century. Moreover, he believes that "complex problems need the disparate skills of people from the arts, humanities, sciences, and engineering for solution."[20] This was characteristic of the historical Renaissance, as men and women carried on discussions across what are now called disciplinary boundaries. And the greatest geniuses of the period made significant contributions in more than one field.

VITRUVIAN MAN. AROUND 1492 LEONARDO DA VINCI DREW THIS MAN OF IDEAL PROPORTIONS INSIDE A CIRCLE. IT IS BASED ON THE TREATISE "DE ARCHITECTURA" WRITTEN IN THE FIRST CENTURY AD BY VITRUVIUS. BECAUSE THE DRAWING ALSO CELEBRATES HUMAN POTENTIAL, THE RENAISSANCE COMPUTER INSTITUTE AND OTHER ORGANIZATIONS HAVE ADOPTED IT AS A LOGO. [PHOTO CREDIT: ALINARI/ART RESOURCE, NY.]

Renaissance Icons

An icon is an image, figure, representation, or picture instantly recognized and whose meaning is understood by all. Some Renaissance works of art are so well-known that they have become icons. Because they are universally recognized, they are wonderfully useful for expressing emotion and commenting on contemporary life. They also lend themselves to parodies.

Leonardo da Vinci's painting *Mona Lisa*, a portrait of a woman with a half-smile on her face, means allusive mystery. In 1949, Jay Livingston and Ray Evans created the popular song "Mona Lisa" to express bewildered longing for love.[21] The narrator sings to Mona Lisa as a way of lamenting his love mysteriously lost. The verse establishes the mood: "In a villa in a little old Italian town lives a girl whose beauty shames the rose. Many yearn to love her but their hopes all tumble down. What does she want? No one knows." The refrain addresses the painting as a way of giving voice to a broken heart: "Mona Lisa, Mona Lisa, men have named you. You're so like the lady with the mystic smile. Is it only 'cause you're lonely they have blamed you for that Mona Lisa strangeness in your smile? Do you smile to tempt a lover, Mona Lisa? Or is this your way to hide a broken heart? Many dreams have been brought to your doorstep. They just lie there, and they die there. Are you warm, are you real, Mona Lisa? Or just a cold and lonely, lovely work of art?"

The song is written in the keys of B flat major and E flat major but with much chromaticism (musical half steps) and many accidentals (sharps and flats to indicate deviations from the scale) in order to give it a melancholy tinge. In 1950, Nat "King" Cole (1919–1965), one of the best-known male vocalists, made a recording that became a huge hit. His silky baritone made the song a wistful lamentation for unrequited love. There has been no sequel. Rock and roll in its many variations has had no interest in Mona Lisa or the Renaissance.

LEONARDOUGH MONEY LISA CONNECTICUT LOTTERY TICKET. [REPRODUCED WITH PERMISSION OF THE CONNECTICUT LOTTERY CORPORATION.]

Mona Lisa is such an icon that she is a natural for parodies and political commentary. She can be used for less lofty purposes than lost love. In 1998, the State of Connecticut used Mona Lisa to encourage people to participate in the Connecticut Lottery. For $1, the buyer got a "Leonardough's Money Lisa" lottery ticket adorned with a picture of Mona Lisa. Buying three tickets gave one a chance to win up to $1,000.[22]

Mona Lisa was reborn as "Monica Lisa" or "Mona Lewinsky" on the cover of *The New Yorker* of February 8, 1999. The face of

Monica Lewinsky, the White House intern with whom President Bill Clinton had an affair that led to his impeachment, is superimposed on the *Mona Lisa* painting. "Monica Lisa" has a slight, enigmatic smile, just like the woman in the painting. The accompanying commentary in *The New Yorker* is entitled "Our woman of

"MONICA LISA" COVER OF *THE NEW YORKER* ON FEBRUARY 8, 1999. THE FACE OF MONICA LEWINSKY, THE WHITE HOUSE INTERN WHO HAD AN AFFAIR WITH PRESIDENT BILL CLINTON IS INSERTED INTO THE MONA LISA PAINTING OF LEONARDO DA VINCI. THE ACCOMPANYING STORY CONCLUDED THAT, UNLIKE THE PAINTING, THERE WAS LITTLE THAT WAS MYSTERIOUS ABOUT "MONICA LISA." [COVER-ART "MONICA LISA" BY DEAN ROHRER. © 1999 CONDÉ NAST PUBLICATIONS, INC. ALL RIGHTS RESERVED. UNDERLYING PHOTOGRAPH OF MONICA LEWINSKY REPRINTED WITH PERMISSION OF AP IMAGES.]

secrets." It wryly reflects on the U.S. Senate's and the public's fascination with Monica Lewinsky. Written just before she testified before the Senate impeachment committee, *The New Yorker* story compares Monica Lewinsky to the mysterious woman in the painting. Like Mona Lisa, Monica Lisa "suits all interpretations." Like Mona Lisa, she is universal: "She is featured in everything from law journals to porn zines." But unlike the mysterious woman in the painting, Monica Lewinsky is not unfathomable: "Monica is the woman of secrets who no longer has any. Her eyes are not windows but mirrors, and what we see in them is awful. Yet we go on staring."[23]

On the other hand, Savonarola is not a mysterious icon. Girolamo Savonarola (1452–1498) was a fire-and-brimstone preacher who dominated the Florentine government for a little over three years, December 1494 until April 1498. He denounced Florentines for their immorality and organized a bonfire of the vanities on February 7, 1497, in which the Florentines voluntarily, and in some cases under coercion, threw into the flames books, paintings, and other "vanities" considered sinful. Today commentators use Savonarola as an epithet with which to condemn moral zealots who use, or want to use, the power of government to impose censorship in order to protect the public from indecency.

On February 1, 2004, the entertainer Janet Jackson bared one of her breasts to tens of millions of viewers during the half-time show of the Super Bowl. The Federal Communications Commission reacted by decreeing large monetary fines on broadcasters who violated public decency, as the FCC sees it. A year later Frank Rich, a columnist with *The New York Times,* reflected on the consequences of Jackson's bared breast. He called Michael Powell "the Savonarola of the Federal Communications Commission" and gave many examples of how the Republicans in Washington and their conservative allies outside had launched an era of censorship and intimidation of the media.[24]

On the same day, Maureen Dowd, another *New York Times* columnist, made some of the same points by referring to Shakespeare and Savonarola. A friend invited her to a production of Shakespeare's *Romeo and Juliet*. But she hesitated, asking herself, "Doesn't that play promote suicide?" "I don't want to get on the wrong side of the Savonarolas." Then Dowd pointed out that Shakespeare's plays are full of actions denounced by moralists. In *Romeo and Juliet,* the apothecary helps Romeo commit suicide. In *Hamlet,* Ophelia drowns herself; in *Othello,* the Moor kills his wife, then commits suicide. In *Julius Caesar,* Brutus runs on to his sword held by his servant, another assisted suicide. Dowd worries about the consequences for art in today's "hypermoralistic atmosphere."[25]

The iconic meaning of Hamlet is someone who cannot make up his mind. The most widely quoted reference to Hamlet of the recent past was "Hamlet on the Hudson," the amusing description of New York governor Mario Cuomo who debated with himself about whether he should campaign actively for the Democratic presidential nomination in 1992. He eventually decided not to. Cuomo probably did not find the reference amusing. But he did know something about the Renaissance, because he sprinkled references to Thomas More, political servant of Henry VIII who condemned war and inequitable distribution of wealth but lost his head for his faith, in his speeches.

The year 1992 was a kindlier and gentler time in American politics. Now political commentators use Shakespeare's plays to draw lessons about war and the killing of prisoners. After visiting the Oregon Shakespeare Festival in August 2004, Nicholas D. Kristoff, a columnist for *The New York Times*, wrote a soliloquy about what lessons George W. Bush might learn from Shakespeare's plays.[26] Kristoff points out that some see Bush as Shakespeare's Prince Hal, the feckless young man who, after sobering up, becomes Henry V, a warrior king of England. The real Henry V was king of England from 1413 to 1422. He invaded France, defeated the French forces at the Battle of Agincourt (October 25, 1415), and would have become king of France as well if not for his sudden death at the age of thirty-five. Shakespeare's *Henry V* shows many attractive features of Henry V and celebrates the victory at Agincourt. Laurence Olivier directed and starred in a well-known 1944 film version that makes Henry V an even more attractive ruler (see chapter 10).

Kristoff cautioned that Americans who want to see George W. Bush as a personification of Shakespeare's Henry V should look more carefully at the play and Shakespeare's mixed messages about war. Following modern scholarship, Kristoff points out that the play is not an unqualified celebration of a great leader and military success but "an unblinking examination of the brutality and inevitable excesses of war."[27] For example, in the play Henry V ordered the murder of French prisoners. (This is in scene IV.vii.66–68; Henry did this because the French sacked the English baggage train and killed the boys therein. Thus, it was an act of vengeance, one unjustified murder for another.) The play also includes eloquent speeches lamenting the brutal cost of war. Kristoff went on to list other lessons that Bush might learn from Shakespeare's plays. From *Othello* he might learn not to trust the intelligence of others, as Iago's lies convinced Othello to kill Desdemona. Above all, Kristoff pointed out that many of Shakespeare's plays demonstrate how pride, self-assurance, and the conviction of their own moral rectitude led rulers to self-destruction.

Another iconic name from Renaissance Florence that has become a part of American writing is "Medici," the family that ruled Florence from 1434 until 1737, with two short interruptions. The iconic meaning of Medici is an extremely wealthy supporter of the arts and learning. *The New York Times Magazine* made this point with a picture spread about "Manhattan's young Medici types." They are very wealthy young women who sit on the boards of New York's museums of modern art or support art in other ways.

Each "young Medici" is photographed in her home in front of a work of modern art and wearing a fabulous dress costing $875 to $2,560.[28] The Medici women of Florence, who also dressed well, would have understood.

The political right has a modern Medici. In May 2005, the John M. Olin Foundation announced that it was going out of business. *The New York Times* article called the John M. Olin Foundation "part Medici, part venture capitalist," because it spent all its money "financing the intellectual rise of the right."[29] Founded by John M. Olin (1892–1982), a midwestern industrialist who began by making explosives and bullets, it gave out about $380 million to conservative think tanks and right wing intellectuals in thirty years. It closed its doors because Olin decreed in his will that the foundation had to spend its money within a generation. The foundation has had a large impact on American politics, law, and economics, but possibly not the kind of effect that Lorenzo de' Medici would have preferred.

The historical Medici supported creative people in many fields. The "Medici effect" expresses the belief that bringing these people together will break down barriers between disciplines and unleash new kinds of creativity. *The Medici Effect: Breakthrough Insights at the Intersection of Ideas, Concepts, and Cultures* (Boston: Harvard Business School Press, 2004) by Frans Johansson, founder of an enterprise software company, makes this argument. According to the author, when the Medici brought creative people together, "they forced a new world based on new ideas—what became known as the Renaissance" (p. 3). The purpose of the book is to show how this same kind of creativity can occur today when people from different disciplines come together and mix ideas. The key conception is "intersection," which is the meeting "of fields, cultures, and disciplines which generates combinations of *different* ideas" [emphasis in the original] (p. 91).

Leonardo da Vinci is an icon of creative success in many areas, including professional football. For twelve years, Joe Gibbs was a very successful coach of the Washington Redskins professional football team, as the team won three Super Bowls. He left in 1992 and the team foundered. When in summer 2004 he resumed coaching the Redskins, fans and sportswriters hailed his return. A story in the *Sporting News* enthused: "He'll win again because he knows how to . . . compile brilliant game plans and paint da Vincis on Sundays."[30] Gibbs did not paint as well as Leonardo in the 2004–2005 season and the team had a losing record. This is just one of many references to the Renaissance and its icons in sports magazines and the sports pages of major newspapers. Because sports writers are often well read and cover "the toy department of life," to borrow the words of former sports broadcaster Joe Garagiola, they are freer to engage in flights of literary fancy and employ metaphors and icons than journalists reporting on government or international affairs.

Michelangelo's statue David has the iconic meaning of perfection. The cover of the April 2004 *The Atlantic* magazine shows the head of David with the words "The Case Against Perfection. What's wrong with designer children, bionic athletes, and genetic engineering." The cover story argues that it is not wise to try to make perfect people through genetic engineering, or to mold perfect children by a constant stream of lessons, but that we should be open to the unbidden.[31] In other words, do not try to make people like Michelangelo's David.

Michelangelo's painting in the center of the Sistine Chapel ceiling depicting God creating Adam has several iconic meanings, including creativity and religious devotion. Readers opening the business section of *The News & Observer* of Raleigh, North Carolina, on Sunday, December 20, 1998, were probably surprised to see a color reproduction of Michelangelo's God the Father bringing Adam to life by touching his finger. But Adam is fully clothed in

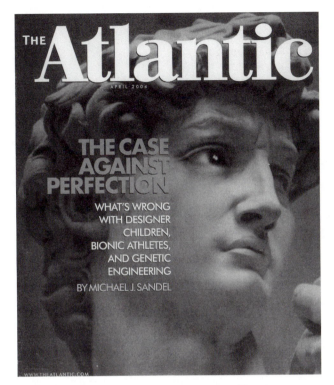

HEAD OF MICHELANGELO'S DAVID FROM THE COVER OF *THE ATLANTIC*, VOL. 293, NO. 3, APRIL 2004. DAVID REPRESENTS HUMAN PERFECTION. THE COVER ILLUSTRATED A STORY WHICH WARNED AGAINST ATTEMPTS TO PRODUCE PERFECT PEOPLE THROUGH GENETIC ENGINEERING OR PERFECT CHILDREN BY A CONSTANT STREAM OF LESSONS. [REPRODUCED WITH PERMISSION OF *THE ATLANTIC MONTHLY*.]

a gray suit, white shirt, and conservative tie, and ready to go to the office. The title of the story is "Divine Touch," which refers both to the painting and the story. The latter describes the many weekly Bible classes that hundreds of (mostly male) CEOs, politicians (including U.S. Senator John Edwards), bankers, developers, real estate brokers, stock brokers, and other business people attend in Raleigh and its suburbs, and probably elsewhere in America. They meet every week, except in the summer, for one hour and forty-five minutes to discuss an assigned selection from the Bible, typically a chapter from the New Testament. The participants pledge to

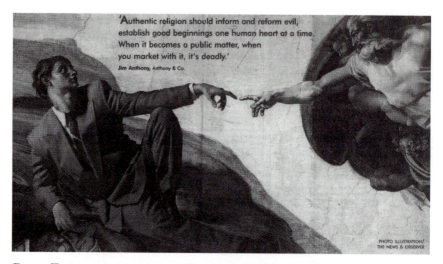

DIVINE TOUCH GRAPHIC BASED ON GOD CREATING ADAM IN MICHELANGELO'S SIS-
TINE CHAPEL CEILING IN *THE NEWS & OBSERVER* OF RALEIGH, NORTH CAROLINA,
DECEMBER 20, 1998, PAGE E1. IT ILLUSTRATED A STORY ABOUT WEEKLY BIBLE
CLASSES ATTENDED BY PROMINENT BUSINESSMEN, POLITICIANS, AND CIVIC LEADERS.
[REPRODUCED WITH PERMISSION OF *THE NEWS & OBSERVER* OF RALEIGH, NORTH
CAROLINA.]

discuss only the Bible. They are not even allowed to talk about
Atlantic Coast Conference basketball. Nothing indicates their seri-
ousness of purpose so well as foregoing the pleasure of debating
the merits of the Duke Blue Devils, the North Carolina Tar Heels,
and the North Carolina State Wolfpack. The Michelangelo image
conveys the theme of the story, that studying the Bible is very
important to business leaders in a major metropolitan area.[32]

Cartoonists take advantage of the wide knowledge of
Michelangelo's painting to use it to poke fun at different aspects of
modern life. For cat lovers, the strip *Rhymes with Orange* showed
"The Cat View of Creation." God the Father is creating Adam,
except that God has the face of a cat and he says to Adam "I grant
you life, so you will forever do my bidding." In a strip in *Funky
Winkerbean,* the painter is painting a mural on the walls of Tony
Montoni's pizza parlor. Tony complains to the painter that "it only

took Michelangelo four years to paint the entire ceiling of the Sistine Chapel," while you have been painting for eight years. The painter responds, "Some guys just don't give a darn." The strip may be inspired by the 1965 film *The Agony and the Ecstasy* in

"THE CAT VIEW OF CREATION" FROM *RHYMES WITH ORANGE* COMIC STRIP, MAY 30, 1999. THIS IS ANOTHER USE OF MICHELANGELO'S FAMOUS FRESCO AS SEEN BY A CAT WHO CREATES MAN WHO DOES THE CAT'S BIDDING. [© *RHYMES WITH ORANGE*— HILARY B. PRICE. KING FEATURES SYNDICATE.]

ANOTHER HUMOROUS LOOK AT MICHELANGELO'S SISTINE CHAPEL PAINTING. *FUNKY WINKERBEAN* COMIC STRIP OF APRIL 11, 2004 [© FUNKY WINKERBEAN—BATOM, INC. KING FEATURES SYNDICATE.]

THE CARTOONIST USES THE READER'S KNOWLEDGE OF MICHELANGELO'S SCULPTURE OF *DAVID* TO POKE FUN AT THE RELIANCE ON FOCUS GROUPS TO MAKE DECISIONS. *NON SEQUITUR* COMIC STRIP OF NOVEMBER 18, 1999. [*NON SEQUITUR* © 1999 WILEY MILLER. DIST. BY UNIVERSAL PRESS SYNDICATE. REPRINTED WITH PERMISSION. ALL RIGHTS RESERVED.]

which Pope Julius II (Rex Harrison) repeatedly demands to know when Michelangelo (Charlton Heston) will finish, and the painter also answers testily, "When it is done." In a strip of *Non Sequitur,* Michelangelo chips away at a block of marble, while a second character tells him, "There's strong negative numbers on the nudity, Michelangelo, and the consensus is to change the title from 'David' to 'Ralph.'" The caption of the strip reads "The wisdom of focus groups through the ages."[33] There are many other examples of the use of iconic images from the Renaissance for comedic purposes.

Leonardo creating the Mona Lisa has inspired a film cartoon. A 1975 animated film cartoon entitled *Pink Da Vinci* shows Leonardo da Vinci as a short, dark-haired man with a moustache painting the *Mona Lisa*. He paints her with a frown. Once Leonardo leaves the room, the Pink Panther (created by filmmaker

Blake Edwards) enters, paints an enigmatic smile on her lips, and slips away. Leonardo returns; he furiously repaints her with a pout. When the little painter is not looking, the Pink Panther again gives her a smile. And so on. Eventually, the Pink Panther wins. Thus, *Mona Lisa* with her enigmatic smile is a collaboration of Leonardo and the Pink Panther. Henry Mancini's Pink Panther music helps make it a charming six-minute animated feature.

And so the Renaissance lives in the world of advertisers, business, and icons. Businesses and advertisers use the well-known and admired individuals and images of the Renaissance to sell their products. Naturally, they only use those with positive meanings. They do not advertise a Borgia Hotel or Iago Auto Care. Journalists and cartoonists use Renaissance icons that have more varied and sophisticated meanings. They refer to the *Mona Lisa*, Michelangelo, Savonarola, Leonardo da Vinci, Shakespeare's plays, and the Medici to make their points. Even though these men and women lived, and the works of art were created, 500 years ago on a continent some 3,000 miles away, they are familiar parts of twenty-first-century American life.

Part II

RE-CREATING THE RENAISSANCE

Not content with admiring the Renaissance from afar, different sectors of American society have re-created parts of it over the past several decades. They have rebuilt American cities in order to achieve the splendor and cultural amenities of fifteenth-century Florence. Pittsburgh and Detroit call themselves Renaissance cities. Machiavelli has returned to life as a conservative adviser on foreign policy, as well as political commentator, management guru, and social scientist. Americans have re-created the Renaissance with bricks and mortar and political policies.

Chapter 6

AMERICAN RENAISSANCE CITIES

C ities such as Florence were the centers of the artistic, cultural, political, religious, and social life of the European
Renaissance. When American cities sought to revitalize
themselves after World War II, they consciously compared themselves to the great cities of the European Renaissance. They
worked to create a Renaissance in their own cities. Urban renewal
became the Renaissance of American cities.

The Pittsburgh Renaissance

The pioneering and most important American city renaissance was
the Pittsburgh Renaissance. It provided a model to follow.

The city was in terrible shape when World War II ended.
Although its steel mills and labor force had contributed much to
victory, Pittsburgh was losing its own war against urban blight.
A 1944 *Wall Street Journal* survey of the postwar prospects of
American cities judged it a city with a bleak future.[1] Yet by 1960,
a partnership of business and political leaders had revived the
city to an unprecedented degree. This revival, the first and most

influential for American cities in the second half of the twentieth century, is called the Pittsburgh Renaissance.

"The smoky city" was not a pretty sight in 1945.[2] A famous photograph showed automobiles driving through the city at noon on a sunny day with their lights on because the smoke was so thick. Children left for school in the morning in clean clothes and returned coated with soot. Floods regularly inundated the city and made much of the waterfront dangerous and uninhabitable. Antismoke and flood control legislation had been enacted before World War II. But the antismoke ordinances were not enforced during the war, and no funds were provided for flood control. The steel industry dominated the economy even as the central business district deteriorated. Abandoned buildings pockmarked the urban landscape, and debris littered the river banks. Housing was inadequate and often substandard. Population was declining. Corporations considered leaving the city because managerial employees and their spouses did not want to move to Pittsburgh. The city had few cultural amenities.

Pittsburgh's leaders began to organize to deal with the problems. In the last year of the war, they created several committees of business and civic leaders to work toward improvement. The most important was the Allegheny Conference on Community Development (ACCD), formed in 1944 after Richard King Mellon (1899–1970) made it clear that he supported such a group. Its executive committee of ten to fifteen presidents and chief executive officers of the major commercial and financial institutions of the city was a key part of civic renewal. Members were elected as individuals, not as representatives of their companies, and could not send substitutes to meetings. The only exception was Mellon, who was never a member of the executive committee but made his wishes known through others. The ACCD created committees to find solutions for civic problems. Other such committees, sometimes composed of experts, followed in succeeding years.

Things began to move after the war was over, thanks to an unexpected alliance. All accounts attribute leadership of the Pittsburgh Renaissance to two men. The first was Richard King Mellon, the extremely wealthy leader of the Mellon family. He was chairman of the Mellon Bank and had controlling interests in Gulf Oil, a coal company, and other enterprises.

Mellon was Protestant and a Republican, like all other wealthy industrialists of the time. He enjoyed hunting and riding and was a conservationist. He was not an intellectual and lacked interest in the arts. But he believed that a man should live and work in the community in which he made his money. Shy and adverse to publicity, Mellon made his preferences known through conversations with other corporate leaders in the exclusive Duquesne Club of Pittsburgh and relied on associates to communicate and implement them in the ACCD and other groups. In 1947, he created the Richard King Mellon Foundation to make grants for regional economic development and improvement of the quality of life in western Pennsylvania, plus national land and wildlife conservation. It had assets of more than $1.4 billion at the end of 2002.[3]

The other leader of the Pittsburgh Renaissance could not have been more different. David Leo Lawrence (1889–1966) was born in one of Pittsburgh's poorest neighborhoods, the Point, where the Allegheny and Monongahela Rivers come together to create the Ohio River.[4] The son of an Irish laborer, Lawrence had only ten years of school before going to work. An early interest in politics, a talent for organization, and hard work enabled him to become the political "boss," a term that he hated, of the Democratic Party of Pittsburgh and western Pennsylvania. Although he was elected Secretary of the Commonwealth of Pennsylvania in the 1930s, he preferred to exert his influence from behind the scenes by controlling the Democratic Party organization and determining its nominees. However, in the absence of any other acceptable and available Democratic candidate, he ran for mayor of Pittsburgh in the fall of 1945 and won on a platform of renewing Pittsburgh. He served for thirteen years, 1946 through 1958, most of the years of the Pittsburgh Renaissance. He later became the first Roman Catholic governor of Pennsylvania (1959 to 1963) and a king maker in Democratic presidential politics.

Great differences separated the business community and city hall. Nevertheless, the two sides reached out to each other. Lawrence's electoral platform of 1945 listed some of the goals of the ACCD. It was a signal that he was willing to work with the business community for the greater good of Pittsburgh. The business community responded. The Pittsburgh Chamber of Commerce invited mayor-elect Lawrence to speak to it, the first invitation ever tendered to a Democratic mayor, on January 2, 1946, five days before his inauguration. In his speech, Lawrence stressed teamwork between government, business, and labor for the benefit of the city.[5]

If Pittsburgh were to be renewed, cooperation between political and business leadership would have to surmount strong political differences. It is hard to overstate the mutual loathing that separated Democratic politicians and Republican corporation executives of that era. David Lawrence was the Catholic Democratic boss of western Pennsylvania who had enthusiastically supported Franklin D. Roosevelt and progressive labor legislation. Mellon and all members of the ACCD were Protestant Republican corporate executives who had hated Roosevelt and the New Deal with all their being. When he was Secretary of the Commonwealth from 1934 to 1939, Lawrence had been the driving force behind the enactment of a series of laws, such as lowering the work week for women from fifty-four hours to forty hours, which he called "The Little New Deal." Republican legislators under the urging of business leaders repealed most of the laws when they regained political power in Harrisburg. Nevertheless, the two sides, led by

Mellon and Lawrence, were willing to work together for the good of Pittsburgh.

Mellon and Lawrence were never close. Indeed, they communicated infrequently by telephone and probably did not meet privately more than a couple of times in their lives. Intermediaries relayed messages. Nevertheless, they respected each other and shared a common goal of renewing Pittsburgh. They worked together to renew the city.

Initially called the Pittsburgh Program, action to renew the city began in earnest in 1946. Flood and smoke control came first. The Pittsburgh leadership persuaded Congress and President Harry S. Truman to provide the funds for upstream dams and reservoirs on the Allegheny and Monongahela rivers. By September 1953, eight of the nine reservoirs were in operation and flooding had stopped. The battle to enforce the antismoke legislation was tougher. Coal companies opposed it, there were problems of supplying enough smokeless coal, and distributors raised prices by 25 percent. The Pennsylvania Railroad also opposed the smoke legislation, but Mellon, a stockholder, applied pressure and the railroad accepted it. The ordinance fell heaviest on poor people, who had to convert to natural gas or smokeless coal. Hence, labor and many householders were opposed. But Lawrence stood fast and the ordinances were enforced. Consequently, labor leaders and some Democrats accused Lawrence of being the tool of business; another Democrat challenged him in a bitter primary battle in 1949 when he sought reelection. Lawrence prevailed and was reelected mayor that fall with a much narrower margin than in 1945. This victory was seen as a political mandate to proceed with the Pittsburgh Renaissance, and Lawrence was never seriously challenged at the ballot box thereafter.

As flood and smoke control progressed, the city turned to revitalizing and rebuilding the downtown area by means of the

Gateway Center project. To make this work, the city created a new agency. Called the Urban Redevelopment Authority (URA) of Pittsburgh, it served several functions.[6] It gave the city an agency to interact with private groups. It could secure private funding for redevelopment projects, thus avoiding the risk of the voters refusing to approve bonds. And it had the power of eminent domain, meaning that it could acquire individual properties when owners refused to sell, then combine them into a land package and sell the package to private developers. Lawrence chaired URA, but three of the five board members came from the ACCD, the private sector of corporation executives. In other words, an interlocking, closely integrated group led urban renewal. Many other boards and commissions, both public and private, such as an Industrial-Economic Research Council, were created to develop projects and deal with technical and other issues.

The informal name for urban renewal at that time was the Pittsburgh Program. The first use of renaissance (lowercase "r") to describe what was happening in Pittsburgh came from outside the city. In 1949, *Architectural Forum* published an article called "Pittsburgh Renascent." It described the planning and personalities involved in Pittsburgh, with artists' sketches of highways, flood control projects, and buildings, that would remake the city.[7] Then in 1951, an *Atlantic Monthly* article contrasted Pittsburgh "before the renaissance" (lowercase in the original) and after.[8] So far as can be determined, these were the first uses of renaissance to describe American urban renewal.

The *Atlantic Monthly* article stimulated Pittsburghers to think of their program as a renaissance, but for a negative reason. After a very favorable description of the physical renewal of the city, the author voiced mild criticism of the ACCD for neglecting social welfare and cultural development. The criticism stung, partly because the leaders of the city were sensitive to such charges, which had been leveled against Pittsburgh before World

War II, and partly because the criticism was accurate. The ACCD had not paid much attention to cultural renewal and social welfare. City leaders began to think more broadly about their plans and to compare Pittsburgh with the European Renaissance. In a speech of 1952, a leader of the ACCD commented that the "renaissance in Pittsburgh" did call to mind the artistic and intellectual accomplishments of the European Renaissance, but Pittsburgh was deficient in these areas. He urged the group to put greater emphasis on culture.[9] And it did, although it was many years before cultural projects came to fruition. Social welfare in the form of better housing for the city's poorer residents made greater, if sporadic, progress.

In the mid-1950s, the name "Pittsburgh Renaissance" (with an uppercase "R") appeared, as civic leaders consciously linked the renewal of Pittsburgh with the European Renaissance. In 1954, Arthur B. Van Buskirk, who represented Mellon interests in the ACCD, urged his fellow citizens to try to make the Pittsburgh Renaissance like "the great Renaissance of Europe between the Middle Ages and modern world," especially in "the casting off of the shackles upon human beings, and the realization of the meaning of freedom of mind and conscience."[10] Sweeping references to the Renaissance as a period of freedom of the human spirit were common in those days.

In May 1956, Mayor Lawrence addressed a conference on urban design at the Graduate School of Design of Harvard University. He narrated the history of the Pittsburgh Renaissance. He listed its goals, what had been accomplished, and future projects, all of which came to fruition. He described the public–private partnership and emphasized that successful urban renewal should combine good design and livability. Lawrence affirmed that "the people of a city can take pride and glory in it in our own times as the Athenians did under Pericles or the Florentines did under Lorenzo."[11] The reference was to Lorenzo de' Medici, the de facto ruler of Florence between 1469 and 1492, seen as a golden age of the civic Italian Renaissance. And both the mayor and his audience must have known that Lawrence is the English translation of "Lorenzo." The reference may have been more than a speechwriter's flourish. Although his formal education was limited, Lawrence had visited Europe many times and his knowledge went far beyond politics. For example, when accused of corruption in 1940, he cited Machiavelli against his accuser.[12]

A 1959 article in *Holiday* had a slightly different twist. It wrote that "Pittsburghers like to compare their renaissance with that of Florence centuries ago, and the comparison is not inapt, since the great Medici builders were also bankers. But Pittsburgh is Florence without Lorenzo. Her Medici are builders, not dreamers, with a Calvinist mistrust of the humanities and arts."[13] The point was that the Medici, while bankers, also built palaces and strongly supported the arts and scholarship by patronizing artists and scholars. But the leaders of the Pittsburgh Renaissance did not. The gibe may have been particularly directed toward Mellon, who was a Presbyterian. Nevertheless, the Pittsburgh Renaissance did embrace the arts and learning in its second phase.

The Pittsburgh Renaissance continued with many other projects, including a new industrial plant for Jones and Laughlin Steel, new housing, and a Civic Arena. After the needed planning and approvals had been secured, the Pittsburgh Renaissance produced sixteen different projects covering more than a thousand acres in the period 1949 through 1964. The private sector invested $499 million in these projects and the public sector $133 million.[14] When there was opposition, or private and community interests collided, Mayor Lawrence and leaders of the business community proclaimed the principle that, while individual rights were to be respected, the common good had to prevail. In many ways, Point State Park at the tip of the Pittsburgh where the rivers meet was the symbolic conclusion of the Pittsburgh Renaissance.

It was created in an area of abandoned warehouses, railroads, and the slum in which Mayor Lawrence was born. When after many delays Point Park was completed, and the water of its fountain shot 150 feet in the air, Pittsburghers saw it as the culmination of the Pittsburgh Renaissance.[15]

The results were gratifying. The decline of the city had been reversed and Pittsburgh thrived. Smoke and flood control was achieved, the nation's largest urban renewal program was put into place, industry expanded, slums were cleared, several parks were created, and a start was made on improved facilities for arts and cultural activities. The city's population expanded to a peak of about 677,000 in 1950 in a metropolitan area of more than two million. Many corporations erected new headquarters in the city.

A personal note: my wife and I lived in Pittsburgh from late summer 1963 to early summer 1964 when I was a temporary lecturer in history at the University of Pittsburgh. We lived in the Oakland neighborhood within walking distance of the university, the symphony hall (the Syria Mosque, a 1915 building with quirky acoustics), Carnegie Museum, Forbes Field where the Pittsburgh Pirates (baseball) and Steelers (football) played, the Roman Catholic cathedral, and much else. It was clear that Pittsburgh was an attractive city, very different from the smoky past.

The Pittsburgh Renaissance received wide attention. Between 1946 and 1960, eighty-six groups from other towns and cities came to view the Pittsburgh Renaissance.[16] What happened there, especially its public-private partnership, became a model for other cities suffering blight and seeking their own renaissances out of urban decline.

Historians usually date the Pittsburgh Renaissance (later called Renaissance I; see below) from 1945 to 1960 with some projects being completed in the 1960s.[17] Joseph Barr was mayor from 1959 to 1969 during which time the public-private partnership continued. But then Peter Flaherty, running as an independent Democrat, won the mayor's seat in 1970. Flaherty distanced himself from the ACCD, and his relations with the corporate community were frosty.[18] He opposed the public-private partnership that had created the Pittsburgh Renaissance, and he strongly opposed and ultimately defeated a mass transit system endorsed by the corporate community and the majority of Pittsburghers. Urban development stopped; indeed, the Urban Redevelopment Agency issued no reports between 1969 and 1979.

Then came the disappearance of big steel, a real disaster for Pittsburgh. During the recession of 1979 through 1983, Pittsburgh's heavy industry basically shut down. Steel plants that had provided stable employment for nearly a century closed. In a few years, manufacturing employment in Pittsburgh dropped from 37 percent of those employed to 16 percent.[19] The closing of the steel mills meant more than the loss of jobs, devastating as that was. The steel mills had provided the economic foundation for social stability embracing family, neighborhood, church, and community in Pittsburgh and nearby towns. The closings destroyed a way of life that had endured for generations, as son had followed father in the mills. Although many workers stubbornly believed that the blast furnaces would fire again, they were closed for good, the victims of foreign competition and economic restructuring.

When Flaherty left to become deputy attorney general in Washington in April 1977, Richard Caligiuri, the first mayor of Italian descent, succeeded him and was elected in his own right later that year. He held the office until his premature death in 1988. At his inauguration in early 1978, he used the words "Renaissance II" to describe what had to be done, the first person to use the title. Historians of Pittsburgh now divide the Pittsburgh Renaissance into Renaissance I (1945 to 1960) and Renaissance II (the 1980s and early 1990s).

Mayor Caligiuri initially emphasized neighborhood redevelopment and downtown street improvements, with major office expansion in the downtown core following.[20] The mayor, corporate executives, and experts revived the public-private committees of Renaissance I and added some new ones. The renewed public-private partnership had several goals, the most important of which was to encourage a postindustrial economy in Pittsburgh. They also sought to improve the quality of life by adding cultural facilities, improving neighborhoods, and thinking regionally about ways of improving the towns that had been devastated by the closing of the steel mills. Progress was slower and less dramatic than in Renaissance I. The days in which the combined authority of Lawrence and Mellon, supported by the technical expertise of their advisers, could set a project in motion were gone. Consensus had to be built, and urban constituencies had more ways of blocking development than before. Moreover, the corporate world was less stable than in the time of Renaissance I and the executives preoccupied. They now led diversified, worldwide corporations and had less time to give to ACCD and Pittsburgh.[21] Nevertheless, Renaissance II was launched.

It sought to develop a diversified economy based on advanced technology, professional services, and cultural vitality. The committees of Renaissance II did this by encouraging technology development and research; emphasizing Pittsburgh as a center for higher education; promoting the medical, financial, legal, and other professional services of Pittsburgh; and improving the infrastructure with highways and a better mass transit system. The University of Pittsburgh and Carnegie Mellon University were much more involved than in Renaissance I, as they expanded research and added buildings. Renaissance II included a new concert hall, museums, a science center, and public spaces, such as Market Square for food and restaurants. And it paid more attention to housing and preserving neighborhoods than had Renaissance I.

Even historic preservation made a start during Renaissance II, with some notable battles over buildings, not all of which were saved from the wrecker's ball. The goal was to create an economically viable city without steel by attracting other kinds of businesses and professional people and their families.

Although the results were not so dramatic or visually obvious as with Renaissance I, Renaissance II made impressive progress toward its primary goal: a viable poststeel economy. And the emphasis on cultural amenities strengthened the resemblance to the historic Renaissance.

Detroit Renaissance

Other cities paid close attention to the Pittsburgh Renaissance. Its basic arrangement of a public-private alliance to renew a city was frequently copied in greater or lesser degree. Other American cities seeking to renew themselves through urban development sometimes used the term Renaissance. For example, Baltimore called itself "the Renaissance City."[22] Detroit used the term Renaissance in two ways in its urban renewal of the 1970s and 1980s.

In summer 1967, Detroit suffered devastating riots that left 41 dead, 347 injured, and 1,300 buildings destroyed. Three years later, some twenty-six business, industrial, and civic leaders met to plan the economic revival of the city.[23] They created an organization of business leaders and called it Detroit Renaissance. It is a private, nonprofit organization whose primary purpose is to revitalize Detroit physically and economically. Henry Ford II (1917–1987), the chief executive of the Ford Motor Company, became the head of Detroit Renaissance. In 1971, he announced plans for a $500 million project on the riverfront area of the city, the area near the Ambassador Bridge that fronts the Detroit River looking toward Windsor, Ontario. It would be a huge, privately financed project designed to encourage commercial activity in the heart of the city. An architect was hired, the city approved the plans, and construction began in 1972. A contest was held to name the development project. After more than 141,000 entries were processed, the winner was "Renaissance Center."

When completed in 1977, Renaissance Center consisted of five linked buildings, a 73-story prestige hotel with facilities for large conventions and four 39-story office towers; enough retail commercial space for thirteen restaurants, four movie theaters, and numerous shops; and, last but not least, parking space for 6,000 automobiles. The five linked buildings dominate Detroit's skyline. They present a striking modernistic structure of towers to the onlooker best seen from Windsor, across the Detroit River. Like most large-scale urban building projects, Renaissance Center has drawn mixed reactions from architectural and urban critics. At the formal dedication on April 15, 1977, the mayor of Florence, Italy, Detroit's sister city, joined in the ceremonies, making even more clear the image that Detroit wished to project: Detroit through its Renaissance Center and Detroit Renaissance organization was creating its own Renaissance, just as Florence had done five centuries earlier.

In 1974, Detroit elected as mayor Coleman Young (1919–1997), a former union official, the first African American to hold the office. He won four more elections before retiring in 1993. During his tenure, Coleman and Detroit Renaissance pursued development projects, usually with substantial help from the city, often in the form of tax vacations. They included a second phase of the Renaissance Center with two 21-story office towers, a sports arena to keep the city's professional hockey team from leaving for the suburbs, a new General Motors assembly plant in 1985, and a new Chrysler Corporation plant in 1992. Designed to keep about 6,000

THE COMPLEX OF BUILDINGS COMPRISING THE RENAISSANCE CENTER OF DETROIT, COMPLETED IN 1977. IT IS AN EXAMPLE OF THE IDENTIFICATION OF AMERICAN URBAN RENEWAL WITH THE RENAISSANCE. [PHOTOGRAPH © WILLIAM MANNING/CORBIS.]

automotive jobs in the city, the last two projects necessitated the razing of hundreds of homes and businesses and the relocation of thousands of people at the expense of the city.

Despite some impressive buildings, other forces made Detroit's problems worse. The decline of the auto industry in the early 1980s as a result of competition from Japanese automakers was a massive blow. It meant the loss of thousands of automotive and related manufacturing jobs. The efforts of the city to create new jobs could not dam the tide of jobs floating away. This and problems of crime and poor schools in the city helped produce a sharp population decline for Detroit, from 1,670,000 in 1960, to 1,500,000 in 1970, to 1,200,000 in 1980, to about 1,000,000 in 1990.[24] Residents moved to the suburbs.

The greatest part of the population loss was "white flight," the departure of white residents, although large numbers of the black middle class also moved to the suburbs. Detroit, which had been 29 percent minority in population in 1960, was 75 percent black in 1990, while the suburbs were more than 90 percent white in 1990.[25] Unemployment and poverty among Detroit's inhabitants, especially African Americans, reached very high levels, and crime increased. The loss of white residents meant black residents held most political offices in the city. But it also led to tensions between business leaders and Mayor Coleman, who saw what he called "white racism" as a major cause of Detroit's problems. Coleman saw the white suburbs as implacably hostile to the black city, and some of his remarks exacerbated relations.[26] Even though they worked together on several large-scale development projects, relations between the mayor and the city's business leaders, including Detroit Renaissance, were sometimes tense.

Despite considerable successes, especially in the erection of buildings, the overall economic results did not realize the dreams of the founders of Detroit Renaissance. A telling piece of evidence is that Renaissance Center lost money. Hence, the Ford Motor Company and its local partners sold it at a loss to non-Detroit owners in 1982, and it was resold later. Perhaps no program of urban development could have solved the problems that came from global economic change and the human social problems of Detroit of the 1980s and early 1990s.

Nevertheless, Detroit Renaissance continues to work for economic and physical development. It has numerous committees and programs designed to help minority businesses, public education, transportation, and cultural policy. But its primary focus remains economic development through support of strategic projects.[27] And the late 1990s and first years of the twenty-first century have seen significant new development for Detroit.[28] The auto industry made a comeback in the 1990s with the help of Daimler-Benz, the

German manufacturer, which absorbed the Chrysler Corporation in all but name in 1998. Several of the city's most important theaters and concert halls were renovated or restored. In April 2000 Comerica Park, the new home of the Detroit Tigers professional baseball team, opened, while the Detroit Lions, the professional football team, left suburban Pontiac for a new stadium in the heart of the city in 2002, a reversal of the usual direction of development. General Motors bought Renaissance Center and announced in 1999 plans for renovation that would meet criticisms that it was a forbidding fortress to enter and a confusing maze inside. General Motors also announced that it would transform twenty-five acres of adjacent parking lots into a commercial area of shops and restaurants. Despite its problems, the Detroit Renaissance lives on.

Some Renaissance city renewal has been much smaller in scale. For a number of years, Renaissance Kentucky has offered grants of up to $1 million to towns and cities in Kentucky for specific urban projects. Renamed Renaissance on Main in early 2005 with an announcement that there would be greater emphasis on job creation, the program continues.[29] A city applies to the Governor's Office for Local Development (GOLD) of Kentucky for money for a specific project, such as the renovation of a library building, building a solid waste management system, installation of a gas line to an industrial site, or the creation of a recreational trail. The funds come from the state and from federal programs such as the Community Development Block Grants of the U.S. Housing and Urban Development agency. If the application is successful, the city or town gets the money, does its project, and the governor and his office reap good publicity. The projects are useful if ordinary. But attaching Renaissance to the name of the program probably gives them a little more glamour and attracts attention.

The American urban Renaissances had many successes but did not achieve everything that they sought.[30] All of the cities involved used public relations techniques to emphasize their goals and achievements. Adopting the name Renaissance and evoking the historical Renaissance, which began in Pittsburgh in the mid-1950s, certainly generated positive publicity. Nevertheless, city Renaissances, especially in their early phases, received merited criticism for concentrating too much on massive projects and not enough on people, neighborhoods, and jobs. But they also had many positive achievements, which were badly needed. In later years, they helped expand cultural facilities, by building concert halls and sports stadiums. At the same time, the urban Renaissance could not completely arrest the decline of American cities, because global economic transformations were beyond their powers to change. Despite urban Renaissances, older cities lost jobs to the rest of the world and people to the suburbs. They were no longer the centers of American life. But their plight would have been much worse without urban Renaissances.

American Renaissance Cities and European Renaissance Cities

Making comparisons among European Renaissance cities, such as Florence, and American Renaissance cities, as Pittsburgh and Detroit, is not as far-fetched as it seems. There were many similarities. For example, Florence had a considerable building boom in the Renaissance. Many of the buildings (the Medici Riccardi palace, the Strozzi palace, the Pitti palace, the Rucellai palace) that tourists admire today were built in the fifteenth century.[31] Although Florence's cathedral was begun earlier, Filippo Bunelleschi's magnificent dome completed it in 1436. Many other cities from Rome to Paris experienced building booms in the Renaissance. For example, Sixtus V (ruled 1585–1590) and other Renaissance popes tore down buildings in the center of Rome in order to carve out straight streets and large piazzas with obelisks or fountains in the center. Popes and cardinals added new palaces and they built St. Peter's. This was urban renewal, Renaissance style. It was often done to glorify the ruler and his family as well as to improve the city. Even though generating employment was not the stated purpose of Renaissance urban renewal, large building and road projects certainly increased employment for architects, stone masons, brick layers, carpenters, laborers who built roads, and interior decorators, such as Raphael and Michelangelo. And everything was done by hand.

Renaissance cities had their own version of private–public leadership for urban renewal. The big difference was that it was often united in the same person or family. Cosimo de' Medici, who ruled Florence from 1434 to 1464 without holding high office, his son Piero who did the same from 1464 to 1469, and grandson Lorenzo, who ruled Florence from 1469 to 1492, again without holding formal office, were simultaneously the political leaders of Florence and its wealthiest citizens, the Florentine equivalent to Pittsburgh's Mellon and Detroit's Ford. Hence, Cosimo and Lorenzo de' Medici combined the influence of Richard K. Mellon and David Lawrence, of Henry Ford II and Coleman Young. And like Mellon and Ford, they preferred to work behind the scenes through their extensive network of supporters, business partners, associates, friends, relatives through marriage, and those who came to them for favors. A word from Lorenzo de' Medici carried a great deal of weight, just as suggestions from Mellon and Ford did.

The leaders of the historical Renaissance did not have to deal with opposition like the leaders of twentieth-century American cities did, because their cities were not democracies. A Renaissance prince, or a behind-the-scenes ruler like Lorenzo de' Medici, was not voted out of office. But they might be assassinated, the Renaissance equivalent of losing the primary election. In some locales, assassination attempts occurred almost as often as elections in twentieth-century American cities, with the major difference that assassinations were unscheduled. A conspiracy of those who objected to the dominant role of the Medici organized an assassination effort against Lorenzo de' Medici and Giuliano, his younger brother, in 1478. They attacked while Lorenzo and Giuliano were attending mass in the Florentine cathedral, fatally stabbing Giuliano and wounding Lorenzo. But he escaped to rally his supporters who rounded up and executed the conspirators. Lorenzo had no further problems with political opposition. In similar fashion, David Lawrence survived a primary challenge from another Democrat, who objected to his alliance with business leaders, and won a contested fall election in the fall of 1949, but was not threatened again.

A final similarity is that Renaissance leaders and leaders of American urban renewal strongly supported both the arts and mass entertainment. Renaissance leaders paid artists, architects, and musicians handsomely to paint, build, and sing. In so doing, they contributed significantly to the economy.[32] Neither the leaders of the Pittsburgh Renaissance nor the Detroit Renaissance began with any concern for the arts. But they later built or renovated concert halls. Lorenzo de' Medici sponsored tournaments with jousting knights on horseback in Piazza Santa Croce to entertain Florentines. Pittsburgh and Detroit built baseball, football, and hockey stadiums for their fans. Unfortunately, the cost of providing mass sports entertainment is much more expensive than in the fifteenth century.

Chapter 7

MACHIAVELLI: AMERICAN POLITICAL ADVISER

In 1999, a Washington-based neoconservative published a book entitled *Machiavelli on Modern Leadership*. It cites Machiavelli again and again in support of an aggressive American foreign policy, including military action, without concern for whether the policies are morally justified. Many neoconservatives are followers of Leo Strauss, an academic political philosopher whose most important book was *Thoughts on Machiavelli*. On the other side, critics describe the policies of the George W. Bush administration as "Machiavellian," and they do not mean it as a compliment. "Mayberry Machiavellis" is one of the epithets used to describe Bush's political operatives. Historians measure major American statesmen against Machiavelli's precepts. Whatever the point of view, Machiavelli is a major reference point for discussions of American policy and history.

Americans were not very interested in Niccolò Machiavelli early in the twentieth century. But after World War II, he came into his own as an adviser to American policymakers. Today, Machiavelli's influence on political policy may be greater than at any time since he served the Florentine government. Machiavelli has become an American.

The Real Machiavelli

Niccolò Machiavelli was born in Florence in 1469, the son of a lawyer of middling income and status. He received an excellent education in the classics, but little else is known about him until he was appointed head of the foreign policy chancery of the Florentine government in 1498. He was not a policymaker but the key civil servant in the foreign policy administration of the Florentine state. In the next fourteen years, he spent more time out of Florence than in the city, as he traveled, observed, and negotiated with princes on behalf of the Florentine Republic. He visited Italian and foreign states and watched princes rise and fall. But in 1512, the Florentine republican government lost control of the city, and the Medici family returned to power. Machiavelli was dismissed. He was briefly imprisoned and tortured on charges of complicity in a plot to overthrow the Medicis. His innocence having been established, he was released and moved to his small farm outside of Florence. There he wrote all the works that made him famous. He died in 1527.

In the second half of 1513, Machiavelli wrote *The Prince,* the best-known book on politics of all time. It is an instruction manual for a ruler who wishes to gain and hold power. Machiavelli believed that politics could be a science. Observation of the present, study of the past, and the application of reason enabled one to discover the principles of successful politics. He insisted that the prince should base his actions not on what people ought to do but what they were likely to do in the pursuit of self-interest. He did not believe that a ruler could succeed if he did what is morally right. Machiavelli endorsed the use of force against internal and external enemies. He emphasized the importance of the ruler's personal *virtù,* a combination of boldness, stealth, and the ability to manipulate others. He viewed the bulk of men (and women as well, although he did not mention them) as fickle, selfish, and easily duped. But Machiavelli also recognized that rulers were not completely masters of their own destinies. They were at the mercy of fortune, which was a combination of luck, chance, even opportunity. Fortune was the unpredictable element in politics.

Much of Machiavelli's enormous appeal comes from his brilliant and memorable language. Some of his most famous epigrammatic statements are "It is better to be feared than to be loved." "The prince must be both a lion and a fox." "A good man will come to ruin among so many who are not good." "The prince must learn how not to be good." "Fortune is a woman who yields to the young and the bold." "A man will sooner forget the loss of a father than the loss of his fortune."

Machiavelli also wrote *Discourses on the First Ten Books of Livy*, a very large treatise on politics organized as a commentary on the famous history of Rome from its legendary foundation in 753 BC to 194 BC written by the ancient historian Titus Livy. Like *The Prince*, the *Discourses* analyzed past and present political events in order to discover universal principles. Machiavelli wrote most of it between 1515 and 1517, although some scholars believe that he began it in 1513, dropped it to write *The Prince*, then finished in 1520 or 1521. In the *Discourses,* Machiavelli offered analyses of the principles and institutions of successful, enduring republics, that is, states in which the people have large or small participation in government. He paid less attention to individuals and more to groups, such as the nobles and the people. Above all, he discussed the political, religious, and military institutions and laws needed for a successful republic. He endorsed civil religion with the argument that ancient Roman religion strengthened the state by encouraging its inhabitants to fight for it. At the same time, he asserted that governments might manipulate religious rituals in order to get results that would persuade the people that the gods endorsed the government's policies. The *Discourses* differs from *The Prince,* because it studies republics and goes far beyond advising a ruler. But the basic political principles are the same.

In 1519 and 1520, Machiavelli wrote *The Art of War,* which discussed military organization and tactics. He argued that states should develop citizen militias rather than rely on mercenary soldiers. He also wrote comedies, short stories, historical works, numerous letters, and diplomatic reports earlier in his career. None of his works were published in his lifetime; the most important were first published in 1532 and have not been out of print since. There are numerous English translations of Machiavelli's most important works.

Despite condemnation by state and church authorities and being banned more than once, Machiavelli's works have attracted enormous attention over the centuries. Many have responded to Machiavelli, because he posed basic political questions: can a good man survive in an evil political world? Can a state survive without violating common moral principles? The view that a ruler or state cannot is embodied in the expression "reason of state" (a phrase coined after Machiavelli's death), meaning that the good of the state justifies dishonest and evil actions.

Machiavelli: Conservative and Neoconservative

Although he died nearly five centuries ago, Machiavelli is an active political adviser to members of the American government and those who seek to try to influence policy, especially in foreign affairs. Conservatives and neoconservatives make the greatest use of Machiavelli, but opponents pay attention as well. Political operatives and would-be opinion makers, those who offer advice in books, columns, and Web sites, often cite Machiavelli in support of their views.

The love affair between conservatism and Machiavelli began in 1943 when James Burnham proposed a contemporary science of politics based on Machiavelli. The son of a Chicago railroad executive, Burnham (1905–1987) studied English literature and philosophy at Princeton University and Oxford University, then became a professor of philosophy at New York University in 1929, a position that he held until 1953.[1] In the 1930s, he was a Trotskyite Communist and helped form the Socialist Workers Party. But he left the Communist movement in 1940 in the aftermath of the German-Soviet nonaggression treaty of 1939. He began to write for the *Partisan Review*, the leading journal of the non-Communist left. In 1941, he published *The Managerial Revolution*, which argued that a new ruling class, called "the managers," would soon replace both capitalists and Communists. Burnham's book stimulated much discussion in Washington and elsewhere.

In 1943, Burnham published *The Machiavellians: Defenders of Freedom* (New York: John Day). It was his most important book because it explained his geopolitics. Burnham presented an approach to politics derived from Machiavelli plus French and Italian social and political thinkers such as Gaetano Mosca (1858–1941), Georges Sorel (1847–1922), Robert Michels (1876–1936), and Wilfredo Pareto (1848–1923), whom Burnham calls "Machiavellians."

Burnham began by rehabilitating Machiavelli. He pointed out that American and British thinkers have a low opinion of Machiavelli. This is because Anglo-Saxon politics is characterized by hypocrisy and an avoidance of the truth, whereas continental European politicians are more honest. However, Machiavelli and the Machiavellians established several points, which are the heart of Burnham's system of political analysis. The most important division in society is between the ruling class and the ruled, the elite and the nonelite. The elite rules through a political formula containing myths, ideology, and/or religion. Nevertheless, the interests of the elite and the nonelite do sometimes coincide. And understanding this is the key to achieving partial—but not complete—liberty and democracy.

Although Burnham believed in liberty and democracy, he did not think that "the masses" could act scientifically (i.e., select real goals and take practical steps to achieve them). Instead, they believe in myths. By contrast, some elites can act scientifically. Despite the devotion of elites to the maintenance of their own power and privileges, the goals of the masses and elites are sometimes in harmony. Therefore, elites must foster belief in myths for the multitude; in other words, they must sometimes lie. And the ruling class must be prepared to open its ranks to able and ambitious newcomers from below. If these conditions are met, Burnham is cautiously optimistic that civilization will survive. Although there never will be a perfect society, human beings will live in a minimum of moral dignity.

"Freedom" in the subtitle of the book is part of the argument in several ways. When men look realistically at politics and see it as it really is, they are free of myths. Such freedom also protects them from bureaucratic dominance, the rule of the managers. It leads them to oppose rulers, which is a good thing. Capitalism is also a guarantee of freedom from managers, because private ownership means a dispersal of economic power. It prevents the concentration of economic power in the state, which destroys the foundations of liberty. Burnham clearly favored capitalism and opposed big government. Although he may have had the Soviet state system in mind when he wrote, these ideas became basic themes of American conservatism.

At times, the book is brilliantly prophetic. For example, Burnham predicted in 1943 that soldiers would provide a considerable section of the ruling class of the future. After World War II, former military officers did become leaders in American life, and Dwight D. Eisenhower became president in 1952. Military planning and operations became an essential part of American foreign policy at the same time and show no signs of diminishing in the early years of the twenty-first century. On the other hand, some of Burnham's book was unconvincing and inconsistent. For example, it is hard to see how rule by elites could produce greater freedom than an elected democracy.

The Machiavellians was Burnham's most important book because it presented his political-historical method of analysis. He used that method to become America's primary intellectual advocate of the Cold War against the Soviet Union. In 1944, two years before George Kennan and Winston Churchill warned about Soviet aims and the Iron Curtain dividing Europe, Burnham identified Soviet-inspired actions in an uprising in Greece as a sign of the Soviet commitment to rule the Eurasian landmass. He sounded the alarm about Soviet expansionism. In three books and many articles published between 1944 and 1952, Burnham proposed a strategy to fight back. He did not favor a policy of containment because, in his view, that would mean Communist victory. Rather, he argued for "the policy of liberation." He wanted the United States to undermine Communist power in Eastern Europe, Iran, Afghanistan, Manchuria, North Korea, and China. He argued that the United States should mount a propaganda offensive against Communism; it should create economic difficulties for the Soviet Union, stimulate discontent among the Russian masses, and encourage resistance movements in Soviet satellite states. Burnham proposed a strategy of political, psychological, and economic warfare to defeat Communism, and the United States adopted much of what he proposed. Burnham's policies were the application to global politics of the principles of realist policies outlined in *The Machiavellians*. As a result of these positions, Burnham broke with his former colleagues at the *Partisan Review* in the early 1950s and found a new journalistic home in William F. Buckley Jr.'s *National Review,* for which he wrote for more than twenty years.

American anti-Communists revered Burnham because he offered a formula for winning the Cold War. But his books also stimulated considerable opposition inside and outside of government from those who believed that Burnham's proposals were reckless, unrealizable, and/or wrong. Burnham saw the Communist movement as unified. Critics correctly pointed out that the Communist world comprised separate peoples and nations with conflicting aims. Burnham did not recognize the depth of the differences between China and the Soviet Union. Burnham's consuming passion about the Communist threat meant that he supported congressional investigations of domestic communists and refused to condemn U.S. Senator Joseph McCarthy's excesses and violations of civil rights. And Burnham continued to propound his own view of a realist foreign policy. In 1962 he predicted that America could not win in Vietnam with limited military action. But he also denounced the peace movement.

Burnham was a key figure who provided an intellectual rationale for vigorous tactics in the Cold War. Burnham certainly had considerable intellectual prominence. He lectured to many government groups and was a consultant for the CIA. But how much direct influence on policy he had is impossible to say. His most important achievement was to become the major intellectual of the anti-Communist movement. President Ronald Reagan recognized this by awarding him the Presidential Medal of Freedom in 1983. And his use of Machiavelli became part of American conservatism.

Leo Strauss, a very influential academic conservative, also studied Machiavelli carefully. Born in Germany, Strauss (1899–1973) received a doctorate in philosophy in 1921 and held a research position at the Academy of Jewish Research in Berlin from

1925 to 1932. He left Germany in 1932. He arrived in the United States in 1938 and became a member of the New School for Social Research in New York. In 1949, be became a professor of political science at the University of Chicago. After retirement in 1969, he was a scholar-in-residence at St. John's College in Annapolis, Maryland. He apparently was an inspiring and stimulating teacher. He also wrote fifteen books and about eighty articles.

Strauss never summarized his political philosophy in one place. Rather, he wrote books about Plato, Aristotle, Maimonides, Machiavelli, Thomas Hobbes, John Locke, Friedrich Nietzsche, and others, in which he indicated his views through his commentary.[2] His complex and involuted way of reading texts, with long turgid sentences, minimal paragraphing, and lack of topic sentences and summaries, makes his thought difficult to grasp. Moreover, Strauss often argued from silence; that is, he took what authors did not say to indicate their true positions. Any attempt to present Strauss' thought must use "it seems" and "apparently." Strauss had a large circle of students, admirers, and followers. After his death, his former students and followers, almost all of whom are political conservatives, organized conferences devoted to analyzing and extending his insights. As they interpret Strauss' works, they sometimes act like a circle of initiates, the limited few who understand the master.

Several themes are central to Strauss' thought. The most important is a rejection of liberal democracy. It comes from his conviction that liberalism inevitably leads to nihilism, the lack of belief in anything. His interpretation of the failure of the Weimar government in Germany (1918–1933) may have influenced him greatly. The Weimar democracy was Germany's first fully democratic government. But in the view of Strauss, it lacked the fundamental values and beliefs that would have enabled it to withstand the assaults from right and left that overwhelmed it. In his view, the weakness of Weimar democracy opened the door to Nazi tyranny. (Many historians do not view the Weimar government so negatively. Some see it as a period of considerable political, artistic, and cultural achievement. But then it was undermined by problems it inherited, overwhelmed by inflation and economic depression over which it had no control, and finished off by street violence.) Strauss seemed to see some of the same weaknesses in American liberal democracy but hoped that it might become stronger through commitment to eternal values and truths, as he understood them.

Strauss rejected relativism, the lack of belief in eternal and unchanging truths and values. He saw relativism as a key element of modernity and very close to nihilism. Strauss criticized modernity, by which he meant twentieth-century liberalism characterized by relativism and a susceptibility to being exploited by democratically elected demagogues. Plato, probably Strauss' favorite philosopher, offered an alternative to modernism and liberalism. Like Plato, Strauss almost seemed to endorse government by philosopher kings, an elite not elected by the people but worthy to rule others because they have special insight into what is good for man and society. In short, Strauss is popular with conservatives for three reasons: his criticism of modern liberal democracy, his rejection of relativism, and his appeal to a knowledgeable few, an elite of wise men.

In 1958, Strauss published *Thoughts on Machiavelli*, possibly his most important book.[3] Reviewers were baffled and unimpressed, because it broke no new historical ground on Machiavelli. Some pointed out that Strauss ignored recent scholarship on Machiavelli and the history of Renaissance Italy. But that was not the intent of the book. *Thoughts on Machiavelli* was not primarily a study of Machiavelli as he was, but of his position in the evolution of modern political philosophy as Strauss saw it.

Strauss criticized Machiavelli for rejecting old values and a limited perspective. In Strauss' view, Machiavelli was the first modern, the man who turned civilization in the wrong direction of liberalism and relativism. Machiavelli was a "fallen angel," because he understood ancient Greek philosophy and its search for the good, but rejected it. The discovery of truth and the embrace of good principles by the state and its people, as Plato sought, are most important in politics. But Machiavelli saw politics only as a means to political success. In renouncing the right path, Machiavelli became the first modern philosopher. After Machiavelli came Thomas Hobbes, John Locke, and eventually Friedrich Nietzsche, all of whom followed Machiavelli on the road to modern liberalism, the wrong road.

Strauss also disapproved of Machiavelli's attitude toward religion, even though Strauss' views may not have been very different. He correctly noted that Machiavelli viewed organized religion, both Christianity and ancient Roman paganism, as a useful tool to strengthen the state. Religion helped make the citizenry a cohesive body. Moreover, Machiavelli approved of rulers who manipulated religious rituals in order to win the support of the people. Strauss lamented what Machiavelli said about religion, especially Christianity. But he also criticized Machiavelli for saying it openly. In other words, Strauss did not so much object that Machiavelli advocated using religion for political purposes but that he told the world about it. That religion can be used by rulers for their own, higher purposes should have been left unspoken. Elsewhere, Strauss did not think that the elite needed to believe in religion. But he did posit that religion provided a set of beliefs and principles that the mass of people should accept and believe in order for a stable society to exist. The Renaissance philosopher Pietro Pomponazzi (1462–1525) made similar arguments in his famous *On the Immortality of the Soul* of 1516.[4]

Part of the complexity and attraction of Strauss' thought is his notion that great philosophers write in an exoteric way that protects an esoteric inner message. In other words, Machiavelli had one message for the superficial reader, and another for the careful, very attentive reader who puzzled out what he really meant. Naturally, Strauss' followers believe that he also wrote exoterically in order to protect an inner, real message. This is one reason why they devote time to interpreting him and are able to use him for various purposes.

Alan Bloom (1930–1992), a Strauss student and disciple who also taught at the University of Chicago, popularized some elements of his thought in *The Closing of the American Mind: How Higher Education Has Failed Democracy and Impoverished the Souls of Today's Students* (New York: Simon & Schuster, 1987). It attracted a lot of attention. The book was a diatribe against the ills of American higher education, which Bloom attributed to several causes. The immediate problems were the dumbing down of the curriculum and its cafeteria-style lack of structure, in which the study of Shakespeare and of basketweaving receive equal credit. Behind them are cultural and moral relativism, the same evils against which Strauss objected. In place of cultural standards have come rock music, affirmative action, feminism, and much else in Bloom's colorful *j'accuse* book. Bloom's solution was a return to intense study of the great minds of the past, those whose ideas challenged readers of all epochs. He mentioned Machiavelli many times in his book, although not so often as his favorite, Plato, nor his *bête-noir,* Nietzsche.

Some of Strauss' disciples have risen to positions of considerable influence and high office in Washington. Irving Kristol (1920–), arguably the father of American neoconservatism, was probably the first important Strauss follower. More recently, admirers of Strauss attained key positions in the administrations of Ronald Reagan, George H. W. Bush, and George W. Bush. They also populate conservative think tanks and write for conservative journals, newspapers, syndicated columns, and Web sites. The list includes Paul Wolfowitz, deputy secretary of defense in the first

George W. Bush administration, now head of the World Bank; John T. Agresto, formerly deputy chairman of the National Endowment for the Humanities; former conservative presidential candidate Alan Keyes; former judge Robert Bork, former chair of the National Endowment for the Humanities and former secretary of education William Bennett; U.S. Supreme Court justice Clarence Thomas; and William Kristol, son of Irving Kristol, campaign manager for Dan Quayle and now a syndicated columnist. It has been argued that the "Vulcans," the self-chosen nickname of officials in the first George W. Bush administration who promoted the war against Iraq and the policy of using military force to promote democracy worldwide, have been influenced by Strauss.[5] To be sure, it is difficult to know the extent to which these stars in the neoconservative galaxy consider themselves Straussians or how closely they follow him. But their books and articles usually include references to Strauss and Machiavelli.

Machiavellian Foreign Policy

Although some conservatives see Machiavelli as the point in history at which modern political philosophy took the wrong turn, toward liberalism and relativism, others use Machiavelli in a more traditional way, as the supporter of a strong, realist, and aggressive politics unchecked by the restrictions of moral or international law.

Probably the strongest neoconservative statement of an aggressive, warlike Machiavellian foreign policy comes from Michael A. Ledeen. In 1999, he published *Machiavelli on Modern Leadership: Why Machiavelli's Iron Rules Are as Timely and Important Today as Five Centuries Ago* (New York: St. Martin's Press). Born in 1941, Ledeen obtained a Ph.D. in history from the University of Wisconsin in 1969, where he wrote his Ph.D. dissertation on Fascist Italy. After teaching at Washington University in St. Louis, he became Rome correspondent for *The New Republic* from 1975 to 1977, was a visiting professor at the University of Rome, served as a consultant for Italian military intelligence and, allegedly, had links with a right-wing Italian clandestine military organization accused of plotting to overthrow the Italian government. Returning to the United States, he was a senior staff member of the Georgetown University Center for Strategic and International Studies from 1977 to 1981, then a special antiterrorism adviser to Secretary of State Alexander Haig in 1981 and 1982, followed by a return to the Center for Strategic and International Studies. Ledeen served as a consultant to the National Security Council, the Department of Defense, and the Department of State through the Reagan years. He may have been involved in the attempted exchange of arms for American hostages in Beirut, which came to be known as the "Iran-Contra affair." Like many other conservatives who strongly support military action, Ledeen never served in the American armed forces.

Ledeen is currently the "Freedom Scholar" of the American Enterprise Institute for Public Policy Research, an important conservative Republican think-tank, which includes among its resident scholars Newt Gingrich, the former speaker of the House of Representatives, and Lynn Cheney, former director of the National Endowment of the Humanities, who denounces university professors for their alleged left-leaning scholarship and wants her former agency abolished. Ledeen has written some ten books, mostly on foreign policy. He is a frequent contributor to National Review Online and other conservative newspapers and media outlets.[6] Although Ledeen is not thought to be a prominent adviser to the administration of George W. Bush, the invasion of Iraq looks like the logical result of the militaristic and violent foreign policy that he has been advocating for years with the help of Machiavelli.

The central message of the book is a call for strong leadership without concern for moral or other restrictions. Ledeen praises political, business, and religious leaders who take strong, ruthless, and decisive action: leaders who play to win. He calls the late Vincent Lombardi (1913–1970), coach of the Green Bay Packers professional football team, a leading Machiavellian of modern times, because he said that winning is the only thing. (But Lombardi did not endorse winning by dishonest means.) Ledeen's political heroes are Margaret Thatcher, Ronald Reagan, Lee Kwan Yu, the former authoritarian leader of Singapore, and Pope John Paul II. All of them moved swiftly to take advantage of historical opportunities, another Machiavellian principle, to reshape the world. They did not worry about how they did it, and they ruled by fear. He also praises Bill Gates for fighting ruthlessly to dominate the personal computer market.

A key theme is corruption. Machiavelli devoted a number of pages to corruption, by which he meant governments and leaders who subverted the good customs and laws of a state and brought it to ruin. Ledeen's definition of corruption is a ruler who is both given to personal vices and weak. He reserves his strongest words for what he sees as the connection between personal corruption and a contempt for the value of the military and its standards. He sees President Bill Clinton, who was in office when the book was published, as proof. He begins his attack on Clinton with a quote from Machiavelli's *Art of War* in which Machiavelli denounced unnamed Italian princes of his time for their corrupt politics and for keeping "many lascivious women around." Ledeen then couples Clinton's "obsessive and compulsive sexual misbehavior" with his alleged "lifelong contempt for the military, whose total devotion to the common good is the opposite of his own."[7] Much condemnation of Clinton for his corruption and his weak foreign policy follows.

This leads to a denunciation of women in the American armed forces. The presence of women has led to a dilution of standards for military performance and a "demoralization (in the fullest sense of the term) of the armed forces produced by constant close contact

163

between men and women."[8] The rising pregnancy rates of female members of the armed forces has been the result, according to Ledeen. His attack on women in the military does not seem relevant in a discussion of political corruption. And it has no connection with Machiavelli, who never mentioned female soldiers. Indeed, Ledeen fails to mention that the Machiavelli he admires had adulterous sexual affairs.

Ledeen agrees with Machiavelli that strong, ruthless, and dictatorial measures are needed to purge corruption and to restore a state to health. Only strong leaders can restrain the ruinous impulses that drive human actions. Only dictatorial measures can force men to act for the common good. Ledeen believes that the strong leader acting for the common good may commit evil. According to Ledeen, Machiavelli's tests of acceptability for evil deeds were that the actions had to make things better, and that "evil actions must be limited to meeting a specific crisis and must not become an integral part of the government or regime." Ledeen lists several twentieth-century leaders and groups that met these standards. For example, Kamal Ataturk, an army officer, used the Turkish army and dictatorial means in order to defeat a foreign enemy and then to create a secular Turkish state in the 1920s. When Turkey was threatened by a wave of mass terrorism in the 1970s, the army followed Ataturk's example and seized power, defeated the terrorists, and restructured the state. In 1997, the Turkish army again intervened to topple a government. Ledeen also praises General Douglas MacArthur who as temporary dictator of Japan after World War II "purged the warlords and imposed a democratic constitution."[9]

Like Machiavelli, Ledeen believes that it is better for a ruler to be feared than loved. If the ruler is loved, he becomes the personal symbol of the government and the target when things go wrong. Further, a leader who rules by love gives up the initiative.

The leader who rules by fear can act decisively and quickly, leaving his opponents fearful. Ledeen praises Ronald Reagan as a politician who ruled by fear after he fired the striking air traffic controllers in 1981. He cites Yassir Arafat as a ruler who successfully combined fear with deception. According to Ledeen, Arafat projected an image of moderation while having potential Palestinian challengers killed.

Ledeen accepts and endorses perpetual warfare. He argues that "Peace is *not* [italics in the original text] the normal condition of mankind. War and the preparation for war are the themes of human history." Conflict flows from corrupt human nature; people will not do what is right. Hence, all attempts to solve problems peaceably are destined to fail. He cites Machiavelli in support of the proposition that leaders "who fail to prepare for the next war—on the battlefield, at the ballot box, or in the marketplace—are likely to be defeated."[10]

Accepting Machiavelli's principle of perpetual warfare, Ledeen strongly criticizes leaders and military men who pursue cautious, peaceable policies. Ledeen criticizes President Jimmy Carter for banning political assassinations by U.S. government agencies. Carter's moralistic policies only made murder more likely, because it stopped America from killing terrorists. Ledeen criticizes the Caspar Weinberger–Colin Powell doctrine of the 1980s that a nation should not go to war unless it can support it, win it, and has an exit strategy. Ledeen criticizes the first President Bush for halting the first Iraq war in 1991 just when the American army was ready to destroy the regime of Saddam Hussein.

Ledeen's knowledge and understanding of Machiavelli's works is reasonably good. But he misuses Machiavelli in some ways. Ledeen writes that Machiavelli praised free enterprise, private property, and minimal taxation. Machiavelli had nothing to say about these. The quote from the *Discourses* that Ledeen cites in support is ambiguous and does not address these points.[11] Indeed, many scholars have pointed out that Machiavelli's greatest omission was his failure to discuss economic factors in politics and war. For example, he never discussed how a prince should raise the money to pay for war.

Despite occasional misrepresentations, the book is a bold attempt to apply some of Machiavelli's principles of strong leadership and military action to contemporary politics. But it leaves hanging some of the same questions that Machiavelli did not answer. Ledeen, echoing Machiavelli, argues that sometimes the corruption of the state is so bad that it is necessary for a strong ruler to take matters into his own hands for the common good. When the times are this bad, the strong leader may employ evil means to overthrow the current government and establish a new one. But who decides when such action is necessary? Machiavelli leaves it up to the strong individual, and Ledeen never raises the issue. A related question is, what constitutes political virtue and corruption? For Ledeen, political virtue is conservatism and acceptance of perpetual warfare. The final question is, will the strong leader who seizes power for the common good later transfer power to the people and step down? Neither Machiavelli nor Ledeen provide answers. The evidence from the twentieth century is that few strong leaders willingly step down. In the final analysis, Ledeen's advocacy of strong leadership and militarism based on Machiavellian principles has eerie echoes of the rhetoric and actions of Benito Mussolini.

Although it never argues for preemptive war, the book might be read as offering a political philosophy justifying the Iraq and Afghanistan wars. Ledeen's most recent book, *The War Against the Terror Masters: Why It Happened, Where We Are Now, How We'll Win* (New York: St. Martin's Press, 2002) argues that the United States should seek to topple regimes that sponsor terrorism, especially Iran. He repeats some of the themes of *Machiavelli on Modern Leadership* and again uses Machiavelli, but the emphasis is on fighting terrorism. Ledeen condemns the Clinton administration for its intelligence failures and weak leadership against terrorism. He endorses "anticipatory self-defense." He argues that the United States should support dissident movements within Iran and should proclaim America's message of freedom to the people of Iran. But he stops short of advocating military invasion of Iran.

Although neoconservatives, or at least some of them, endorse Machiavelli's amoral politics, one very successful amoral ruler presents a problem: Fidel Castro. *Is Fidel Castro a Machiavellian Prince?* (Miami: The Endowment for Cuban American Studies, 1999) was written by a Florida professor of political science, Alfred G. Cuzán, with ties to neoconservatives, and was published by a conservative Cuban-American organization.[12] Cuzán presents a profile of the prince as described by Machiavelli in *The Prince* and to a much lesser extent in *The Discourses*. Next, he summarizes Castro's life and career: his origins and early life, the seizure of the Cuban state in 1959, the repulsion of the invaders at the Bay of Pigs in 1961, the establishment of a socialist state, his attempt to export his policies, the execution and imprisonment of opponents and allies, and the suppression of dissent.

The author runs through a list of Machiavelli's qualities for an effective prince. Does Castro exhibit *virtù*, defined as audacity, courage, energy, and strength? The answer is yes. Does he study history? Yes. Does he imitate the ferocity of the lion and the deception of the fox? Yes. Does he understand military matters and rely on his own resources in his military campaign? Yes. Has he been favored by *fortuna*? Yes. Does he manipulate alliances with foreign powers to his advantage? Yes. Does he instill fear in his subjects? Yes. Is he loved by his subjects? The answer is that it is difficult to tell, because Cubans lack freedom of speech. Of twenty-three qualities and actions defining Machiavelli's prince, Castro fulfills nineteen of them, does not fulfill two, and the answer is unknown on two others. The reader expects the author to conclude that Castro is a Machiavellian prince.

But in a surprising about face, Cuzán concludes that Castro is not a Machiavellian prince. The reason is that Machiavelli described a prince but not a tyrant. Cuzán points out that Machiavelli did not use the word "tyrant" in *The Prince*. But Machiavelli did present some examples of tyrants in *The Discourses* and he disapproved of them. Thus, Cuzán argues, Machiavelli made a distinction between prince and tyrant. The latter made the rich poor and the poor rich, built and unbuilt cities, moved people from one place to another, revolutionized everything, and allowed no rank, institution, or wealth to exist that does not depend on the tyrant. The tyrant uses such extreme cruelty that his subjects flee or withdraw into private lives. All these Castro has done. Hence, the author concludes that Castro, while resembling Machiavelli's prince in most respects, "is fundamentally different. . . . Machiavelli's prince is not a tyrant as the ancients understood the term. Fidel Castro is."[13] The conclusion does not seem consistent with the rest of the book.

Machiavelli has been a theme in American conservative political discussion since the 1940s. It is likely that the use of Machiavelli has contributed to the combative mentality that characterized American Cold War politics, the belligerency of American conservatism, and the take-no-prisoners tactics and language employed against liberalism and Democrats. Or maybe Machiavelli just served as the excuse.

Criticism of Machiavellianism in American Policy

Critics of the dominant themes of American politics and foreign policy, and especially of conservative politics, also employ Machiavelli to make their points. They charge that an ideology of power moves the actions of American governments, especially its foreign policy decisions. Their definition of Machiavellianism is that American dominance is the goal, and this end justifies evil means. They argue that many American leaders tell lies to the American people and the world to cover up their actions, just as Machiavelli recommended.

The leftist historian Howard Zinn (1922–) provides an example of this tradition. After serving as a bombardier on B-17 Flying Fortresses in World War II, Zinn earned a Ph.D. in American history at Columbia University. He taught history at Spelman College, political science at Boston University, participated in civil rights actions and anti-Vietnam protests, and wrote *A People's History of the United States* (1980), which has sold 800,000 copies. Another work addresses Machiavellianism in recent American history: *Declarations of Independence: Cross-Examining American Ideology* (New York: HarperCollins, 1990). The book is partly a discussion of key episodes in twentieth-century American history and partly personal reflection on these episodes.

The first chapter, "Machiavellian Realism and U.S. Foreign Policy: Means and Ends," provides the theme for much that follows. Zinn points out that the goal of Machiavelli's *The Prince* was not the welfare of the citizenry, but power, conquest, and control, in order to maintain the state. It is the same in America, Zinn declares. The Declaration of Independence hangs on the walls of schoolrooms, but American foreign policy follows Machiavelli. The interests of those who run the government and the interests of the average citizens are not the same. The former engage in Machiavellian power politics and camouflage their actions through a technique of deception called "plausible denial." Machiavelli advised the prince to use force to achieve his aims when necessary. A democratic state often does the same, writes Zinn. But a democracy with an elected president instead of a prince must present national power as serving liberty, justice, and humanity. Hence, presidents and their advisers often lie to the people. This chapter and much of the book give examples, such as the justifications advanced for dropping atomic bombs on Japan in 1945 and governmental deception during the Vietnam War. Zinn rejects this aspect of American ideology. But he also notes the existence of "Anti-Machiavellians" in American history, meaning people who think for themselves and reject the dominant ideology. Sometimes even those close to power ignore Machiavellian advice and summon the moral strength to dissent. When there are enough of them, "history has its splendid moments."[14]

Other critics link some of the ruthless political tactics of Republican officeseekers of the past fifteen years to Machiavelli. In Nelson A. Blue's book *Machiavelli's The Republican: The best possible America and how to achieve it* (2000), Machiavelli himself offers political advice to conservative Republicans. Machiavelli explains that although he "lost his corporeal capacities in 1527," he still follows politics with great interest and wants to help conservative Republicans. He admits that some changes have occurred between the sixteenth and the twentieth centuries: "We will have to restrict our assassinations to mere character assassinations." Machiavelli then provides ample examples of Republican deceptions and lies. The book is a political satire with serious points to make.

Machiavelli endorses as an example of how to win elections through deception the television advertisement of Republican U.S. Senator Jesse Helms in his 1990 North Carolina senatorial campaign against Democrat Harvey Gantt, an African American. In the ad, a pair of white hands holds and then crumples a job rejection letter, as the voice-over narrates:

> You needed that job, and you were the best qualified, but they had to give it to a minority because of a racial quota. Is that really fair? Harvey Gantt says it is. Gantt supports Ted Kennedy's racial quota law that makes the color of

your skin more important than your qualifications. You'll vote on this issue next Tuesday. For racial quotas—Harvey Gantt. Against racial quotas—Jesse Helms.[15]

The television ad distorted Gantt's position; he supported an equal rights bill but not quotas. But noncorporeal Machiavelli praised the commercial and endorsed the timing. The Helms campaign filled the airwaves with the ad a few days before the election, preventing the Gantt campaign from mounting an effective response. Helms won the election.

Machiavelli also praises the "Willie Horton" political commercial used by George H. W. Bush in the last days of the 1988 presidential campaign. It claimed that Governor Michael Dukakis of Massachusetts was responsible for releasing a black convict on a weekend furlough, during which he raped a white woman. The ad did not mention that a previous Republican governor had created the furlough program, which Dukakis had ended. Machiavelli concluded that these kinds of techniques produced "many of our greatest successes." Indeed, the late Lee Atwater, who planned both television ads, boasted that he read *The Prince* every year.[16] The last chapter of the book is entitled "Exhortation to Liberate America from the Liberal Yoke," a parody on the last chapter of Machiavelli's *The Prince,* entitled "An Exhortation to Liberate Italy from the Barbarians." *Machiavelli's The Republican* does not delve into political philosophy. But it does quote extensively from congressional records and other sources. It is a political satire with some funny lines, even though the actions that the incorporeal Machiavelli describes and endorses are not funny.

Machiavelli and the Bush Family

Critics regularly describe the actions of the administrations of George H. W. Bush (1988–1992) and especially that of George W.

Bush (2000–2008) as Machiavellian. They charge that Republication strategists have read Machiavelli and imbibed a Machiavellian mentality. For opponents of the Bushes, "Machiavellian" means political manipulation, deception, lies, and ruthlessness in the pursuit of political advantage.

On October 24, 2002, John J. Di Iulio wrote a seven-page letter to Ron Suskind, a former political correspondent for *Esquire Magazine*. A professor at the University of Pennsylvania and Bush supporter, Di Iulio was the director of the White House Office of Faith-Based and Community Initiatives. He was charged with drafting legislation that would provide federal funding for community service projects that would include church participation. But Di Iulio was frustrated by the "Mayberry Machiavellis" in the White House. He meant the political staff led by chief White House adviser for political affairs Karl Rove, "who consistently talked and acted as if the height of political sophistication consisted in reducing every issue to its simplest black-and-white terms for public consumption, then steering legislative initiative or policy proposals as far right as possible. These folks have their predecessors in previous administrations (left and right, Democrat and Republican), but in the Bush administration, they are particularly unfettered." "There is no precedent in any modern White House for what is going on in this one: a complete lack of a policy apparatus. What you've got is everything—and I mean everything—being run by the political arm. It's the reign of the Mayberry Machiavellis."[17]

Mayberry refers to the fictional southern town in which the homespun television series "The Andy Griffith Show" was set. Some identify Mayberry with Mount Airy, North Carolina, Griffith's birthplace. In the show, Griffith is the good-hearted sheriff who resolves problems with humor and by honoring traditional values. Hence, the combination of Mayberry and Machiavelli is a shorthand description of what critics see as the Bush administration's combination of deceptive talk about concern for all Americans and traditional values, which masks a ruthless quest for political advantage and policies benefitting the wealthy.

Kevin Phillips' *American Dynasty: Aristocracy, Fortune, and the Politics of Deceit in the House of Bush* (2004) is a full-throated denunciation of several generations of the Bush family. It charges family members with great ambition successfully realized by means of unsavory connections with the energy business, the military, the CIA, the religious right, and autocratic foreign regimes.

Phillips compares the actions and deceits of members of the Bush family with Machiavelli's politics of amorality, fraud, and the manipulation of religion, especially in the last chapter, entitled "Machiavelli and the American Dynastic Moment." He writes: "As the 2004 presidential election took shape, another such Machiavellian moment was at hand. U.S. president George W. Bush, while hardly a Medici (the ruling family of Florence through much of the Renaissance), was a dynast whose family heritage included secrecy and calculated deception." Phillips adds that Karl Rove, chief political strategist of George W. Bush, is a devotee of Machiavelli. But Phillips also uses the example of Renaissance Italy to voice his fear for America. Expressing alarm about the wars of the George W. Bush administration, he points out that "warfare destroyed most of the remaining municipally centered republics, such as Florence and Siena, as it spread across fifteenth- and sixteenth-century Italy. The republican institutions of the United States could also be expected to suffer."[18]

Machiavelli the Political Commentator

The national elections of 2004 unleashed a flood of references to Machiavelli, as pundits and observers used "Machiavelli" and "Machiavellian" to comment on what was happening.

For example, in the vice-presidential debate, Vice President Richard Cheney attacked the senatorial attendance record of U.S. Senator John Edwards by saying that the debate was the first time that he had met Edwards. Practically the day after the debate, it was revealed that Cheney's statement was a lie: he had met Edwards before. This lie plus misrepresentations about intelligence on Iraq by Cheney and President Bush prompted columnist Richard Reeves to criticize Cheney and Bush by writing a column quoting Machiavelli to the effect that a prince does not have to be honest and keep his word, he only has to seem to do so, a famous passage from chapter 18 of *The Prince*.[19]

A more nuanced use of Machiavelli came from Robert Wright, a senior fellow at the New America Foundation. Shortly after U.S. Senator John Kerry won the Democratic nomination for president, he wrote a column entitled "What Would Machiavelli Do?"[20] The topic was how Kerry could convince the voters that he would win back the friendship of nations alienated by Bush's war policies while simultaneously pursuing terrorists vigorously. Wright noted that Kerry would have a difficult time convincing right-wing Americans, "who have Machiavelli's dictum—better to be feared than loved—tattooed across their chests," that he would be willing and able to do this. But Machiavelli also suggested the solution: while it was better to be feared than loved, the best solution was to be both feared and loved. And if a leader could not do this, he "ought to inspire fear in such a way that, if he does not win love, he avoids hatred," a passage from chapter 17 of *The Prince*. Wright concluded that Bush was "too macho for Machiavelli," and hoped that Kerry would be able to convince Americans that he could make America both feared and loved—or at least respected—in the world. As the election results showed, Kerry did not succeed in convincing a majority of Americans. Or perhaps the voters were not interested in Machiavelli's solution.

Machiavelli was certainly busy in 2004. In addition to advising national candidates, his name played a role in a political scandal in New Jersey. Then Governor James E. McGreevey used the word "Machiavelli" in a tape-recorded conversation with a fund-raiser and contributor. According to the fund-raiser, "Machiavelli" was a code word that signaled that the governor agreed to a deal: he would help the fund-raiser in a land dispute in exchange for $40,000 in campaign funds. The governor said that his use of "Machiavelli" was entirely innocent. Whatever the truth of the matter, Governor McGreevey resigned his office on August 12, 2004, as he disclosed that, although married, he was a homosexual who had had an extramarital affair with a man.[21]

The American election year finally ended, and a new year of different elections opened. But commentators continued to evoke Machiavelli to explain political events. In April 2005, Cardinal Joseph Ratzinger was elected Pope Benedict XVI. The choice surprised those who thought that he was too conservative and too European to be elected. Machiavelli provided the explanation. E. J. Dionne Jr., a nationally syndicated columnist for *The Washington Post*, concluded that the cardinals chose the 78-year-old Ratzinger because they did not believe that he would be pope very long. Disappointed *papabili* (cardinals who want to be pope) would soon have another chance at the prize. "One need not be Machiavelli to suggest that potential popes sitting in the Sistine Chapel decided that they did not have the votes or the standing to make it this time, and would use a Ratzinger papacy to prepare for the next."[22] One wonders if Machiavelli, who disliked the papacy because he believed that it kept Italy politically divided and weak, would have agreed with such a strategy, if that is what it was.

Machiavelli as a Reference Point

The above uses of Machiavelli are part of debates about the conduct of American politics; that is, what course of action should be followed now, or what course of action must be condemned now. Machiavelli is also a reference point for the historical and scholarly study of American politics. Historians have used what Machiavelli wrote as an analytical tool to understand American policies and as a standard against which to measure major American statesmen.

A well-known example was the prize-winning political biography of President Franklin D. Roosevelt called *Roosevelt: The Lion and the Fox* (New York: Harcourt, Brace, & World, 1956), written by James MacGregor Burns, a professor of political science. The title comes from Machiavelli, and the book begins by quoting the famous lion-and-fox passage from chapter 18 of *The Prince*: "A prince . . . must imitate the fox and the lion, for the lion cannot protect himself from traps, and the fox cannot defend himself from wolves. One must, therefore, be a fox to recognize traps, and a lion to frighten wolves. . . . Therefore, a prudent ruler ought not to keep faith when by so doing it would be against his interest, and when the reasons which made him bind himself no longer exist. If men were all good, this precept would not be a good one; but as they are bad, and would not observe their faith with you, so you are not bound to keep faith with them."[23]

Burns argued that this was an apt description of Roosevelt the politician: he was as brave as a lion but also as shrewd and shifty as a fox. In Burns' judgment, Roosevelt was a profoundly moral man who believed that government had a positive responsibility to promote the general welfare, and Roosevelt showed the courage of a lion in pursuit of this goal. But he was also devious, manipulative, sometimes cruel, shifty to an extreme degree, and "willing to use Machiavellian means" to achieve his goal.[24]

A recent example is John Lamberton Harper's *American Machiavelli: Alexander Hamilton and the Origins of U. S. Foreign Policy* (Cambridge: Cambridge University Press, 2004). Harper is a professor of American foreign policy and European studies at The

Johns Hopkins University Paul H. Nitze School of Advanced International Studies in Bologna, Italy. The book is a generally favorable evaluation of the foreign policy views and actions of Alexander Hamilton (1757–1804) in the 1780s and 1790s when the new American state was cautiously charting its way. The comparison with Machiavelli is appropriate, Harper writes, because the American republic was a new state at the time, and Machiavelli wrote *The Prince* for a new ruler.

Harper argues that there was a profound affinity between Machiavelli and Hamilton. Although it cannot be proved that Hamilton read Machiavelli, he probably did, and he certainly studied the works of followers of Machiavelli, including David Hume (1711–1786), the Scottish skeptical philosopher, historian, and political commentator, and Frederick the Great of Prussia (1712–1786). Frederick wrote a book about Machiavelli's statecraft while he was still a prince, then disavowed it as ruler, even as he followed Machiavelli's precepts in order to expand Prussia by fair means and foul. Even more important, Harper argues that Machiavelli and Hamilton inhabited the same moral and intellectual world. Both were born as modest outsiders to the corridors of power. Machiavelli came from an old but down-at-the heels Florentine family and his rise to prominence is hard to explain. Hamilton was born out of wedlock in the West Indies and only came to the United States as a boy. Both were bright and active and rose quickly because of their abilities.

Harper argues that Hamilton and Machiavelli inhabited the same moral and intellectual world. Both were able to step back from a current crisis in order to look at issues through the eyes of history and to search for appropriate solutions. They shared identical, mostly negative, views about human nature and politics. Both were political realists. Although Hamilton did not completely eschew an ambitious foreign policy, he advocated a prudent, realistic, and "cautious accommodationist" approach to the outside

world. Part of Hamilton's realism was his realization that sometimes America had to learn not to be good in foreign policy, as
Machiavelli had argued centuries earlier. Harper approves of
Hamilton's approach to foreign policy, especially in comparison
with that of Thomas Jefferson, who believed that America's mission was to reform the world.

Although the book is an evaluation of Hamilton and American foreign policy of the 1780s and 1790s, it offers lessons for
today. Harper pleads with contemporary Americans and their
leaders to see themselves as others see them and to avoid overcon-
fident and reckless foreign policy actions. The book has been
favorably reviewed as a thoughtful, revisionist study of Hamilton
and the foreign policy of the young American state. Like many
other works, the book demonstrates that the Machiavelli who lived
in Renaissance Florence long ago remains an active participant in
American political thought and historiography.

Machiavelli the Manipulator in Comedy and Love

Not every reference to Machiavelli is deadly serious. Machiavelli is
also the master manipulator in matters of comedy and love (or sex).
In the long-running television comedy series "M.A.S.H.," Hawk-
eye Pierce calls Corporal Max Klinger "A Lebanese Machiavelli in a
garter belt." Klinger, the hairy company clerk of a Lebanese family
from Toledo, Ohio, dresses in women's clothes in an effort to persuade the army to give him a Section 8 discharge for psychological
unfitness. He is a Machiavelli because he tries to manipulate the
army into letting him go.

Machiavellian manipulation may be useful in the war of the
sexes. Nick Casanova, a suspicious name, wrote a book entitled *The
Machiavellian's Guide to Womanizing* (Edison, NJ: Castle Books,

1995). It begins with the announcement that "Machiavelli wrote *The Prince* about how to gain and keep political power. Had Machiavelli focused his energies on womanizing, this is the book he would have written" (p. xiii). Chapter One, "The Big Lie," begins with a quote from Machiavelli about how to succeed by lying, then discusses seduction techniques. Nick advises the reader about how to get into a woman's apartment and how to talk her into bed. He offers techniques for seducing one woman, then seducing her roommate in the next room without awakening the first. Machiavelli might have appreciated Nick Casanova's book. His brilliant comedy *La Mandragola* ("The Mandrake Root") has an unscrupulous young man seducing the beautiful and virtuous young wife of a gullible elderly husband. It is a comedic masterpiece that is still performed. And it is more witty by far than Nick Casanova's weak effort.

The real Machiavelli offered this advice about women. "Fortune is a woman; she must be beaten in order to keep her down. . . . Being a woman she is the friend of young men who are not cautious but bold and aggressive in mastering her."[25] Women have been outraged by this remark ever since. But Machiavelli wrote it as an analogy to describe the role of fortune in politics, not as advice for men in their personal relations with women.

A Renaissance Criticism of Machiavelli

Those who offer positive political advice based on Machiavelli and those who condemn Machiavellian methods share two assumptions. They accept Machiavelli's view that strong, even brutal, methods work, because human beings are not good. And they believe that lessons learned from elsewhere, especially the past, can be applied to the present. But are they right? A major political philosopher and historian from the Renaissance had his doubts.

Francesco Guicciardini (1483–1540) was a Florentine aristocrat, a successful lawyer, and a governor of cities; he had vastly
more practical political experience than Machiavelli. He was also
the ablest historian of his own times. And he was the friend and
correspondent of Machiavelli. After Machiavelli died in 1527,
Guicciardini had access to a manuscript copy of the former's *Discourses* before it was published. In 1530, he began to write a commentary on his friend's work, which he called *Considerations on the
'Discourses' of Machiavelli on the First Decade of T. Livy*. But he
never finished the work, and it remained unknown until the nineteenth century.

Guicciardini was often skeptical about his friend's positions.
He did not accept Machiavelli's view that men were fundamentally
evil. "It is advanced too absolutely that men never do good except
when forced to . . . for there are many who, even when they could
do ill, do well, and all mankind is not wicked. . . . In this context
one should consider that all men have a natural inclination to
goodness and, all other things being equal, like good better than
evil."[26] Guicciardini believed that the fundamental problem was
that men were weak. Knowing this, the wise man removes the
opportunity to do evil. This is a more pragmatic and cautious
approach than that of Machiavelli.

Guicciardini thought that Machiavelli loved violent methods
too much and often overlooked their weaknesses. One should not
"take as an absolute rule what the author (Machiavelli) says, who
was always extremely partial to extraordinary and violent methods." "For violent methods, though they make one safe from one
aspect, yet from another . . . involve all kinds of weaknesses.
Hence the prince must take courage to use these extraordinary
methods when necessary, and should yet take care not to miss any
chance which offers of establishing his cause with humanity, kindness, and rewards." In other words, Guicciardini qualified Machiavelli's absolute approach. Finally, he was not so sure that one

could apply the lessons of the past to the present "because the cases are so different, and the author (Machiavelli) does not distinguish properly between the examples." In other words, Machiavelli did not always get his history right. While Guicciardini agreed with much of what Machiavelli wrote, he added qualifications and nuances to his most important and strongest statements. Perhaps contemporary politicians and advisers enamored of Machiavelli should do the same.

Even though he died nearly 500 years ago, Niccolò Machiavelli may be more popular, more cited, and more respected as a political genius today than at any time in the centuries since he died. All pay attention to the cashiered public servant with the big ideas.

Chapter 8

MACHIAVELLI: MANAGEMENT EXPERT AND SOCIAL SCIENTIST

Machiavelli does more than advise politicians and pundits. He tells American business people and corporate executives how to make money and how to win the race to the CEO's office. He is an inspiration to social scientists engaged in research on primate intelligence and the evolution of human intelligence.

Management Machiavelli

In 1967, the British business management expert Antony Jay published a book entitled *Management and Machiavelli: Discovering a New Science of Management in the Timeless Principles of Statecraft*.[1] The author was both a consultant and an experienced manager. Jay's basic argument is that the modern international corporation is like an Italian Renaissance city-state, such as Florence or Milan, perennially at war, except that corporation CEOs do not try to kill each other. Because modern business resembles Renaissance warfare, Renaissance statecraft provides the best lessons and principles for managing a corporation. Management case studies and political history "are two very similar branches of the same subject. Each illuminates the other," according to Jay.[2] And the modern CEO is like a Renaissance prince who leads his city-state in war and peace while surrounded by internal and external enemies. To survive, the CEO must exercise leadership as Renaissance princes did. Thus, Renaissance political theory taught by Machiavelli is a much richer source for teaching successful management than the case analysis method, in Jay's view. He starts with Machiavelli, then expands his analysis to include many other Renaissance examples in order to teach corporate leadership principles.

Jay argues that he presents a realistic view of modern corporations and business operations as they are, not what they should be, just as Machiavelli presented a realistic description of Renaissance politics. Machiavelli did not discuss whether it was right or wrong for a prince to assassinate rivals and break his word, and Jay does not discuss the morality of the actions of CEOs and corporations. Jay argues that the Renaissance prince deployed power and resources in order to increase the wealth of the landowning classes and the safety and prosperity of the people of the state. The CEO and executive board take actions to increase the wealth of the shareholders and to provide employment. Neither the Renaissance state nor the modern corporation sees dispensing justice or helping the poor and the weak as goals.

The book follows the outline of Machiavelli's *The Prince*. Jay begins by discussing "the right way to treat a firm when you have taken it over."[3] He takes his cue from chapter 3 of Machiavelli's *The Prince*, a discussion of how to rule foreign states that have just been conquered. Machiavelli wrote that the prince could go to live in the new state, thus being ready to nip trouble instantly. But Machiavelli realized that this was seldom practicable, so he recommended a better solution: sending a limited number of colonists into one or two places in the new state. The loyal colonists will act for the prince.

Jay seizes on this as the right solution for securing control over a new firm. "Put small management teams of your own into one or two key factories." A small management team costs far less than bringing in many new people. And it will limit resentment, because the only ones upset will be the few managers who lose their jobs. Even better, a few firings will have a salutary effect on the other old managers, who should be warmly welcomed. The combination of the promise of reward and fear of losing their jobs will make them eager to serve. But Jay warns that there is no middle way: you must either sack or welcome the old managers. If you just downgrade them, they will be resentful and determined to get even. Jay concludes by saying that he has spoken with managers who had to cope with takeovers, and they agree that Machiavelli was right.

Jay concentrates on leadership (i.e., ruling the corporation). He rejects the view that the application of management science will produce industrial success. There must be an individual of courage, vision, and experience at the head. He writes for the ruler, someone high in the corporation with the power to make decisions that will bring success or failure to the corporation, just as Machiavelli wrote for the prince.

By contrast, Jay paints a bleak picture of the lives and careers of other employees of the corporation. The junior manager in General Motors or British Petroleum lives like a courtier or servant of a Renaissance prince, in a state of dependence without rights or powers. If anything, the modern corporation employee is worse off with none of the freedoms that matter. The corporation, far more than the laws of the nation in which he lives and holds citizenship, determines his fate. It can order him to live in another part of the country or another part of the world. Like the servant of a Renaissance prince, the employee has no right to independent speech or publication, as everything must be cleared by the corporation. If an employee says aloud that management is incompetent, he will be fired or he will not rise higher. Even if he does not offend his superiors, a hostile senior manager can blight his career on a whim, just as the prince can dismiss a courtier or execute a servant. But Jay never condemns the behavior of the corporation, just as Machiavelli did not condemn the prince who lied, cheated, and killed.

Jay uses many historical examples to illustrate principles of corporate leadership. The most interesting is an elaborate theory of corporate Renaissance, Reformation, and Counter Reformation. A Renaissance occurs when one department, division, or region suddenly achieves great success. It is then showered with corporate largess: a larger budget, more lab space, quick promotion for young employees, very high salaries, and the opportunity to recruit more people. This can lead to a Reformation, which is a bid for power harnessed to an idea. Some employees propose a new idea with which to reform the entire corporation. However, Jay insists that the bid for power by the employees is always more important than the idea. (The historical analogy is interesting, because Martin Luther certainly had some powerful religious ideas, including the priesthood of all believers. But the Protestant Reformation also quickly became a power grab when rulers turned Protestant, then seized the lands and wealth of the Roman Catholic Church.) Jay's chief example of a Reformation in international business was the seizure of the management of oil fields in the Near East by the oil-producing countries at the expense of the great oil companies. OPEC then engineered large price rises in the 1970s.

What should a corporation do when faced with an internal Reformation movement? The rulers of the corporation can decide to follow the model of the Counter Reformation and crush the revolt. (A historical correction: the Counter Reformation never crushed Protestantism; it only stopped the spread of the Protestant Reformation in some parts of Europe.) But crushing the corporate Reformation is likely to be costly, because the reformers usually include some of the ablest employees of the corporation. They will leave and organize a rival corporation, just as sixteenth-century Protestants founded new churches. Or the rulers of the corporation can try to accommodate the Reformation. The difficult decision is to know how much to give to the reformers without losing control. Jay favors making some accommodations to corporate reformers through decentralization and greater local autonomy.

Jay also uses Renaissance examples to discuss business creativity. In his view, there are two stages. First comes a period of prolonged discussion, the time in which the creative person seeks ideas, guidance, and practical suggestions from others. In the second period the creative person needs to be left alone to produce a creative business idea, his work of art. Jay cites Michelangelo and his sculpture of the Medici Tombs in Florence to illustrate his point. Before Michelangelo began sculpting, he engaged in extensive discussions with others and exchanged fifty letters with Pope Clement VII, who commissioned the work and paid the bills. Jay believes that the exchange of ideas with Clement was an essential part of the creative process. But then Michelangelo worked alone on the tombs and created masterpieces.

The book's message is twofold. The first is that the successful management of a corporation involves a lot more than knowledge of product development, marketing, and cost control. The book is partly a polemic against management science and the case analysis approach of business schools. Second, the author argues that personal leadership is the most important part of managing a corporation, because the corporation is a living organism fighting for its life in commercial wars, just like a Renaissance state fought to conquer its neighbors or to avoid being conquered by them. Good leadership is essential for both the prince and the CEO. Many readers must have agreed, because the book has had enormous success. The dust jacket of the revised edition claims that it sold 250,000 copies in hardcover, was translated into eleven other languages, and became required reading at the Harvard Business School and elsewhere.

Jay's book stimulated a wave of management Machiavelli imitations, often written by successful businessmen. Some followed his lead by emphasizing that individual leadership is essential to business success and that following Machiavelli is the best way to become that leader. The titles express the enthusiasm for Machiavelli: *The New Machiavelli: The Art of Politics in Business*; *The Mafia Manager: A Guide to the Corporate Machiavelli*; *The Boss: Machiavelli on Managerial Leadership*; *The Modern Machiavelli: The Seven Principles of Power in Business*; *Modern Management and Machiavelli*; and *Machiavelli on Management: Playing and Winning the Corporate Power Game*.[4] The titles are repetitious because publishers try to insert "Machiavelli" plus "management" or "business" into the titles. All present Machiavelli's ideas and examples as found in his books, then try to adapt them to modern corporate culture. All emphasize individual leadership. They also implicitly or explicitly endorse Machiavelli's view of human nature as selfish and greedy, expressed in the maxim that "men are quicker to forget the death of a father than the loss of a patrimony."[5] Many include a picture of Machiavelli on the title page or dust jacket. An exception is *The Boss*, which reproduces a sixteenth-century portrait of Cesare Borgia (1475–1507), the prince whose ruthless actions Machiavelli cited as examples to emulate.

A slight variation is to link Machiavelli with entrepreneurship. Alan F. Bartlett, who boasts that he "created a revolution in catering" and became a member of the boards of twenty-one corporations, published *Profile of the Entrepreneur or Machiavellian Management*, which views Machiavelli as an entrepreneur. "Machiavelli was himself an entrepreneur. . . . Machiavelli understood why the entrepreneur succeeded, why he failed and, therefore, his motivation. His comprehension of power was itself a marketable product and this he certainly exploited."[6]

MANY MANAGEMENT EXPERTS TELL AMBITIOUS CORPORATE EXECUTIVES WHO WISH
TO RISE TO THE TOP TO FOLLOW THE PRINCIPLES OF NICCOLÒ MACHIAVELLI
(1469–1527). BOOK COVER FROM *WHAT WOULD MACHIAVELLI DO? THE ENDS JUSTIFY
THE MEANNESS* BY STANLEY BING. [COPYRIGHT © 1999 BY STANLEY BING. REPRINTED
BY PERMISSION OF HARPERCOLLINS PUBLISHERS.]

An exaggerated form of management Machiavelli is found in
What Would Machiavelli Do? The Ends Justify the Meanness by
Stanley Bing, an employee of an unidentified multinational corporation and a columnist for *Fortune* magazine. Bing tells readers that
they have a choice, to do things the mediocre way or to do them
Machiavelli's way. He notes that those who choose to do the decent
thing get nowhere. But if the reader wants to get ahead in business, he should always ask himself, what would Machiavelli do?

189

The answer is, whatever is necessary. To help readers know what Machiavelli would do, the author digests and presents Machiavelli's principles in nuggets of corporate wisdom. The overall theme is that the ends justify the meanness. Bing tells the reader that if he doesn't like it, he should get over it, "you sniveling tree hugger," because that is the way things are. If you haven't got the stomach for true success, "go be a folk singer or a graphic designer or a social worker."

If Machiavelli were a corporate executive, he would be unpredictable and gain the advantage. He would acquire his neighbor and fire his own mother if necessary. He would delegate all the crummy tasks, lie when necessary, be proud of his cruelty and see it as strength, kick ass and take names, and permanently cripple those who disappoint him. He would upset other people's weekends, wedding plans, or open-heart surgery. Above all, he would have fun.[7] The book seems to exaggerate the meanness.

Or maybe it does not. Criminal trials, lawsuits, and scholarly studies reveal that all too many CEOs have behaved in Machiavellian ways. For example, the biography of Michael D. Eisner, the CEO and board chair of the Disney corporation for twenty-one years until ousted in 2004, shows that he practiced deceit on a massive scale. He promised promotions with no intention of keeping his word. He praised, then knifed associates. He developed "a staggering number of gambits to rattle subordinates and competitors, all in order to dilute their authority and enhance his own." He bullied, humiliated, and accused associates and rivals. Eisner apparently believed that "everyone has a dark side," and it was just a matter of finding out what it was and exploiting it. A thoughtful review of Eisner's biography is appropriately entitled "Machiavelli in the Magic Kingdom."[8]

Machiavelli is also viewed as a guide for success in dealing with supranational organizations and looking for an edge when competing with foreign economic powers. Rinus van Schendelen, a Dutch professor of political science and lobbying, published *Machiavelli in Brussels: The Art of Lobbying the EU*. According to the author, lobbying has become a science called "public affairs management." It involves political science, which is the study of influence, and management science, the study of how to get what one wants done. Machiavelli is the guide and model for both, because he wrote about how influence is really exerted and how to get what one wants. Machiavelli is a useful guide when lobbying the European Union.[9]

The book provides a detailed analysis of how the bureaucracy of the European Union works and how to manipulate it to achieve the desired ends. Most of the book is technical, careful, and bland. However, it does include some bits that echo the amoral Machiavelli. The author points out that it is important to understand the officials who make decisions. It offers the dry observation that "background information about the hobbies and life styles of the high officials is for sale in Brussels." The book emphasizes the importance of language and gives an example of deliberate mistranslation of an EU document in order to secure economic advantage. Elsewhere van Schendelen writes of "ruler analysis," which means finding ways to influence the person or persons who make decisions, and it cites Machiavelli's *The Prince* favorably. Finally, he admits that in European Union politics—which the author describes as more complicated than chess—luck sometimes prevails. The lobbyist needs Machiavelli's *fortuna*.

Experts in global economics call on Machiavelli for help in meeting the economic threats from abroad. In 1993, Daniel Burstein published *Turning the Tables: A Machiavellian Strategy for Dealing with Japan*. The author is an expert on global economics, with particular experience with Asia, as well as adviser to a Wall Street investment bank. The Machiavellian message is that America must realize that the U.S.-Japan relationship is a competition about economic power and interests. America must look to what is in its own best interest, just as Machiavelli sought the best interest of Florence. Another part of the Machiavellian message is that America needs to be very smart about improving its performance. It must have *virtù*, defined as intelligent economic policies.

The book argues that the competitiveness gap between America and Japan is only 10 percent the result of unfair Japanese economic practices. Ninety percent of the problem is the consequence of American failures, which the administrations of Ronald Reagan and George H. W. Bush made worse by protectionist policies and reliance on *laissez-faire* marketplace economics. The solution is to follow Machiavelli and "get smart" about economic competition. Getting smart means improving American education and promoting self-interested cooperation with Japan, such as encouraging Japanese automakers to establish plants in the United States in order to provide jobs to Americans. Most important, Burstein advocates strategic planning, such as a government-business planning partnership in the United States and the creation of a Trans-Pacific Community to provide a political structure to encourage economic cooperation between America and Japan. Burstein cites the familiar ruthless Machiavelli management expressions (e.g., arguing that America must be both a fox and a lion when protecting its interests). But the overall message is that Machiavelli was more smart than ruthless, and he had a higher goal. He was "a liberal and a humanitarian" who overstated his case in order to arouse the Florentines to see the enemies from abroad and to do something about weak leadership within.[10] The author notes that Machiavelli wanted leaders to adapt to circumstances. America should follow Machiavelli by adapting its economic policies to today's times.

Machiavelli has become so important to management studies that he is included in *The Ultimate Book of Business Gurus: 110*

Thinkers Who Really Made a Difference. The book presents short biographies of 110 business leaders and management thinkers, including Henry Ford, the founder of the Ford Motor Company, Peter Drucker, the founder of modern management studies, and Machiavelli. The Florentine is hailed as "the most influential business strategist ever born," even though he was himself "a useless businessman."[11] Machiavelli championed business leadership through cunning and intrigue.

Although Machiavelli claims most attention in management studies, business people can also learn from other individuals and actions of the Renaissance. Queen Elizabeth I (b. 1533; reigned 1558–1603) has much to teach corporate executives according to Alan Axelrod in *Elizabeth I CEO: Strategic Lessons from the Leader Who Built an Empire*. Elizabeth's actions and words provide lessons on how to develop a leadership attitude, communicate effectively, establish priorities, manipulate others ethically, create loyalty, nurture creativity in subordinates, know one's enemy, and boost production. "The career of Elizabeth I is an example of vision, of creating vision, of communicating vision, and of realizing vision. Who will learn the most from *Elizabeth I, CEO?* Those men and women who want to grow their enterprise, grow their career . . . and are ready now to build what they dream."[12] The book goes through many episodes of Elizabeth's life in order to show how she acted intelligently and successfully and to draw the lessons for today's business people. Machiavelli makes a cameo appearance in the section that argues that Elizabeth believed that honesty was the best policy but not the only policy.

The use of Machiavelli and other individuals and examples from the Renaissance to teach would-be corporate leaders how to be successful has become a large phenomenon. The reasons are several. The idea that business is like Renaissance warfare is original and clever. The clear and sprightly writing found in most of the management Machiavelli books underscores the message.

Management Machiavelli offers a magic bullet: follow Machiavelli and you will be successful. The concept also takes advantage of the fact that Machiavelli and the Renaissance are well-known and attractive parts of Western history. Probably every white-collar corporate employee has read Machiavelli's *The Prince* in secondary school or university. He or she quickly grasps the historical analogies.

There are deeper reasons as well. Management Machiavelli argues that exercising individual leadership will lead to corporate success. It is an article of faith with many American businessmen that the free individual matters most. Most of them want limited regulation, low taxes, and small government so that they may conduct their businesses as they see fit. Management Machiavelli offers historical justification for the political and social beliefs of many, probably most, American businessmen, especially small entrepreneurs.

Most important, the major theme of management Machiavelli, that the individual can and should be a leader, coincides with a fundamental value permeating American culture: belief in the individual. If leadership is the primary quality for corporate success, then the individual is essential. The books do not endorse collective leadership or group decision making. Instead, they argue that a creative and dynamic individual leader can move a large organization.

Machiavellian Intelligence in Primates

One expects politicians and political commentators, political philosophers and historians, to use Machiavelli. But scholars far from these fields also find him a stimulus to their research. In 1988, a group of comparative primatologists studying the evolution of intelligence in primates (apes, baboons, chimpanzees, monkeys, and man) coined the term "Machiavellian Intelligence" to explain certain kinds of primate behavior. They discovered that baboons and monkeys purposefully deceived and manipulated others in their communities in order to obtain desired personal ends. The researchers call the intelligence that enables primates to deceive and to manipulate others for selfish ends "Machiavellian Intelligence."[13] They see it as an essential part of the evolution of intelligence in primates, including man.

In a typical example of Machiavellian Intelligence, an adult baboon is eating.[14] A young baboon, who wants the food, approaches and begins to scream loudly. In baboon language, screaming means that he is threatened. His screaming attracts a second adult baboon who chases away the one eating. The baboon who comes to the rescue presumably believes that the first adult baboon was threatening the young baboon and acts accordingly, even though this is not true. The screaming of the young baboon announcing a threat is a lie. It is a tactical deception enabling him to achieve his end. With both adult baboons out of the picture, the youngster takes the food. To put it in other words, the young baboon lies, and the lie enables him to manipulate the other two baboons and get the food.

Another example. An adult male attacks a juvenile baboon, who screams. His scream is legitimate, because he is under attack. Several adult males come running to the rescue. But the attacker then stands on his hind legs and stares off into the distance as if there are predators out there. The adult males who have come to rescue the juvenile and to punish the attacker stop and also look into the distance. But there are no predators to be seen, even when the human observer sweeps the area with binoculars. Thanks to the distraction that he creates by looking into the distance, the attacker avoids punishment for his misbehavior. Again, the clever baboon uses deceit to achieve his end. His behavior causes others to change their intended actions. A good part of Machiavellian Intelligence involves the study of how primates manipulate the attention of others before or during striking. As Machiavelli wrote, the prince must be a fox.

The cornerstone of Machiavellian Intelligence in primates is the use and manipulation of the behavior of a third party for personal gain. This occurs whether or not the third party is interested in cooperating. The name Machiavellian Intelligence is appropriate, because Machiavelli argued that princes can and should lie and behave deceitfully in order to achieve their ends. Another key aspect of Machiavellian Intelligence is the ability of primates to make and keep alliances with the right individual. Again the term is apt. In chapter 21 of *The Prince,* Machiavelli explains how to handle alliances. He advises that the prince must not remain neutral when two neighboring states go to war. He should ally himself with the state that will win. If he remains neutral, both sides will despise him. The victor will not trust him because the prince did not come to his aid during the conflict. The loser will hate the prince because he was unwilling to risk battle for his sake. Primates must be equally clever in their personal alliances.

Machiavellian Intelligence is a variety of social intelligence, that is, intelligence exercised by an individual in interaction with others. It is linked to social living and the problems that come with it. It includes the individual mental abilities needed to cope with living with others, especially the ability to change tactics as the social situation evolves. Machiavellian Intelligence postulates that the strategies of primates are oriented to achieving personal gain. It might be called social problem solving unchecked by morality. If the hypothesis and research are correct, animals who solve problems created by social complexity through Machiavellian

Intelligence will flourish through evolution. Hence, Machiavellian Intelligence is important to evolutionary biologists.

The concept of Machiavellian Intelligence differs from and is opposed to the behaviorist tradition in the study of animal and human learning. It also differs from the intelligence exhibited by monkeys manipulating laboratory objects in order to get food or other satisfaction. It is a more sophisticated intelligence than the pursuit of, or fighting for, a sexual mate, or the estrus female advertising through display behavior that she is available for mating.

Some scholars have expressed reservations about Machiavellian Intelligence and believe that there are limits to its usefulness. An important reservation is that not all animals behave in the same way. Big apes do not behave the same way as monkeys and baboons. Moreover, its application is limited to primates. Some animals, especially adult big cats, such as the leopard and the mountain lion, are quite solitary. Therefore, it does not appear that social intelligence plays a large role in the evolution of their intelligence. When applied to the study of human behavior, it might be argued that Machiavellian Intelligence puts too much emphasis on deception and exploitation of others and not enough on acts of cooperation and helping. The latter might be as important, or more important, in the development of human intelligence.

Machiavellian Intelligence postulates that intelligence begins in cunning, deceit, and manipulation. Hence, it has implications for other fields, including social psychology, social anthropology, modern advertising, and perhaps news broadcasting. In social psychology literature, Machiavellianism is sometimes seen as a personality trait that can be tested. An individual might be a "high-Mach" or a "low-Mach." Researchers are interested in contrasting the preferences for immediate self-interest against attitudes of unselfishness and altruism. They wish to understand how and why an individual chooses one or the other.[15]

Machiavelli the Postmodernist

Some postmodernist and poststructuralist theorists have appropriated Machiavelli, the ultimate writer about reality, in support of their theories. The basic notion of postmodernism is that there is no reality outside of discourse (i.e., speaking and writing). Postmodernism argues that the individual can understand and experience reality, especially the reality of the past, only through discourse. But discourse is socially determined through relationships of power, a concept borrowed from the French historian and cultural critic Michel Foucault (1926–1984). Words are subjected to every kind of influence, especially the influence of power, which always changes their meaning. Communications theory, an offshoot of postmodernism, makes a distinction between lived experience and mediated experience, which is how the experience is perceived. Mediated experience, which is more important than lived experience, comes from the mass-communication culture, which uses symbolic language. Moreover, it employs discourse, which is "socially determined" through power relationships. As with all language theories currently popular in the academic world, a pebble of insight has been turned into a slagheap of exaggerations, and the obvious nugget of wisdom floats on a sea of jargon.

How does Machiavelli fit into postmodernism? Machiavelli was a postmodernist communications theorist 500 years ago because he stated that men pay attention to the appearance of things rather than the reality.[16] Machiavelli wrote that men can be fooled by appearances, and the prince should take advantage of this. In addition, Machiavelli realized the importance of symbolism. He described how the ancient Romans manipulated auspices (examining the behavior of birds to discover whether the auguries for success were favorable) in ancient Roman pagan religious rituals in order to get the result that they wanted.[17]

As management Machiavelli and Machiavellian Intelligence demonstrate, Machiavelli is treated like a respected contemporary scholar and researcher even though he lived and wrote nearly 500 years ago. Learned, serious, and influential people call on him for support. They are eager to follow his advice and to appropriate his name to their research because they believe that his insights are valid. Machiavelli's influence shows no sign of diminishing.

Part III

THE RENAISSANCE IN FICTION AND FILM

B ecause the Renaissance is such an integral part of American culture and life, it is not surprising that novelists have written many works of fiction, and filmmakers have produced numerous films on the Renaissance. Contemporary values and concerns play a large role in the view of the Renaissance found in both. For a long time, writers and directors saw it as a period of talented individuals who achieved great deeds. Although that vision remains, some now see the Renaissance as a period of religious fanaticism and the persecution of minorities.

Chapter 9

THE RENAISSANCE IN FICTION

Since 2003, readers have been buying Dan Brown's *The Da Vinci Code*, in which Leonardo da Vinci and the *Last Supper* play key roles. Its popularity has amazed book-trade analysts who marvel that a work of fiction about the far-off Renaissance could generate such commercial success and attract so much attention. But there is nothing new or remarkable about a book on the Renaissance, except for the poor quality of *The Da Vinci Code*. And despite the estimated 25 million copies sold as of May 2005, it is not close to being the best-selling fiction on the Renaissance. That prize belongs to Irving Stone's *The Agony and the Ecstasy*, which has sold more than twice as many copies. Brown's book is not unique but one of many, many recent works of fiction about the Renaissance. It is more evidence of the enthusiasm of American readers for fiction about the Renaissance, an inexhaustible appetite that has been around for a long time.

For nearly 150 years, American and English authors have been writing fiction about the Renaissance. They do so because they find it an intriguing and attractive subject and the books sell. Authors create attractive fictional characters who live and love against the background of an era of exciting events and colorful people. Real men and women from the Renaissance, most often the great rulers and artists, move through the novels. Other books make a real person from the Renaissance the central character and add fictional people and incidents.

There are three kinds of Renaissance fiction. The novelistic biography of a famous figure is the first. The author employs the known historical facts about the subject, then adds invented material not part of the historical record in order to give a fuller picture. The invented material ranges from the inner thoughts and words of the historical figure to fictional love interests. Next comes the traditional historical novel. It creates attractive imaginary characters who live and love, fight and die, in the historical Renaissance, while surrounded by real kings, queens, and artists who enter and leave the novelistic stage. The greatest number of fictional works about the Renaissance are traditional historical novels. The third form is the Renaissance mystery. The story is set in the present. But it is based on a powerful and mysterious secret of the Renaissance that must be unraveled.

Irving Stone's *The Agony and the Ecstasy*

On January 29, 2005, Robert Osborne, host of Turner Classic Movies, introduced a showing of the film *The Agony and the Ecstasy* by announcing that the book with the same title on which it is based sold 53 million copies across the world. It is hard to confirm or disprove that figure. Nevertheless, it is clear that Irving Stone's book, published in 1961, is probably the most widely disseminated book on the Renaissance in any language.

Irving Stone (1903–1989) was a hardworking writer with wide interests. Born in San Francisco as Irving Tannebaum (he later changed his name), Stone studied economics and political science at the University of California at Berkeley where he acquired a bachelor's degree in 1923. He obtained a master's degree from the University of Southern California in 1924 and then returned to Berkeley for two years of doctoral studies. But he quit to write detective stories and never looked back. He was drawn to biography and developed the biographical novel genre.

The biographical novel, or fictional biography, combines a recitation of what is known about the subject with invented material. The author examines in detail the historical record. He looks at the subject's letters and other works. He studies eyewitness accounts, reads widely in historical studies about the period, and visits the places in which the subject lived in order to retrace his steps.

But unless the subject leaves an explicit record, such as a diary, it is impossible to know what the subject felt, thought, and said. According to Stone, at this point "the novelist's creative imagination has to take over." "The author slips slowly and authentically into his (the subject's) bloodstream, the millions of cells in his brain, the feelings in his gut and nervous system."[1] If the scholarly novelist has studied the subject carefully enough, he can then "identify with him and with such honesty, that when you come to the point where documentation leaves off, and you must put yourself inside the heart and mind of this man or woman, you can think and feel as he or she would have in the given circumstances. This is the creative part of the book, and if you are honest, if you are sincere, if you have worked hard, if you are determined to be true and to achieve exact identity and to plumb the depths of a man's feelings, I think you have a good chance of doing the job proudly."[2]

Stone published his first biographical novel on painter Vincent Van Gogh in 1934 under the title *Lust for Life*. In 1956, it became a motion picture starring Kirk Douglas and Anthony

Quinn. Stone also wrote biographical novels about the author Jack London, Jessie Benton Fremont, wife of the Western explorer John Charles Fremont, the American socialist Eugene V. Debs, Rachel and Andrew Jackson, Mary Todd and Abraham Lincoln, Abigail and John Adams, Sigmund Freud, Charles Darwin, and the painter Camille Pissarro. And he published conventional biographies of Clarence Darrow and Earl Warren.

His most ambitious book by far was *The Agony and the Ecstasy*, a biographical novel of Michelangelo Buonarotti (1475–1564) published in 1961. Bestseller does not begin to describe its commercial success. The book has had at least fifty paperback printings in English and has been translated into at least twenty-one languages. Stone followed with illustrated editions of 1963 and 1977, a partial version entitled *The Story of Michelangelo's Pietà* in 1964, an abridged juvenile edition published as *The Great Adventures of Michelangelo* in 1965, and other spinoffs.[3] There have also been many partial translations and condensations in English and other languages. Thanks primarily to *The Agony and the Ecstasy*, Stone received honorary degrees and many other awards, including two from the Italian government.

Stone took advantage of the fact that there are more surviving letters, poems, and contemporary information about Michelangelo than for any other Renaissance artist and probably for any artist who lived before the nineteenth century. Two men who knew him wrote useful biographies while he was still alive. At least twenty-two modern scholars have published biographies of Michelangelo. An enormous amount of primary source material has been edited and printed. Stone hired a professor of Italian to translate into English the approximately 500 surviving letters of Michelangelo, plus his art contracts and other records.[4] His poetry was already available in English translation. Stone then had assistants translate scholarly works about Michelangelo from Latin, German, and Italian, while he read those in French. Stone also spent several years "living and researching the source materials of Florence, Rome, Carrara, and Bologna." He retraced Michelangelo's steps in Italy, visited the marble quarries in Carrara, and learned how to cut and sculpt marble. All told, Stone spent five years researching and writing *The Agony and the Ecstasy*. Although this may be a long time for a novelist, it is short compared with the decade and longer that scholars often devote to a major study. But they are researching and writing original works, while Stone was writing a fictional biography based on the scholarship of others.

Stone parts company with conventional biographers when he begins to write. He creates scenes in which Michelangelo and others speak. He often transfers words from Michelangelo's letters and poems into his conversation so that Michelangelo can reveal what is in his mind and heart. Stone invents dialogue for Michelangelo's family, associates, and patrons, then puts all the words, transferred and fictional, inside quotation marks as in a novel. Stone tries to make the fictitious conversations authentic in several ways, including putting Tuscan proverbs into the mouths of Michelangelo and others. This is legitimate, because Florentines then and now do use proverbs. As Michelangelo walks around Florence, Stone names and locates the streets.

The book begins when Michelangelo Buonarotti is thirteen years old. The boy loves to draw. Over his father's objections, he persuades the painter Domenico Ghirlandaio, a real Florentine, to take him on as an apprentice. But Michelangelo wants to be a sculptor, and before long he moves to the sculpture garden, really a training school for young sculptors, sponsored by Lorenzo de' Medici, the ruler of Florence.

Lorenzo brings Michelangelo into his household where he listens as the famous and real humanists Marsilio Ficino, Cristoforo Landino, Giovanni Pico della Mirandola, and Angelo Poliziano speak about their enthusiasm for the ancient world. This enables

Stone to work in a definition of Renaissance humanism as seeing man as a noble, creative, free-thinking individual, now freed from intellectual constraints.[5] It is a very simplified and inadequate understanding of humanism, but one that resonates in popular conceptions of the Renaissance. Stone takes the reader through the upheavals of the expulsion of the Medici in 1494, Savonarola's meteoric rise and fall, Michelangelo's move to Rome, his stormy relations with Pope Julius II and other patrons, and everything else. The historical events are seen from the point of view of Michelangelo. A great deal of what Stone writes is accurate or plausible.

But not all of it. For example, Stone creates a puppy love affair between Michelangelo and Contessina de' Medici, Lorenzo's youngest daughter who is Michelangelo's age. Although she enters an arranged dynastic marriage, their friendship continues. As she lies dying, they profess their true love for each other.[6] There is no historical documentation for any of this. Elsewhere Stone creates a brief sexual affair for Michelangelo in Bologna. In the aftermath of the expulsion of the Medici from Florence in 1494, Michelangelo spent a year in Bologna as the guest of a nobleman. There, according to Stone, he falls in love with Clarissa Saffi, the mistress of an important Bolognese nobleman, writes a sonnet to her, and makes love to her once.[7] She then disappears from the story. There is no documentation for an affair.

Other aspects of Michelangelo's emotional life as described by Stone have a more solid foundation. In Rome, Michelangelo has a deep and enduring friendship with a handsome young Roman named Tommaso Cavalieri, to whom he wrote poetry and letters. Stone describes this and notes that their friendship caused tongues to wag. But Stone does not address whether Michelangelo's love for Cavalieri, who later married, was homoerotic. Finally, Stone describes Michelangelo's relationship with Vittoria Colonna

(1492–1547), a widow and great poet, as platonic. Scholars agree; like Stone, they see it fueled by their similar religious views and love of poetry.

Although Stone does not take a stand on Michelangelo's possible chaste or actual homosexuality or ambisexuality, it has to be said that scholars are not certain either. Michelangelo wrote a great deal of love poetry and many letters to both Colonna and Cavalieri, and he sometimes addressed the same words to a woman and to a man. It is possible that some of his poetry expressed homoerotic yearnings. But it is hard to interpret Michelangelo's poetry and letters as expression of his own views, because much of it followed Renaissance conventions. For example, Michelangelo often used the language and ideas of Renaissance Platonism, in which earthly love for a man or a woman stimulates the lover to contemplation of divine love, the ultimate goal. On other occasions he followed the conventions of Renaissance Petrarchanism (poetry inspired by Francesco Petrarch) in which the lover analyzes his feelings for the unattainable female beloved with complex metaphors. In other words, it is hard to take Michelangelo's words at face value, which makes his sexual preferences very difficult to determine. But adding a fictional romance with Contessina de' Medici and an affair with a courtesan do not help to understand Michelangelo.

Stone provides a great deal of information about Michelangelo's major art works, a story for which there are many documents and numerous critical studies. Michelangelo and Pope Julius II did quarrel over his frescoes of the Sistine Chapel vault, just as Michelangelo battled with other patrons. Stone tends to see the Sistine Chapel ceiling as the crowning achievement of Michelangelo's career, but he does not neglect the other works. On the other hand, the very long book (750 pages in the paperback edition) gives more attention to his early life and less to the last years, in which he did many masterpieces.

The book usually handles historical matters accurately. However, sometimes Stone's dramatizations of incidents in Michelangelo's life create historical error. For example, early in his career Michelangelo wished to dissect human corpses in order to learn more about human anatomy. But how to do it? According to Stone, Michelangelo knows that the monastery of Santo Spirito in Florence runs a charity hospital for the ill and dying. Some of the corpses are not claimed. So Michelangelo asks the prior of the monastery if he may dissect the unclaimed corpses. The prior will not even discuss it, because dissecting corpses is forbidden by ecclesiastical authorities, and both Michelangelo and the prior would be severely punished if they were involved in this. Nevertheless, the sympathetic prior not quite accidentally leaves the key to the death room with the unclaimed corpses in a place where Michelangelo can find it. In the middle of the night Michelangelo steals into the hospital, finds the key, unlocks the door, enters the death room, and dissects corpses by candlelight. (One wonders how he could see what he was doing.) Afterward he retches a dozen times on his way home. Despite the danger and his nausea, Michelangelo continues his clandestine dissecting night after night.[8] In Stone's hands, Michelangelo's dissecting becomes a dramatic episode done in secret because dissecting was forbidden by the church.

Stone's dramatic account is rubbish. Giorgio Vasari (1511–1574) in his life of Michelangelo (1550) writes matter-of-factly that the prior of Santo Spirito "placed some rooms at his disposal where Michelangelo very often used to flay dead bodies in order to discover the secrets of anatomy."[9] In Vasari's account, there is no danger, no subterfuge, no secrecy, no darkness, and no nausea. Vasari does not mention an ecclesiastical ban against dissecting human bodies, because it did not exist. The reality is that dissection was a common practice in Italian medical schools and in autopsies since about 1300 with no objection from the church. Moreover, Michelangelo was not the first nor the last Renaissance artist to dissect bodies in order to improve his knowledge of human anatomy. In supplementing and dramatizing the event, Stone created two historical falsehoods, that dissecting bodies was unusual and that ecclesiastical authorities forbade it. The latter is a common popular misconception still around today.

Another example. In Rome in the late 1530s and early 1540s, Michelangelo hears members of the circle around Vittoria Colonna discussing religious reform, especially their desire to improve the lives of corrupt clergy and to focus on inner religious experience. Stone then extrapolates: "Michelangelo realized that he was in the midst of a revolutionary group. . . . The Inquisition in Spain and Portugal had taken thousands of lives on charges far less serious."[10] This is an exaggeration. The group around Colonna, sometimes called "the spirituals" (*gli spirituali*) by contemporaries and later scholars, was not very revolutionary. As their nickname indicated, they concentrated on inner spiritual renewal, rather than outward action. Only one of them became a Protestant. And they were in no danger at the time. Moreover, the inquisitions in Spain and Portugal put people to death for more serious reasons, such as being false Christians.

Stone portrays Michelangelo as an individual who triumphs over all obstacles. He is every man's hero. As Stone explained, "My goal always is to tell a universal story, meaning it's about a person who has an idea, a vision, a dream, an ambition to make the world somewhat less chaotic. He or she suffers hardships, defeats, miseries, illnesses, poverty, crushing blows. But ultimately that person accomplishes a big, beautiful, gorgeous job of work, leaving behind a testimonial that the human mind can grow and accomplish fantastic ends."[11] As a result, Stone does not show Michelangelo as ill-tempered, miserly, or misanthropic, all of which he was.

Nor do his good relations with the powerful, nor the hard bargaining that produced extraordinarily high payments and made him wealthy, come under scrutiny.

Stone's picture of Michelangelo is typical of a tendency to see the Renaissance as an age of heroic figures. Michelangelo is the quintessential American hero because he is the lone individual who achieves greatness through his personal efforts. He is the person with a vision who triumphs over doubters, a kindred spirit to the lone man of integrity who overcomes the bad guys in Western films. When this conception is combined with Michelangelo's story and Stone's craftsmanship, it is easy to account for the success of *The Agony and the Ecstasy*. The story has intrinsic interest: Michelangelo created an extraordinary body of artistic work known to the whole world. Stone tells that story in clear prose, and he includes a great deal of interesting information based on the research of scholars. Overall, Stone produced a fictionalized biography that has probably introduced more nonscholars to the Italian Renaissance than any other book. Stone deserves full credit for his accomplishment.

Historical Novels About the Renaissance

Far more common than the biographical novel is the traditional historical novel. Numerous American and English, famous and obscure, writers have written historical novels on the Renaissance in the past 150 years. All emphasize individual stories. But the most recent novels see the Renaissance more darkly and introduce twenty-first-century judgments and values. They show that the novelist's conception of the Renaissance has somewhat changed.

The great Victorian novelist George Eliot (Mary Anne Evans, 1819–1880) in 1863 published *Romola*, a historical novel set in

Renaissance Florence.[12] Eliot conceived the book when she and her husband visited Florence for two weeks in May 1860 and a month in May 1861. Once she had the idea, she poured over the available primary and secondary sources, including works available only in sixteenth-century printings. Scholars have identified about 110 titles in Italian, French, German, and Latin that she consulted.[13] And she apparently did not need a translator. In addition, she used to good purpose her knowledge of the classics in her description of Florentine humanism.

The action of the novel occurs in Florence in the turbulent six years between the death of Lorenzo de' Medici in April 1492 and the hanging of Girolamo Savonarola in May 1498. As the novel begins, Romola is the sixteen-year-old daughter of a blind humanist. She falls in love with and marries Tito Melema, a Greek who is handsome and clever but also weak and deceitful. Distraught upon learning that he has been unfaithful, she decides to leave Florence. But just outside the gates, she encounters Savonarola, who persuades her to stay and becomes her spiritual adviser. Much of the story revolves around the rise and fall of Savonarola. The fiery Dominican preacher calls on Florentines to repent their worldly sins, and he and his followers rule the city for a short time, all of which is historically accurate. Romola admires Savonarola for his courageous calls for individual and church reform. The Protestant Eliot probably saw Savonarola as the precursor of Martin Luther and the Reformation. Although there are some superficial similarities, the differences between the two and between Florence and Germany are too great for historians to accept this view. But Romola also realizes that Savonarola goes too far. She watches as his reforming zeal becomes fanaticism and his egoism exceeds rational limits. After Tito is killed, Romola breaks loose from the influence of Savonarola and her father. She devotes herself to caring for the unfortunate of the city, including Tito's destitute mistress and children.

The work achieves a high degree of historical authenticity. For example, Eliot's account of Savonarola's preaching incorporates material from printed versions of his sermons. And it displays remarkable psychological perception. But critics complained that the erudition overwhelmed the human story, and today *Romola* is probably the least read of her novels. It was made into a silent film, *Romola*, in 1924, starring Lillian Gish, William Powell, and Ronald Colman.

Many other authors wrote historical novels about the Renaissance in the first seventy-five years of the twentieth century, including some well-known ones. The Italian-born but English resident Rafael Sabatini (1875–1950) wrote *The Strolling Saint: Being the Confessions of the High and Mighty Agostino D'Anguissola, Tyrant of Mondolfo and Lord of Carmina in the State of Piacenza* (New York: Houghton Mifflin, 1924). It is a colorful tale of an imaginary northern Italian adventurer born in 1525 who has many adventures, battles, and loves, although sexual activity remains discreetly off stage, as was the convention at that time. Another Sabatini historical novel is *Columbus: A Romance* of 1942.

The distinguished British author W. Somerset Maugham (1874–1965) published a historical novel about Niccolò Machiavelli called *Then and Now: A Novel* (Garden City, NY: Doubleday & Company, 1946). The year is 1502. The Florentine government has sent Machiavelli to deliver messages to and to observe Cesare Borgia, then creating a state in central Italy through arms, brutality, and duplicity. The novel does a good job of portraying Machiavelli as he was in real life: astute political observer, good fellow, loyal friend, witty dinner companion, and pursuer of women. He watches Borgia's actions, which serve as material for the portrait of the ruthless and successful ruler in *The Prince*. He and Borgia have long conversations in which one or the other gives voice to Machiavelli's political philosophy. On the lighter side, Machiavelli's unsuccessful attempt to seduce the young wife of a local merchant gives him the idea for his comedy *La Mandragola* ("The Mandrake Root"), although it was not written until about 1517. Maugham wrote a clever historical novel.

The most popular and commercially successful historical novelist of the Renaissance in the middle of the twentieth century was the American Samuel Shellabarger (1888–1954). After receiving his Ph.D. at Harvard, he taught English at Princeton University and later served as headmaster of a private school. His real career was writing. Among his many works were three historical novels of the Renaissance. The best-known is *Captain from Castile* (Boston: Little, Brown, 1945), an account of Hernán Cortés' invasion of Mexico (1519–1521). A young Spanish soldier fleeing from the Spanish Inquisition joins Cortés' expedition and participates in the conquest of Mexico. It was made into the color film *Captain from Castile* (1947), with Tyrone Power as the young captain from Castile, Jean Peters as the servant girl whom he loves, and César Romero as the swashbuckling Cortés who dares his men to follow him to glory. It is full of action, as the Spaniards conquer Mexico. The music composed by Alfred Newman includes the rousing march for orchestra *Captain from Castile*, which is still occasionally heard.

Shellabarger followed with *Prince of Foxes* (Boston: Little, Brown, 1947). It is the story of a young man of low birth who takes the noble name of Andrea Orsini in Italy in 1500. He first serves the evil Cesare Borgia, but then works to thwart his schemes, which imperil him and his beloved. The black-and-white film *Prince of Foxes* (1949; director Henry King) is a free adaptation of the novel. It concentrates on the rivalry between Cesare Borgia (acted by Orson Welles) and Orsini (Tyrone Power) for the love, or the body in the case of Borgia, of Camilla Verano (Wanda Hendrix), who against her will is promised to Borgia. It has abundant sword-play and chases.

The most memorable scene in the novel occurs at a banquet presided over by Borgia. He has captured Orsini. After beating him, he commands that he be brought before the diners, including Camilla. Borgia announces that he will put him to death. But one of Borgia's captains, a secret friend of Orsini, protests that death would be too easy. Rather, blind him and turn him out to wander helpless in the world, he argues. Let me put his eyes out; I will do it with my thumbs. Borgia, knowing that this would horrify Camilla and shock his dinner guests, agrees. The captain advances menacingly to the bound Orsini. He shouts loud threats as he leans over Orsini. But he also whispers to Orsini to pretend to scream in agony. Orsini does as bidden, while his friend mashes with his thumbs two grapes instead of his eyes and then holds up the pulp for all to see. None of the horrified onlookers can bear to look closely, so the deception works, and Orsini is turned loose unharmed.[14] He later triumphs over Borgia and gets the girl. The film includes this scene.

Shellabarger's third Renaissance novel is *The King's Cavalier* (Boston: Little, Brown, 1950), which is set in the France of Francis I (ruled 1515–1547). It lacks the panache of the first two. But as in the other two, Shellabarger manages to include a considerable amount of historical information.

Historical novels of the Renaissance, written in the late nine-teenth century and much of the twentieth, see the period as one of action and strong personalities, and of achievement and excess. Larger-than-life individuals stride across the pages of the books. They conquer lands, rule kingdoms, and sometimes do cruel deeds. They are memorable and leave historical marks. With the exception of *Romola*, the novels focus on real and fictional male figures of the Renaissance.

Feminist Novels of the Italian Renaissance

This changed at the end of the twentieth century. A bumper crop of best-selling historical novels of the Italian and English Renaissances appeared. They share some characteristics of earlier novels but are also very different in ways that reflect contemporary interests and concerns. Many focus on women and show a dark side of the Renaissance.

The Secret Book of Grazia dei Rossi: A Novel (New York: Simon and Schuster, 1997) by Jacqueline Park is a good example. The author wrote scripts for Canadian television and film and taught dramatic writing at the Institute of Film at New York University for many years. *The Secret Book* is her first major novel. The novel is a large, sweeping story (572 pages) that has as its central figure a fictional Jewish woman from Mantua. It begins in 1487 when Grazia is nine years of age and ends in late May 1527, after the Sack of Rome. There is much tumultuous history and many fictional and real characters. It has received generally favorable reviews and has been reprinted in paperback and translated into German, French, and Italian.

The book begins in 1526 as Grazia writes the story of her life in the form of a *ricordanza* (a secret or private memoir of the family) to be read by her young son after her death. The *ricordanza* is an authentic Renaissance literary form often used by Florentine merchant fathers. Grazia, born in 1479, is the daughter of a Jewish banker and pawnbroker of Mantua. Although she is fictitious, Mantua had at the time a large and important Jewish community, including an extended Rossi family of Jews in Mantua, although they were not prominent bankers. Many Jews lived in the area of the city near what is now the state archive; Park describes the neighborhood accurately. Grazia is lively, outspoken, determined, and intellectually precocious. She learns the pawnbroking and banking business under her father's tutelage. She has a command of Latin and later adds Hebrew, ancient Greek, and a little French. Grazia easily and aptly quotes Vergil and Catullus' love poetry. She frequently refers to her favorite classical heroine, Dido, the queen of Carthage, who fell in love with Aeneas in the *Aeneid*, the famous poem of Vergil. After Aeneas abandoned her, Dido killed herself because her love for Aeneas had caused her to betray her own people. In similar fashion, Grazia is torn between love and loyalty to her Jewish heritage.

The overarching historical theme is the deteriorating position of Jews in Catholic Italy. The lives of Grazia and those she holds dear are disrupted as hostility toward Jews grows during a period of war and dynastic rivalries. In the novel, in 1487 the preaching of the Franciscan friar Fra Bernardino da Feltre (1438–1494) against Jews for lending money at interest inflames popular emotions and causes the Gonzaga duke of Mantua to withdraw his protection from the Jews of Mantua. Although Fra Bernardino was real and a notorious preacher against the Jews, it was another Franciscan whose preaching in Mantua in 1496 caused trouble for Mantuan Jews. The Rossi family flee to Ferrara.

In Ferrara, Grazia, now thirteen, meets and falls in love with Pirro Gonzaga, about seventeen, a fictitious character from a cadet branch of the Gonzaga family. No shy virgin she, Grazia immediately makes passionate love with Pirro, who wants to marry her. Princess Isabella d'Este Gonzaga (1474–1539), wife of Duke Francesco Gonzaga and a formidable figure both historically and in the book, will endorse the marriage if Grazia will convert to Catholicism. She tries. She enters a house of catechumens, a residence where those who are considering becoming Catholics can be instructed. But it turns out to be a very unpleasant place presided over by a bullying priest. When Pirro is suddenly sent away and ordered to marry a princess, Grazia returns to her family and Judaism with relief. But her love for Pirro continues.

A distinguished Jewish physician named Judah (Leone in Italian) del Medigo, some fifteen or more years older, marries Grazia when she reaches the ripe old age of fourteen. (Although some Renaissance women married at fourteen, the majority did not marry until their later teens.) He is calm, learned, rational, and a great friend of the humanist Giovanni Pico della Mirandola (1463–1494), whom he tutored in Hebrew. Judah del Medigo may be inspired by Elia (or Elijah) del Medigo (c. 1450–c. 1497), the Jewish scholar who taught Pico Hebrew and translated texts for him. Although not in love with Judah, Grazia is happy to have him as a husband and determined to be a good wife to a man who encourages her thirst for learning. They move to Florence where he becomes part of a learned circle of humanists. However, he harbors a chaste love for Pico, and it is not until after Pico's death in 1494 that his marriage with Grazia is consummated. It produces a daughter, who dies at birth.

Meanwhile, military and political events upset their lives and the political balance of Italy. Grazia and Judah move to Venice where she becomes an editor and translator from Greek for the famous humanist printer Aldo Manuzio (c. 1450–1515). She also begins to write a book about famous heroines in imitation of *The Lives of Illustrious Women* of Giovanni Boccaccio (1313–1375), a pioneering work celebrating women. However, whereas almost all of Boccaccio's illustrious women came from the ancient world, Grazia's heroines are Renaissance women. She celebrates them for their courage and boldness, qualities honored by twentieth-century feminists, rather than for their virtue, which the Renaissance honored. Meanwhile, Judah is physician to the high, including two kings of France. He relieves their syphilis symptoms so that they may fornicate and fight with abandon, as they lead armies up and down the Italian peninsula. Judah becomes ill and is sent back to Venice in 1515 in the care of no less than Pirro Gonzaga, who suddenly reappears as a soldier. Pirro and Grazia enjoy a single night of passion before he must return to soldiering.

The rising tide of anti-Semitism sweeps over them. The Venetian government forces all Jews of the city to live in a restricted area, the first ghetto of Italy and the world. The far-seeing Judah predicts that this will be the first of many ghettoes, because Jews have now been declared outcasts. Centuries later, attempts will be made to exterminate those declared to be outcasts, he prophesizes. It is a twentieth-century editorial interjection by the author. Nevertheless, Judah and Grazia are filled with joy, because Danilo, the fruit of her night of love with Pirro, is born in March 1516. He is the first child born in the first ghetto. Grazia is a mother at age 37, not unusual among twenty-first-century American women, but very old by Renaissance standards.

Judah becomes physician to the new pope, Leo X (1513–1521), and the three move to Rome at the height of the Renaissance. Isabella Gonzaga is also in Rome, and she invites Grazia to become her secretary. As the war clouds gather again in the 1520s, Judah decides it is best to leave Italy altogether and secures a position as physician to the Sultan Suleiman I (the Magnificent, ruled 1520–1566) in Constantinople (Istanbul). But Grazia is fearful of moving to the strange land of Islam. They agree on a compromise. He will go on ahead to scout the ground. If all goes well, she and Danilo will follow in six months' time.

But the ravenous armies of Emperor Charles V move more quickly. They fall on Rome in the terrible Sack of May 1527. Grazia and Danilo take refuge with Isabella Gonzaga, who raises an enormous sum of money to ransom everyone in her house. Pirro Gonzaga, now a widower, suddenly reappears, and again he and Grazia make love. This time Grazia decides that she will become a Catholic and marry Pirro. Thanks to the intervention of Isabella, Grazia and Danilo escape Rome on a ship bound for Genoa. But the ship is taken by pirates. Danilo, showing the daredevil nature of his soldier father, taunts the pirates from his perch high in the sails. A pirate seizes a musket to shoot him. But Grazia throws herself at the pirate and the gunshot kills her. The chastened pirates bury her at sea and set sail to Constantinople in order to sell their captives as slaves. But in honor of Grazia they permit Danilo to write a note to his nominal father, Judah, so that he may quickly be ransomed. The novel ends as the eleven-year-old Danilo descends the gangplank at Constantinople clasping the portrait of Grazia earlier done by the famous painter, Andrea Mantegna (1430/31–1506), and her unread secret book, saying to himself, "carpe diem," seize the day.

The major historical theme is the growing persecution of the Jews because of religious fanaticism in unsettled times. A secondary theme is that everyone, Jew and Christian alike, was dependent on the favor of the mercurial and double-dealing aristocrats who ruled Italy's small states. Isabella Gonzaga, mistress of manipulation and power in real life, is well portrayed. So many exciting, momentous, and calamitous real events take place in the forty years covered by the novel that the author does not need to create many fictitious ones.

It is a feminist novel with the strong women and weak men typical of the genre. Grazia is strong, loyal, and extremely learned at a young age. She is very courageous even when making foolish mistakes. By contrast, all the male characters are flawed. The dashing Pirro is the absent male of the late twentieth century. All the other men, even Grazia's beloved father, have character defects.

The historical research is thorough. The author spent time in Italy and has made good use of Shlomo Simonsohn, *History of the Jews in the Duchy of Mantua* (Jerusalem: Kiryath Sepher Ltd., 1977), a storehouse of information about Mantuan Jewry. There is a considerable amount of description of the lives, commerce, religious practices, and social customs of the Jews in their own communities, not always flattering. The author makes reasonable extrapolations from the documentary record when describing the reactions of her characters to events. She deserves praise for featuring Mantua, Ferrara, and Bologna, instead of limiting herself to the better known Florence, Rome, and Venice. Park describes well the sharp contrasts between rich and poor, fine palaces and dirty bodies, intellectual achievement and rampant superstition, between greatness of spirit and petty meanness, between acceptance and persecution. The novel works well, because the central character and the historical situation are intensely realized.

But there are errors of historical balance because Park exaggerates the atmosphere of anti-Semitism. The Jewish characters in the book often express the fear that having carnal relations with Christians will lead to death by burning. This was not true. Italian inquisitions persecuted Jews thought to be false Christians (i.e., outwardly Catholic but secretly practicing Judaism). And the punishments were often mild. The author repeats stories about the cruelty of Roman and Spanish inquisitions, which scholars have disproved or modified. Overall, her picture of relentless persecution of Jews in Italy is overdrawn. Although persecution existed, it waxed and waned. There were significant differences from place to place and often considerable tolerance of the minority. Another sign of the author's point of view is that the book never presents a Catholic clergymen in a favorable light. Overall, Park's vision of the Renaissance is a period of persecution of a minority group, of wars, and of sharp contrasts.

Another feminist Renaissance historical novel is *Birth of Venus: A Novel* (New York: Random House, 2003) by the English author, broadcaster, and critic Sarah Dunant. Although she has written seven previous novels, this is the first set in the Renaissance.[15] Like Park's *Secret Book of Grazia dei Rossi*, it is the story of a very intelligent and determined young woman who manages to take control of her life despite society's restrictions.

The title comes from the name of Sandro Botticelli's wonderful painting of that name created in Florence about 1484. The novel is the story of the fictional Alessandra Cecchi, the daughter of a wealthy Florentine wool manufacturer and merchant. Well educated, she reads and speaks Latin and reads Greek from an early age. The story really begins in 1492, when she is fourteen. It concentrates on 1492 to 1498 in Florence, the years of the rise and fall of Savonarola, but from a different perspective than Eliot's *Romola*. Alessandra's father hires an emaciated and reclusive Flemish painter, whose name is never given, to paint the ceiling and walls of the family chapel. Alessandra already draws and wishes to learn to paint but has great difficulty communicating with the painter, who speaks no Italian at first and is beneath her socially. At the age of sixteen (1494) she is married to Cristoforo Langella, age 48, a lover of art and literature who appreciates her mind. But Cristoforo is a homosexual. His lover is Tomaso (which should be "Tommaso" in Italian), Alessandra's older brother. For Cristoforo the marriage is a screen to protect him against denunciation as a sodomite (i.e., homosexual) by Savonarola's rabble-rousing vigilantes. Indeed, one of Alessandra's brothers is a fanatical follower of Savonarola. (The Cecchi family is the dysfunctional family found in numerous contemporary novels.) But Alessandra does not learn of her husband's sexual preference until after they are married.

As intolerance toward sin and art grow, the married Alessandra and the unnamed painter make love in 1497. This produces a daughter the following year. Meanwhile, religious and political events threaten them. Cristoforo fakes his own death, and he and his lover disappear from Florence and the novel. The Flemish painter flees to Rome. Freed of her husband and bereft of her lover, Alessandra becomes a nun, and she and her newborn daughter settle in a very civilized and easygoing convent in rural Tuscany. There she paints the convent's chapel while raising her artistic daughter, who also speaks and writes three languages at the age of twelve. When the daughter is fourteen, the now prosperous painter finds them. He and Alessandra now openly make love in her convent cell. Although discipline at some Italian Renaissance convents was lax and scandalous before the tightening of rules after the Council of Trent (1545–1563), the behavior at this fictional convent looks like an episode from *Sex and the City*. Alessandra decides that her daughter should go with her father so that she may develop her artistic talent. Alessandra remains in the convent in reasonable contentment until she decides to end her life with a suicide disguised as cancer at the age of 50 in 1528. At her death, the other nuns discover that she has tattooed her body with a long lascivious serpent whose tail begins at her collarbone and whose male head licks her vagina.

The novel moves along well and uses Florentine material. There was an extended Cecchi family in Florence, and some of its members were in the wool trade. Alessandra Cecchi may be inspired by the real Alessandra Scala (1475–1506), a Florentine woman who was extraordinarily skilled in classical Greek and entered a convent after her husband, a Greek soldier and poet, was killed in battle in 1500. On the other hand, the name "Langella" for the homosexual husband does not sound Florentine. The book includes many excerpts from Savonarola's fiery sermons, and it summarizes the historical circumstances of his rise and fall pretty well on the basis of limited research. But some plot turns are unconvincing, and the serpent is bizarre. A Renaissance nun tattooed like a NBA basketball player?

The tension of the novel comes from the struggle of the heroine to realize her dreams and to find her own way despite society's restrictions and religious fanaticism. *Birth of Venus* might be read as the birth of Alessandra's sexual awareness, as she decides what is sinful and what is not. She takes control of her life despite the constraints of society. She is a strong female character, while the men are weak, deceitful, fanatical, or absent when she needs them. The author's conception of the Florentine Renaissance is that of a cultural flowering of the arts and the mind that is threatened by religious fanaticism. But Alessandra Cecchi is a multitalented Renaissance woman.

The Real and Imaginary Artemisia Gentileschi

Another feminist novel, this time based on a real woman, is Susan Vreeland's *The Passion of Artemisia* (New York: Viking, 2002). Vreeland is a San Diego–based teacher turned novelist best-known for *The Girl in Hyacinth Blue*.[16] The release of *The Passion of Artemisia* coincided with the opening of a major exhibition of the paintings of Orazio and Artemisia Gentileschi at the Metropolitan Museum of New York in February 2002. It was a selection of the Book of the Month Club and the Quality Paperback Book Club.

The historical record on Artemisa Gentileschi (1593–1652/53) offers rich material for both historian and novelist.[17] Born in Rome on July 8, 1593, she was the daughter of Orazio Gentileschi (1563–1639), a well-known artist who taught her to paint. Her first signed and dated painting, done when she was seventeen, demonstrates that she had great ability.

But then her life changed. Agostino Tassi, a painter and collaborator of her father whom Orazio had hired to teach her perspective, raped her in May 1611. This seems undeniable. But the rape was followed by consensual sex for several months, because Agostino promised to marry her, which would have restored her honor. And perhaps affection played a role. In any case, in early 1612 Orazio brought suit against Tassi for raping his daughter. A lengthy series of interrogations (a judicial proceeding but not a trial in the modern sense) of the principals and witnesses began in March 1612. Tassi, who had a history of womanizing and abuse, denied the charges and said that Artemisia had had previous lovers. Artemisia insisted that she was a virgin until raped. In order to convince the court of the veracity of her testimony she voluntarily underwent the pain of torture by means of a form of thumbscrew, whose strings bit into the fingers of her flesh. In November, the magistrates decided that Tassi had raped her and gave him the choice of five years of hard labor in prison or five years of banishment from Rome. This was in addition to his imprisonment during the eight months of the interrogations. Tassi chose banishment but managed to get it revoked after four months, probably through influential contacts.

Immediately after the decision was rendered, Artemisia married a Florentine painter, Pierantonio Stattessi (b. 1584), and the couple moved to Florence. There Artemisia's career blossomed. Thanks initially to her father's contacts in Florence and then her own ability, she found patrons and began to produce some remarkable paintings. She later painted in Genoa, Rome, London, and Naples, before dying in late 1652 or in 1653. Like her father, Artemisia was much influenced by Michelangelo Merisi da Caravaggio (1571–1610) and is seen as one of the painters who carried on his style. But she brought to the best of her paintings a dramatic intensity and a preference for female subjects, including female nudes, and the ability to paint them well, which made her an original artist and the first influential female painter of modern Europe.

Her most noted paintings are several versions of Judith slaying Holofernes, a story found in the Book of Judith, chapters 10–13, in the Old Testament. Judith was a beautiful widow who vowed to rescue Israel from the Assyrian army threatening Israel. She goes to the camp of the general, Holofernes, posing as a disillusioned Jewess and pretending to offer herself to him. Smitten by her beauty and wishing to have sex with her, Holofernes invites her to dine with him. She agrees. Holofernes drinks too much wine and falls into a drunken slumber. When the others have left, Judith, who has eaten and drunk little, takes his sword, cuts off his head, puts it into a bag, and leaves the camp with her maidservant. She takes the head to the Israelites, who put it on a rampart. The next morning the Jews attack the Assyrians. The Assyrian soldiers rush to the tent of their general only to discover his headless body. Leaderless, they are routed, and Israel is saved.

In 1613 and 1614, shortly after the rape interrogation and her marriage, Artemisia painted a dramatic and very realistic version of Judith in the act of sawing at the neck of Holofernes as blood spurts from the wound. The painting is sometimes interpreted as her personal act of revenge against her rapist and her father for her humiliation in Rome. Artemisia did other paintings of biblical and classical era women dealing with the effects of the evil actions of men. They include several other versions of Judith and Holofernes, the Roman wife Lucretia who kills herself after being raped, Susanna and the elders who spy on her in her bath, Bathsheba who becomes King David's lover, and Cleopatra with the asp. This subject matter has led some art historians and feminist scholars to see Artemisia as an heroic feminist of the past. They argue that her art, and the art of all women, is radically different from that of men, not only because life experiences differ from person to person, but because all women have different social experiences from men.

Other art historians are skeptical. They note that patrons in the decades in which Artemisia was most active wanted paintings of dramatic and horrific scenes, and that Artemisia, like male artists, gave them what they wanted. For example, Artemisia's *Judith Beheading Holofernes* has many similarities to Caravaggio's painting of the same title done in 1598 and 1599. And there are numerous other contemporary paintings by male artists of the scenes that Artemisia painted. In other words, these art historians

227

suggest that the preferences of art patrons and her need to sell paintings influenced her choice of subjects more than her life experiences. Because Artemisia Gentileschi has attracted intense scholarly attention only recently, the jury is probably still out. Art historians have much work to do determining attributions (i.e., which paintings were hers), searching for more information on her life and her patrons, and interpreting the paintings. In the meantime, Artemisia has become a key figure in feminist historiography.

All the above information is the historical record. Vreeland's novel uses it freely. The author makes Artemisia a heroic and virtuous figure who wants only to paint and to love. The novel begins with her torture and concentrates on key episodes in her life. It focuses on three relationships: Artemisia and her father, whom she cannot forgive for subjecting her to the humiliation of the trial and for continuing to paint with Tassi; her marriage, which she tries hard to make work; and her loving and protective relationship with her daughter Palmira. The passion in the title is her passion to paint, and much of the novel deals with her determination and perseverance to be a good painter. At times she becomes the modern career woman trying to balance job, marriage, and child. When she has to choose between art and wife and mother, she painfully chooses art. Although there are some supportive males in the novel, those closest to Artemisia are not very sympathetically drawn. Her closest confidants are fictional women.

The book presents an attractive and well-written personal story at the expense of many omissions and considerable historical inaccuracy. Vreeland eliminates other family members in order to heighten the daughter-father, wife-husband, and mother-daughter relationships. The author portrays Artemisia as the only child of Orazio, whereas she had three younger brothers, one of whom was also a painter. Palmira is the much-loved only child of Artemisa in the novel. In reality, Artemisia gave birth to four children, two daughters and two sons, between 1613 and 1618, of whom only a daughter lived to adulthood. The novel writes that her husband became embittered because of Artemisia's greater success as a painter. It is true that she was inducted into the prestigious Florentine Accademia dell'Arte del Disegno in 1616, the first woman so honored, whereas he never was. According to the novel, when she was honored he immediately began to drink and see other women. He soon abandoned Artemisia and their daughter. The historical record shows that they remained together for at least another six years, through Lent 1622, after which he departed, and she lost track of him. There is no information on the reason for his departure. In addition, further research suggests, without proving, that Artemisia had love affairs with some of her patrons and may have given birth to an illegitimate daughter after the departure of her husband.[18] Finally, on the basis of one surviving letter, Vreeland portrays Artemisia and Galileo Galilei as good friends and has her writing to Galilei warning him about the nefarious priests in Rome. This is a considerable exaggeration of the record. The novel does not begin to measure up to Stone's fictional biography of Michelangelo.

Meanwhile, Artemisia Gentileschi is a growth industry in both scholarship and entertainment. The French film *Artemisia* (director Agnes Merlet; cast Valentina Cervi, Miki Manojlovic, and Michel Serrault) appeared in 1998. It shows Artemisia and Agostino Tassi as voluntary and passionate lovers until Orazio, for his own reasons, brings charges of rape. According to the film, the blameless Tassi is her artistic teacher and accepts the false charge of rape to protect Artemisia's reputation. The film argues that Artemisia's love affair with Tassi awakened her creativity. When the film opened in New York City in May 1998, its American distributor advertised that it was the true story of Artemisia. Gloria Steinem and others appeared at the opening to distribute a fact sheet prepared by art historian Mary D. Garrard that corrected the misrepresentations of the film.[19] We will hear much more about Artemisia Gentileschi.

The Variety of the Renaissance Novel

Although some prominent recent historical novels feature a feminist heroine in an Italian Renaissance filled with war, persecution, and religious fanaticism, other novels take advantage of the diversity of the Renaissance in order to offer a greater variety of perspectives.

Another recent novel starring women is Michael Ennis, *Duchess of Milan* (New York: Viking Penguin, 1992). It features two brilliant and vivacious historical characters, each with good reason to call herself duchess of Milan. Isabella d'Aragona (1471–1524) is married to Giangaleazzo Sforza (1469–1494), the duke of Milan. However, because he came to the throne at the age of seven, his uncle Ludovico "Il Moro" Sforza (1452–1508) is the regent and de facto ruler of the duchy. Consequently, Isabella is duchess of Milan in name only. In 1491, Ludovico il Moro marries the gifted and lively Beatrice d'Este (1475–1497). Because her husband exercises practical control, she can also claim to be duchess of Milan.

The two women are cousins and good friends at first, as they share a love of balls, riding, and the pain and joy of childbirth. Together they cope with the intrigue, awkwardness, and laughter of court life. But their friendship wanes, as they are caught up in the competition between their husbands, and each willingly supports her spouse. The novel concentrates on the years 1491 through 1497, just before and after the French invasion of Italy in 1494, which began a long period of turmoil in Italy. Intrigues, diplomacy, double-dealing, rivalries, poisonings, torture, competition with mistresses for the affection of husbands, earthy humor, and many turns of fortune mark their lives. The novel stresses the role that women played in dynastic politics, not just through their arranged marriages, but as willing players in the game of politics. Much of the novel is based on the life of Beatrice d'Este, which has been carefully studied by historians.[20]

Because the book is faithful to the historical record, it does not have a happy ending. Isabella d'Aragona sees her son taken to France at the age of ten and never sees him again. Her daughter becomes a queen in faraway Poland. Beatrice d'Este dies in childbirth, while Ludovico's schemes come to naught, and he dies in a French prison. But their effigies are united in a magnificent Renaissance funeral monument in the Certosa of Pavia, a monastery a few miles south of Milan, which should not be missed. The novel is filled with real historical characters, including Leonardo da Vinci, and it quotes documents. But it is difficult to keep track of the many characters and the intrigue.

The vision of the Renaissance presented in *Duchess of Milan* is more traditional and more accurate than that found in feminist historical novels. It is a novel of politics, a game played by everyone at the court, by fair means and foul. Although the chief protagonists are women, there are important male figures as well. The Italian Renaissance is seen as a period of strong personalities competing for power.

Some recent novels about the Renaissance emphasize blood and gore. *Loredana: A Venetian Tale* (London: Jonathan Cape, 2004), by the American-born but London-based Lauro Martines (b. 1927), begins with a scene of torture and has several additional episodes of torture, as well as incest and much else in a tale of sixteenth-century Venice. Although the author is a distinguished historian of Renaissance Florence, his rendition of government and society in Renaissance Venice is not particularly reliable. Another novel with a great deal of bloodshed and intolerance is Richard

Zimler, *The Last Kabbalist of Lisbon* (Woodstock, NY: The Overlook Press, 1998). It centers on the riot that produced a massacre of a number of Jews in Lisbon in 1506. They had been forcibly converted to Christianity in 1497 but were secretly practicing Judaism. The novel focuses on the adventures of one Jew who escapes the massacre. Zimler is an American living in Portugal; his book has been a bestseller in English and has been translated into at least eight other languages.

After the novels about bloodshed and persecution, it is a pleasure to turn to those that describe some of the accomplishments of the period. These books depict the same years of the Italian Renaissance as the novels of war and persecution but show a brighter side. A clever and light-hearted book is *Carnival of Saints* (New York: Ballantine Books, 1994) by poet, actor, director, playwright, and theater critic George A. Herman (b. 1928).[21] It offers a humorous account of the origins of an important Renaissance creation, the *commedia dell'arte*, improvisational comic theater, which spread across Europe and influenced many playwrights including Shakespeare.

The year is 1503 and the place is Aosta in the extreme northwestern corner of Italy. Harlequin, a man of unknown background and empty pockets, meets Colombina, a lady of uncertain virtue who is past her prime but owns a wagon. Together with a juggler (Scarpino) and thief (Pantalone) on the run, they tumble into the wagon and escape the town. The novel narrates their adventures as they journey south. Along the way they pick up other raffish or forlorn characters, including a blustering captain, a befuddled assistant to Leonardo da Vinci, a sharp-tongued tart, a handsome and vain young man, and the illegitimate daughter of a future pope. Assorted villains, including Cesare Borgia, chase them. Niccolò Machiavelli makes a cameo appearance as the Florentine ambassador observing and writing down Borgia's schemes.

Princes, cardinals, duchesses, and even Leonardo da Vinci enter and exit.

The impecunious travelers decide to try to earn a little money by entertaining villagers with some playacting in which they will use their various skills. But they have no text to follow. So, they borrow situations from other authors, such as the Roman comic dramatist Plautus (c. 254–184 BC) and improvise their own dialogue and action. Their comic skits involve generational domestic conflicts, such as young lovers who are thwarted by parents but helped by shifty servants. Mistaken identities further confuse matters, but threatening situations are always overcome. Harlequin and his fellow travelers engage in physical action, slapstick, and clowning, and add new characters, such as the pompous scholar who spouts meaningless Latin phrases and a blustering but mentally challenged captain. Thus was born *commedia dell'arte*. Audiences loved it.

Herman cleverly works in all the stock characters of Italian Renaissance *commedia dell'arte* including Isabella (probably inspired by the real Isabella Andreini [1562–1604], a gifted *commedia dell'arte* performer and poet), and Tristano, a character originating in medieval chivalric romances. Herman's chronology is probably premature, because the earliest document about a *commedia dell'arte* company is dated 1545. Nevertheless, by the 1560s it was extremely popular, and several companies toured Italy. In the last third of the century, Italian companies brought their improvisational comedic art to France, Germany, England, and even Poland. *Commedia dell'arte* had considerable influence on English theater in the late sixteenth and seventeenth centuries.

Herman's historical novel uses historical characters and events to tell his story without worrying too much about chronological or any other kind of accuracy. He makes room for broad wordplay. At one point, a speaker describes the alleged sins of Lucrezia Borgia. His listener is appalled: "Lucrezia has been sleeping with her father, the pope, and with her brother Cesare?" The first speaker responds deadpan: "They are a very close family."[22]

Herman has also written Renaissance detective stories starring Leonardo da Vinci and a very intelligent fictional dwarf, Niccolo da Pavia. *A Comedy of Murders* (New York: Carrol & Graf, 1994) begins in 1498. The duke of Milan survives an assassination plot in a monastery in Pavia thanks to Niccolo da Pavia. The duke brings him to Milan where the dwarf wins the friendship of Leonardo da Vinci. When cardinals start to die under mysterious circumstances, Leonardo and Niccolo attempt to solve the murders with the aid of Leonardo's anatomical studies and wonderful machines. The adventures of Leonardo and Niccolo continue in *The Tears of the Madonna* (1995), *The Florentine Mourners* (1996), and *The Toys of War* (2001), as they solve the theft of a diamond necklace and various murders involving the Borgias, the Medici, and other princely families. All are set in Italian courts around 1500. The novels of Ennis, Herman, and others offer a variety of views about the Italian Renaissance, which is appropriate, because it was a broad and complex society.

The English Renaissance in Fiction

After Italy, England is the favorite setting for historical novels of the Renaissance. Novelists produce book after book about sixteenth-century England and its four monarchs (Henry VIII, reigned 1509–1547; Edward VI, reigned 1547–1553; Mary I, reigned 1553–1558; and Elizabeth I, reigned 1558–1603). The reasons are clear: all but the boy king Edward VII were strong figures with compelling life stories. Three recent examples come from the English author, Philippa Gregory.

The first of her trilogy is *The Other Boleyn Girl* (London: HarperCollins, 2001). The other Boleyn girl is Mary Boleyn (1508?–1543), the younger sister of Anne Boleyn (1507?–1536) who became the wife of Henry VIII. (These are the most frequently mentioned birth dates. A recent historical study argues that Anne was born about 1501, and Mary about 1499, thus making her older than Anne.) [23] It is a novel of deadly sexual politics. It is known that Mary Boleyn was Henry VIII's mistress before Anne, but nothing is known about the relationship. Gregory makes Mary into a major character and the narrator of a book that tells the story of how Henry VIII falls in love with and marries Anne Boleyn and then has her executed.

In Gregory's story, senior male members of the Boleyn/Howard clan, a powerful and real noble family, dangle Mary, who is already married, before Henry VIII in the hopes of getting her into Henry's bed. They want to improve the position of the family, because monarchs often showered titles and favors on the family of a favorite mistress. And if she can produce a son for Henry, and get him legitimized, the family would be part of the monarchy. At first Mary simply obeys her father and uncle, but then she falls in love with Henry, and has a daughter and a son by him. But they are bastards, unacknowledged by their father, because Henry is still married to Catherine of Aragon (1485–1536). Moreover, when Mary becomes pregnant and, thus, not very attractive to Henry VIII, the Boleyn/Howard clan thrust the bright, vivacious, and extremely ambitious Anne into Henry's path. He is infatuated with her, but she holds out for marriage. At the same time, the smitten Henry becomes convinced that because Catherine did not produce a son, his marriage to her was unlawful and must be annulled. After he breaks with Rome and establishes the English church, Henry and Anne become lovers. They marry after the cowed English church dissolves his marriage to Catherine.

After Henry and Anne are married, Queen Anne gives birth to a daughter, the future Elizabeth I (b. 1533; reigned 1558–1603). But then she has a miscarriage. Henry becomes disenchanted with her and takes up with another woman of the court, Jane Seymour. According to the novel, Anne, desperate to produce a son, sleeps with her homosexual brother George Boleyn. This union produces another miscarriage, a malformed male fetus, in January 1536. The story moves to its tragic conclusion. Anne is arrested on charges of multiple adulteries, plotting to secure the king's death, incest, and witchcraft. After a brief trial, whose result is predetermined, Anne is beheaded on May 19, 1536. Her brother George and other men accused of committing adultery with Anne Boleyn are also executed. But Mary Boleyn survives. After her first husband dies of illness in 1528, she remarries. After the fall of the Boleyns, she moves to the country with her new husband and children, the two by Henry and a third by her new husband. The book emphasizes personal stories, especially the rivalry between Mary, who is portrayed as loving and good-hearted, but naive about court intrigue, and Anne, who is a thoroughly modern bitch. But the book also makes it clear that both daughters, and women of high status generally, are pawns to be maneuvered and sacrificed if necessary for the advancement of the family. Mary and Anne lament the lack of control over their lives but can do little about it.

The historical reality is that Mary Boleyn married William Carey about 1520, that she was Henry's mistress, probably in the early 1520s, and that she gave birth to a son, Henry Carey, in March 1526, plus a daughter at an unknown date. But it is not clear that Henry VIII fathered either of them. At least one historian is convinced that the children were conceived after Mary returned to her husband's bed.[24] Henry VIII never acknowledged them as his, even though he did recognize an illegitimate son by an earlier mistress. Given the fact that Henry VIII fathered only four living children for certain in his life despite constant attempts with six wives, two known mistresses, and possibly others, it is likely that he was unable to produce many children and did not father Mary Boleyn's son and daughter. In any case, after William Carey died in 1528, Mary secretly married William Stafford in 1534, and they had one or more additional children. She died in 1543.

The novel has Anne Boleyn committing incest and giving birth to a malformed fetus. This is based on a recent historical study that argues that Anne was condemned to death because people at the time believed that illicit sex acts produced deformed children. The combination of the deformed fetus and accusation of incest awakened suspicions of witchcraft, which contributed to her downfall with Henry and others, according to this argument. But other historians are not convinced that the fetus was malformed, or that beliefs about witchcraft helped cause Anne's downfall. They argue that her downfall was the result of the loss of Henry's support and because of changing court politics. Anne had made a powerful enemy in Thomas Cromwell, the king's chief minister, who organized her trial and execution. And the Seymour family was rising in influence. Indeed, on May 30, 1536, only eleven days after Anne Boleyn's execution, Henry VIII married Jane Seymour.[25]

The novel is a well-written page turner, marred only by the consistent grammatical error of substituting "who" for the correct "whom," in the American paperback edition, a mistake found in other novels as well. Dialogue and events are vividly realized. The historical research is thorough and pretty accurate as far as it goes. The novel captures well the sycophancy and machinations of members of the court, as well as the inordinate amount of time spent on games, masques (dramatic entertainments performed in costume), and other amusements. It does a good job of portraying the talented, mercurial, petulant, and vicious Henry VIII. This takes skill, because Henry was both an attractive man and a monster. Of his six wives, he executed two and divorced two. A fifth

(Jane Seymour, c. 1509–1537) died giving birth to Edward VI, while his sixth wife survived him (and quickly produced a child by her next husband, further evidence that the failure to produce more children was Henry's). Henry broke with Roman Catholicism, confiscated monastic properties, and corrupted the law in order to get his way, although the novel does not dwell on these aspects of his rule. He executed people, including practically all of his most able and faithful ministers of state, on trumped-up charges. The trials of Anne Boleyn and many others were nothing more than judicial murders. But concentrating on the personal relations between Mary, Anne, Henry, George Boleyn, Catherine of Aragon, and others, while practically ignoring the growth of Protestantism in England and Henry's grandstanding in European politics, makes for a vivid personal story that is not grim until the end. *The Other Boleyn Girl* has had many paperback reprints and has been made into a BBC film.

Gregory's second Tudor novel is *The Queen's Fool* (London: HarperCollins, 2004). It deals with the rivalry between Queen Mary Tudor (reigned 1553–1558) and her younger sister, Elizabeth, next in line for the throne if Mary has no children. The story is told in the words of Hannah Green, an invented character. Hannah is a young Jewess who flees to England to escape persecution in Spain. Robert Dudley (1533?–1588), a historical figure, discovers that she has a gift of prophecy and brings her to the court as a female fool whose role is to amuse the court. In reality, there was a female fool at the court at this time, but nothing is known about her. Hannah also serves as a spy on Mary for Elizabeth, and on Elizabeth for Dudley. From this vantage point, she narrates the contest between Mary and Elizabeth, a sibling rivalry like that of Anne and Mary Boleyn. Gregory describes how Mary is disappointed in love, because her husband Philip, prince and later king of Spain, spends little time with her, and she does not conceive. At the same time, Elizabeth flirts with Dudley, but craftily remains unattached. The religious conflict is part of the story, as Mary is Catholic, whereas Elizabeth is Protestant. Gregory portrays Mary sympathetically, seeing her as an ill woman who is unlucky, rather than the "Bloody Mary" of popular legend. (It is usually forgotten that Henry VIII and Elizabeth I each executed as many or more English men and women for religious reasons, and in just as cruel fashion, as did Mary.) The book ends in 1558, as Mary dies, and Elizabeth becomes queen. Along the way, Gregory also tells the story of Hannah's life and love.

The third of Gregory's Tudor novels is *The Virgin's Lover* (London: HarperCollins, 2004). It picks up the story in 1558 with some of the same historical characters. Again, it is a novel of sexual politics and a love triangle. Elizabeth I becomes the Protestant queen in 1558 and has many problems, including the question of whom she should marry. Her favorite is the same Robert Dudley, Earl of Essex, who appeared in the previous novel. Dudley is an ambitious and able statesman, who loves her and power, possibly in reverse order, and wants to marry her. The novel asserts that they are lovers, but historians have found no reliable evidence and have doubts, because it would have been extremely difficult to hide an affair from other members of the court. Foreign ambassadors paid ladies in waiting and other court members to report every move that the queen made.[26] If the two were physically intimate, everyone would know. In any case, Dudley is already married, and his wife Amy (1533?–1560) refuses to give him a divorce. Amy then dies under mysterious circumstances. Rivals put it out that Dudley murdered her, thus casting a shadow on him. Elizabeth decides never to marry, possibly the most astute political decision of her reign. Again, the novel is well written and develops the psychological aspects of the three main characters.

Gregory's novels and most other historical novels about the English Renaissance see it as an age dominated by the Tudor monarchs, Henry VIII, Mary, and Elizabeth. One cannot argue with this view. All three were strong monarchs who exercised personal rule and transformed England. Henry VIII and Elizabeth were vivid personalities who ruled for 38 years and 45 years, respectively.

Renaissance England is an ideal setting for historical novels. The novelist needs strong and vivid personalities; they do not have to be invented for England. Unlike some other parts of Europe, Renaissance England also had vital and important women as Elizabeth, Mary Tudor, Anne Boleyn, and others. The strong and well-known historical characters are already in place. So are the personal loves of the chief actors. All the novelist has to do is to add the fictional characters through whose eyes the historical events can be witnessed and other stories told. That Renaissance England was a small place also helps the novelist to create a focused story. England, Scotland, and Ireland together had only 5 million people in 1500, compared with 16 million in France and 11 million in Italy. There was only one court that mattered, and the brightest and most ambitious flocked to it. Because readers never tire of reading about the monarchs who created modern England, there will be many more historical novels about Renaissance England.

The Renaissance as Mystery: Thrillers and Detective Stories

Another flourishing literary genre is the Renaissance mystery, a contemporary story based on something about the Renaissance. Although the story is set in the present, the key element of the plot is a Renaissance secret.

There are two kinds of Renaissance mysteries, the thriller and the detective story. In thrillers, the secret involves something powerful and threatening from the Renaissance that must be uncovered and rendered harmless. Sometimes it is a secret with the potential of doing great evil if it falls into the wrong hands. The hero and heroine—thrillers often feature a man and a woman who in the course of solving the mystery are attracted to each other—stumble onto information that leads them to investigate a mysterious secret or artifact from the Renaissance. They must overcome great danger from an organization that also wants to unravel the secret and use if for evil purposes. The formula is that of most thrillers, but the Renaissance rather than the Cold War or the Nazi era provides important plot information.

For academics, a charming aspect of Renaissance mysteries is that the hero or heroine is often a university scholar rather than a spy, private detective, or adventurer. A favorite device is to feature a scholar reluctantly pulled out of the study. The scholar must call on his or her knowledge to solve the mystery while avoiding the evildoers. This allows the author a credible rationale to insert into the text the needed information about the Renaissance. This can be done so skillfully that the reader barely notices the history lesson. Or the author's research may stick in the throat like a lump of porridge: good for you but barely edible. In either case, part of the attraction of the mystery is that the reader learns something unusual about the Renaissance.

The Overseer (New York: Crown Books, 1998; paperback: New York: Jove Books, 1999), the first novel of Jonathan Rabb, is a good example of the Renaissance mystery thriller. A cabal of right-wing schemers in the United States has trained operatives who blow up buildings and manipulate the markets to create chaos. The stability of the country and the government are at stake. The conspirators are allegedly following the plan of a Renaissance monk named Eisenreich who around 1530 wrote a political treatise that is a blueprint for bringing down a government and taking control of a nation. His manuscript is rumored to be more dangerous, effective, and evil than Machiavelli's *The Prince*. But it has never been found. A female agent of the American government and a male professor, an expert on political theory and conservative groups, learn of the manuscript and try to find it and expose the murderous conspirators. The book inverts the usual roles of hero and heroine. She is the trained operative with the martial skills to fight off the bad guys, while he is the physically hapless scholar thrust into a violent world. Their quest takes them to Florence, other parts of Europe, and then back to the United States, with the right-wing group trying to kill them at every step of the way. Eventually they find the manuscript and thwart the conspirators. The novel has good plot turns and dialogue, attractive central characters, and moves along well.

The author, who has a master's degree in the history of European political theory, provides the text of the Eisenreich manuscript at the end of the book. It is post-Machiavellian. That is, while it uses Machiavelli as a base, it claims to be a better way to take and hold power. It even chides Machiavelli for the weaknesses in his theories. The starting point is that chaos must be created through assassination, rebellion, economic collapse, or some other huge disruption of the life of a nation. These create the conditions for seizing control of the government. But in order to stay in power, the usurpers must achieve cultural power over the people through educational indoctrination. The manuscript postulates that all men are aggressive and want to assert their wills over others. Therefore, the government must offer a common enemy for the people to hate and conquer. In general, the treatise superimposes twentieth-century fascist and totalitarian principles, reminiscent of the permanent war and daily hate exercises imagined in George Orwell's *1984*, on top of Machiavelli's *The Prince*. The view of the Renaissance in the book is that it produced sophisticated political theory that remains effective and powerful today.

A mixture of thriller and detective story is *The Rule of Four* (New York: Dial Press, 2004). It is a first novel by two authors, Ian Caldwell, a recent graduate of Princeton University, and Dustin

Thomason, recently graduated from Harvard University. It focuses on a very famous book of the Renaissance: *Hypnerotomachia Poliphili* ("The dream of Poliphilo" or "The strife of love in a dream of Poliphilo") of the monk and author Francesco Colonna (1433/34–1527). It was published in Venice in 1499 by the famous publisher Aldo Manuzio. The book is unusual, to put it mildly. Poliphilo has a dream about a long journey through gardens, symbolic spaces, and classical ruins. He finds his love, Polia, who leads him to a temple of Venus. But she rejects his physical love, eventually dies, and is assumed into the heavens. The book is a strange mixture of romance, allegory, architectural tour, encyclopedia of the ancient world, and fantasy. Its language increases the complexity. Although the book has a Latin title, it is written in Venetian dialect, but adds numerous Latin, Greek, and invented words. It mixes languages together by adding Latin prefixes and suffixes to Italian words and vice versa. The technical term for this kind of language is "macaronic." A major attraction of the book is its numerous elegant and sometimes erotic illustrations done by an unknown artist. Although most readers then and now find the text confused and tiresome, some readers and scholars have sought hidden meaning in the book. Those who want to find out for themselves may read it in a modern Italian version or in English translation.[27]

In *The Rule of Four,* a Princeton undergraduate is writing his senior thesis on the *Hypnerotomachia Poliphili* in spring 1999. The obsessed student believes that he is close to unraveling the secret meaning of the text. But he fears that a senior professor at the famous Institute for Advanced Study, also located in Princeton but not affiliated with the university, intends to steal his research. There is also a wealthy New York art dealer who supported the student's research in the past but whose current attitude is hard to fathom. And there is a missing Renaissance notebook that may hold the final clues.

This intellectual intrigue takes place in the midst of Princeton undergraduate life, with students searching for meaning and love amidst eating clubs and the Nude Olympics (running naked through campus on the night of the first snowfall, an event that has since been banned). Any resemblance to F. Scott Fitzgerald's *This Side of Paradise* might be real. "The rule of four" refers to the relations between four undergraduates, the obsessed student and his three suite mates, as well as to the secret meaning of the *Hypnerotomachia Poliphili*. Then a graduate student who is also studying the *Hypnerotomachia Poliphili* is murdered. More violence occurs as the student finally unravels the blockbuster meaning of the book hidden for 500 years. The story reaches a fiery climax in an event that recalls the burning of the vanities in February 7, 1497, when Savonarola persuaded Florentines to burn their worldly art and books.

Of recent fiction about the Renaissance, *Rule of Four* is based on the most research and is the most accurate. Some of the information in the book is little known beyond a small number of intellectual historians of the Italian Renaissance. And when the authors depart from the historical record, they say so in an afterward. The authors also demonstrate some knowledge of the process of publishing Renaissance scholarship today. For example, the larcenous professor at the Institute of Advanced Study, where Einstein once pondered the universe, intends to announce his discoveries by publishing an article in *Renaissance Quarterly*. That would be appropriate, because *Renaissance Quarterly* is the leading journal in the world for interdisciplinary studies of the Renaissance and would be happy to publish such an article, if it survived the peer review process. In the three years, 2000 to 2003, during which I served as articles editor of *Renaissance Quarterly,* we did publish an article on the *Hypnerotomachia Poliphili,* but on the relationship between language and illustrations in the book rather than any secret meaning.

The undergraduate who unravels the mystery of the book is amazingly learned for a twenty-two year old. He already reads five languages, including Latin and Greek. He produces scholarship so good and original that a senior scholar with decades of research behind him will kill to steal it. This is an undergraduate fantasy. Nevertheless, the writing, including a funny riff on the Boy Scouts, is good enough, and the central characters attractive enough, to charm readers. And for those who want to learn more, there is Joscelyn Godwin, *The Real Rule of Four* (New York: The Disinformation Company, 2004). Godwin, who translated the *Hypnerotomachia Poliphili* into English, provides additional historical information and corrections, plus maps of Princeton University and the Institute for Advanced Study.

For the authors of *The Rule of Four*, the Italian Renaissance is twofold. First, it is a puzzle palace. The book presupposes that Renaissance intellectuals were enormously erudite men who constructed riddles. Second, the Renaissance was a period of great intellectual openness and accomplishment but threatened by fanaticism. The book praises Renaissance humanism as a quest for earthly knowledge; humanism "teaches men that pagan authorities can rival the Bible, that wisdom and beauty should be worshiped in unchristian things." At the same time, the wonderful world of the Renaissance is threatened by "the worst kind of fanaticism, everything that was wrong with Christianity," which is personified in Savonarola.[28] Like other fictional accounts of the Renaissance, the book makes too much of religious hostility and intolerance.

Dan Brown's *The Da Vinci Code* (New York: Doubleday, 2003) has been wildly successful commercially. As of March 2005, it had sold 25 million copies in 44 languages around the world. Brown has also written *The Da Vinci Code. Special Illustrated Collector's Edition* (New York: Bantam Press, 2004). And a film version starring Tom Hanks is scheduled for release in May 2006.[29] The plot is intricate. The curator of the Louvre is murdered. But before he dies he strips naked, lies down in the position of Leonardo da Vinci's Vitruvian Man, and writes in his own blood a mysterious symbol on the floor of the Louvre. A Harvard professor of religious symbology (the interpretation of religious symbols, a fictitious academic discipline invented by the author) is asked for advice, and he and the curator's granddaughter, an expert cryptographer, try to solve the mystery of his murder. They discover that the curator was the head of a secret religious group called the Priory of Sion, which has guarded the true nature and location of the Holy Grail throughout history. Like Indiana Jones, they search for the Grail. Various churchmen, including a crooked cardinal and a hit man from the conservative Catholic Opus Dei organization, oppose them. Naturally, they unravel more and more mysteries while people get killed along the way. The hero and heroine discover that a number of famous people, including Leonardo da Vinci, were leaders of the Priory of Sion over the centuries.

Their search for the Holy Grail leads them to see Leonardo da Vinci's *The Last Supper* in a new way. They conclude that the apostle John, the blond man at Jesus' right (the viewer's left), is really a portrait of Mary Magdalene, who was Jesus' lover and wife. Pregnant by him at the time of the crucifixion, she bore their daughter, and the two fled to France where Jesus' line continued through the ages. The Holy Grail was not the cup from which Jesus drank at the Last Supper but Mary Magdalene, the human vessel of Jesus' seed. But early Christian leaders and, later, the medieval Catholic Church deliberately suppressed this information and demonized the divine feminine, according to the novel. And so on and so forth.

The historical part of the book is a recapitulation of a number of implausible conspiracy theories that have been around for a long time. Indeed, the author has recently been sued for his alleged unauthorized use of the research of others. Most of the pseudohistorical information comes from exaggerations and misreadings of materials from the first centuries of Christianity. Many scholars have pointed out the inaccuracies and wild statements.[30] Some wonder if the author has an anti-Christian and anti-Catholic agenda.[31] The criticisms of the historical material are justified. A good rule of thumb is to reject 95 percent of the historical information in the book and to view with extreme scepticism the remaining 5 percent.

The amount of material on the Renaissance is limited but just as wrong, especially the interpretation of *The Last Supper*. No scholar believes that the apostle John in *The Last Supper* was really Mary Magdalene. Indeed, the portrait of John was consistent with traditional iconographical representations. In any case, *the Last Supper* is in such bad shape that viewers can hardly make out anything clearly. The faces of Jesus, John, and the rest of the Apostles have been repainted so often in the past five centuries that Leonardo's original intent is impossible to determine. The other secret symbolic meanings in the paintings of Leonardo da Vinci offered in the book are equally fictitious. Even as a work of literature, the book fails. The chief characters and dialogue are wooden, there is almost no character development, and some subsidiary characters exist only to deliver lumps of fictional erudition. The book's combination of conspiracy theory, puzzles, and negative depiction of organized Christianity may explain its popularity.

The use of "Da Vinci" in the title and throughout the book is awkward. The translation is "from Vinci," the town in Tuscany where Leonardo was born. But it is wrong. In his own lifetime, Leonardo called himself and was called by others "Leonardo" or "Leonardo da Vinci." No one in the Renaissance would say "From Vinci painted *The Last Supper*." It would be like saying "From Red Cloud (i.e., Willa Cather) wrote *My Ántonia*."

The Renaissance detective story resembles the thriller but is less feverish. A puzzle involves something from the Renaissance. Again, the story is set in the present but has a good deal of material involving the Renaissance. There are villains but only a limited amount of killing, perhaps a single murder. The tone is lighter, the adventures less frenetic. There is more room for episodes from the human comedy.

Renaissance art is popular subject matter for detective stories. *The Caravaggio Obsession* (Boston: Little, Brown, 1984) by Oliver Banks begins with a series of art thefts in Italy and the murder of an art dealer in New York.[32] "Art cop" Amos Hatcher, who pursues art thieves because he loves art, uses his historical knowledge of the life of Caravaggio in order to find the thief and murderer who is, as the title indicates, obsessed with the paintings of Caravaggio. Much of the story is set in Rome, with quite accurate descriptions of piazzas and churches, plus comments about Italian politics. The author has a Ph.D. in art history and taught the subject before becoming an art consultant and writer.

Iain Pears (b. 1955), author of a scholarly work in art history, a former correspondent for Reuters, and a television consultant has written a series of detective novels about Renaissance art. The first is *The Raphael Affair* (New York: Harcourt Brace Jovanovich, 1990; American paperback: New York: Berkley Books, 1998). The premise of the novel is the sudden appearance of a unknown masterwork by Raphael (1483–1520). Jonathan Argyll, an English art history graduate student, uncovers evidence of the existence of the painting. He concludes that it was painted over in the early eighteenth century by a mediocre Italian painter so that it could be spirited out of the country and sold to an English nobleman. Now the painting miraculously reappears. It is stripped of its overlay, scientifically tested, authenticated, and sold back to the Italian government at the highest price ever paid for a work of art. But is it real? Suspicions rise like fungi after a rain. A well-known art forger dies, leaving a very large sum of cash in his safe deposit box in a Swiss bank. An Italian expert who has doubts about the authentication process is murdered. So, General Taddeo Bottando, the head of the Italian National Art Theft Squad, and his beautiful assistant, Flavia di Stefano, begin to investigate. With the aid of the maladroit Argyll, they set about solving two mysteries: is the painting genuine, and who is doing the killing? There is no shortage of suspects in an art world full of forgers, smarmy dealers, and museum directors willing to sell their souls in order to acquire masterpieces.

The novel's view of the Renaissance is that it was a dynamic period with great artistic achievement. It assumes that readers know and admire Raphael's lovely female portraits picturing the highest ideals of Renaissance beauty. The novel correctly posits that art forgeries happen and gives detailed information about forgery techniques. The book pokes gentle fun at art historians and describes the art world as follows: "Flavia took it for granted that all art dealers were crooked at some level."[33] Bottando marvels at how museum directors win praise and deflect blame in the Machiavellian world of Italian politics. Much of the story is set in Rome, which Pears describes in loving and accurate detail. For example, there really is an excellent ice cream store (*gelateria*) in a tiny street behind the Palazzo Montecitorio, where the Chamber of Deputies, the lower house of the Italian government, meets.

Pears followed with six more Renaissance art history mysteries: *The Titian Committee* (1991), *The Bernini Bust* (1992), *The Last Judgement* (1993), *Giotto's Hand* (1994), *Death and Restoration* (1996), and *The Immaculate Deception* (2000). The dauntless trio of sleuths, Bottando, Flavia, and Jonathan, appear in all three, with the latter two eventually falling in love and marrying.

Whether thriller or detective story, the Renaissance mystery depends on the reader having some knowledge of the Renaissance. Mysteries see the Renaissance as a remarkable age full of extraordinary individuals of great achievement and insight who created great works of literature and art. It is not so grim as portrayed by some historical novels. Mystery novels also assume that books, manuscripts, and paintings from the Renaissance have the power to influence the world today.

Truth and Fiction

Historical novels walk a fine line between the past and the present, between the historical record and contemporary culture. Authors want to tell a good story with gripping individuals and events located in a fascinating era of the past. At the same time, they need to make their characters attractive and sympathetic to today's readers. This means that the author must endow them with some contemporary feelings, attitudes, and views, which are often very different from those of the past. The result is a mixed view of the past, part historical and part contemporary.

The contemporary concerns that appear most strongly in recent Renaissance historical novels are obvious. The books emphasize personal actions and feelings, thus reflecting a dominant feature of today's culture. Important historical events provide the background to the personal stories in the best fiction or hardly appear in the worst. The rise of feminism has had a major impact. Women are often central characters. They are very accomplished and take considerable control over their lives despite the constraints of society. By contrast, male characters are usually flawed and weak. Current attitudes about sex are reflected in the novels. Recent fiction on the Renaissance includes considerable sexual activity outside of marriage, including homosexuality and incest.

Heroines seem to have more children by lovers than by husbands in the novels.

When the novels turn to the larger historical canvas, the Renaissance itself, contemporary attitudes again color the stories. One of the surprising things about recent novels is that they often depict the Renaissance as an age of religious fanaticism. Several feature Savonarola or make far too much of him. In the nearly 300 years of the Italian Renaissance, from about 1350 to about 1620, there was only one Savonarola. He dominated one city for a little more than three years, December 1494 until April 1498. But in the novels he appears frequently as the example of what recent authors see as the dark side of the period, its religious fanaticism and intolerance. These threaten to destroy the learning, achievements, and human tolerance of the Renaissance. The novels seldom portray clergymen sympathetically and tend to see the Renaissance and organized religion as two warring factions. They ignore the fact that churchmen and the papacy were an integral part of the Renaissance and responsible for many of its greatest achievements. It may be that this attitude comes from a broad hostility toward organized religion in a segment of today's culture. The overall fictional picture of the Renaissance is that it was a period of remarkable individuals who achieved great things but were threatened by dark forces.

Many readers get their knowledge of the past from historical novels. And this is often a sensationalized history, because novelists prefer the more exciting, bloody, conspiratorial, and/or mysterious versions of events. They make for a better story. But fiction, however well-crafted, is still fiction. Still, fictionalized history can stimulate readers to learn more by reading real works of history found in school, public, or university libraries. For example, consulting articles on Henry VIII and Anne Boleyn in standard reference works, such as the *Encyclopedia of the Renaissance* and the

Encyclopedia of the Reformation (New York: Oxford University Press, 1996), will give readers factual information and suggestions for further reading. The historical truth is often just as interesting as novelistic accounts.

Chapter 10

THE RENAISSANCE IN FILM ❧

In 1998, Hollywood and British filmmakers released four films on the Renaissance: two on the English Renaissance, one on the Italian Renaissance, and another on the French Renaissance. *Shakespeare in Love* was the smash hit of the year. It received thirteen Oscar nominations and won seven Oscars, including Best Picture, Best Actress in a Leading Role (Gwyneth Paltrow), Best Actress in a Supporting Role (Judi Dench, who played Queen Elizabeth), and Best Screenplay Written Directly for the Screen (Marc Norman and Tom Stoppard). It also received forty-two other prizes from film societies across the world.[1] And it was a huge box office success. Although 1998 with its four films on the Renaissance was unusual, it was only a small chapter in the story of the love affair of the motion picture industry with the Renaissance. It began in 1899 and shows no signs of ending.

Compared with books or the stage, motion pictures have advantages and disadvantages in portraying the Renaissance. They have a great edge in their ability to show historical and fictional characters as living human beings. They can show actions, especially large events such as battles, to which a stage play can only hint and a book only describe in words. Films often are visually wonderful, especially in color. They usually show the characters in historically accurate costumes based on paintings and descriptions from the Renaissance. They can film or re-create actual Renaissance locations, such as church, palace, or piazza, in which the events took place.

The disadvantage is that they usually have only a limited amount of time, typically two hours, to tell the story. So they shorten and simplify. Films dealing with the Renaissance often take a historical story and make radical changes to the plot, characters, events, and motivation. The technical possibilities of movies tempt moviemakers to use light, color, and images to project stronger messages than words can convey. They may introduce contemporary values and concerns that distort the historical record; because these messages are presented in moving images, the impact can be overwhelming. Films about the Renaissance that make no pretense to being historically accurate, but mix together attractive historical material, authentic or authentic-looking settings, good fictional story, sympathetic actors, and fine direction and photography, can be enjoyed by all and achieve considerable commercial success.

For a long time, moviemakers saw the Renaissance as consisting of extraordinary creative and heroic individuals. They mattered more than large events and forces. The chief characters achieved great deeds and had the kind of personal control over their lives that modern men and women do. Many films reproduced great theater from the Renaissance, such as Shakespeare's plays. But recent films often present a Renaissance full of violence and religious intolerance.

Shakespeare on Film

For more than a century, there have been three kinds of feature films, that is, commercial films available in movie theaters across the country, on the Renaissance: film versions of Shakespeare's plays, films inspired by plots from Shakespeare, and films that deal with the Renaissance more generally.

Film versions of the plays of William Shakespeare and films inspired by his plays comprise the largest part of Renaissance filmography. Directors, producers, and hard-headed studio chiefs focused on the bottom line have produced many films of Shakespeare's plays for general audience viewing, even though they are written in soaring Elizabethan-era rhetoric and situated in distant lands. In 1899, an enterprising moving picture maker in London made a four-minute film of a scene from a stage production of Shakespeare's *King John*, one of his least known history plays.[2] Numerous one-reel silent excerpts and a limited number of full-length silent films followed.

Even though much of the enjoyment of Shakespeare depends on hearing his words, the Bard is so much a part of English-language culture that in 1929 a Hollywood studio produced a full-length (68 minutes, a common length at that time) silent film version of *The Taming of the Shrew* starring Douglas Fairbanks and Mary Pickford. The advent of talking pictures produced many more Shakespeare films with major movie stars. In addition, there have been numerous films of Shakespeare works for school use and documentaries, as well as television and video productions. Although American, British, and Canadian filmmakers have produced the lion's share of Shakespeare films, Italian, German, Spanish, Scandinavian, Japanese, and former Soviet Union filmmakers have also produced Shakespeare films. One catalogue lists more than 700 Shakespeare films of all kinds worldwide through 1989, and there have been more since.[3]

Table 10.1 lists the most important films of Shakespeare's plays produced by American and British commercial filmmakers for paying general audiences in movie houses. It does not include hundreds of short films, school-use films, television and video films, and documentaries on Shakespeare.

Table 10.1 - Select List of Major American and British Films of Shakespeare's Plays (in alphabetical order)

As You Like It (1936)
  Director: Paul Czinner, Teddy Baird.
  Cast: Elisabeth Bergner, Laurence Olivier

Hamlet (1947)
  Director: Laurence Olivier.
  Cast: Laurence Olivier, Eileen Herlie, Basil Sydney, Jean Simmons

Hamlet (1969)
  Director: Tony Richardson.
  Cast: Nicol Williamson, Anthony Hopkins, Judy Parfait, Marianne Faithfull

Hamlet (1991)
  Director: Franco Zeffirelli.
  Cast: Mel Gibson, Glenn Close, Alan Bates, Ian Holm, Paul Scofield

Hamlet (1997)
  Director: Kenneth Branagh.
  Cast: Kenneth Branagh, Derek Jacobi

Henry the Fifth (1944)
  Director: Laurence Olivier.
  Cast: Laurence Olivier, Robert Newton

Henry the Fifth (1989)
  Director: Kenneth Branagh.
  Cast: Kenneth Branagh, Judi Dench, Derek Jacobi, Paul Scofield

Julius Caesar (1950)
  Director: David Bradley.
  Cast: Charlton Heston, Harold Tasker, David Bradley

Table 10.1 (*continued*)

Julius Caesar (1953)
Director: Joseph L. Mankiewicz.
Cast: John Gielgud, James Mason, Marlon Brando, Greer Garson, Deborah Kerr. Music by Miklos Rozsa

Julius Caesar (1969)
Director: Stuart Burge.
Cast: Charlton Heston, Jason Robards, John Gielgud, Richard Johnson, Jill Bennett

King Lear (1970)
Director: Peter Brook.
Cast: Paul Scofield, Irene Worth

Macbeth (1947)
Director: Thomas A. Blaire.
Cast: David Bradley, Iain Wilimovsky

Macbeth (1948)
Director: Orson Welles.
Cast: Orson Welles, Jeanette Nolan, Dan O'Herlihy

Macbeth (1971)
Director: Roman Polanski.
Cast: Jon Fitch, Francesca Annis

The Merchant of Venice (2004)
Director: Michael Radford.
Cast: Al Pacino, Jeremy Irons, Joseph Fiennes, Lynn Collins

A Midsummer Night's Dream (1935)
Director: Max Reinhardt.
Cast: James Cagney, Joe E. Brown, Olivia de Havilland, Mickey Rooney, Dick Powell

A Midsummer Night's Dream (1968)
Done in modern setting and dress.
Director: Peter Hall.
Cast: Derek Godfrey, Jack Harris, Barbara Jefford

Table 10.1 (*continued*)

Much Ado About Nothing (1993)
  Director: Kenneth Branagh.
  Cast: Kenneth Branagh, Michael Keaton, Keanu Reeves, Emma Thompson, Denzel Washington

The Tragedy of Othello (1952)
  Director: Orson Welles.
  Cast: Orson Welles, Micheál MacLiammóir, Suzanne Cloutier

Othello (1995)
  Director: Oliver Parker.
  Cast: Laurence Fishburne, Kenneth Branagh

Richard the Third (1955)
  Director: Laurence Olivier.
  Cast: Laurence Olivier, Cedric Hartwicke, John Gielgud, Ralph Richardson, Helen Hayes. Music by William Walton

Romeo and Juliet (1936)
  Director: George Cukor.
  Cast: Leslie Howard, Norma Shearer, John Barrymore, Basil Rathbone

Romeo and Juliet (1954)
  Director: Renato Castellani.
  Cast: Laurence Harvey, Susan Shentall

Romeo and Juliet (1968)
  Director: Franco Zeffirelli.
  Cast: Leonard Whiting, Olivia Hussy, Milo O'Shea, Pat Heywood, Laurence Olivier

The Taming of the Shrew (1929)
  Silent film done in broad slapstick. Re-released with dubbed sound in 1966.
  Director: Sam Taylor.
  Cast: Douglas Fairbanks, Mary Pickford

The Taming of the Shrew (1966)
  Director: Franco Zeffirelli.
  Cast: Richard Burton, Elizabeth Taylor

Table 10.1 (*continued*)
***The Tempest* (1980)**   *Director:* Derek Jarman.   Cast: Jack Birkett, Heathcote Williams, Karl Johnson   ***The Tempest* (1982)** Contemporary dress and setting.   *Directors:* Paul Mazursky and Irby Smith.   *Cast:* John Cassavetes, Gena Rowlands, Susan Sarandon, Molly Ringwald,   Vittorio Gassman
Source: Kenneth S. Rothwell and Annabelle Henkin Melzer, *Shakespeare on Screen. An International Filmography and Videography.* New York and London: Neal-Schuman, 1990; Paul F. Grendler and Stephen Wagley, "The Renaissance in Popular Imagination," in *Encyclopedia of the Renaissance.* Ed. Paul F. Grendler et al. 6 vols. New York: Charles Scribner's Sons, 1999, vol. 5, p. 272; plus other sources.

Many famous directors and actors in motion picture history have done Shakespeare on screen. Some of the films and performances remain in the visual memory of viewers decades later. One of them is surely *Julius Caesar* of 1953 with its star-studded cast, and especially the scene in which Marlon Brando delivers Mark Antony's famous, "I come to bury Caesar, not to praise him. The evil that men do lives after them, the good is oft interred with their bones." So are Laurence Olivier's performances as Hamlet and Richard III. And his production of *Henry the Fifth* of 1944, which pictured English military victories in fifteenth-century France, encouraged hopes of Allied victory in Europe as D-Day approached. Some films are more memorable for their all-star casts than their excellence, such as the 1936 production of *Romeo and Juliet*, starring Leslie Howard and Norma Shearer, who were a little long in the tooth to play teenage lovers. And the films keep coming, including those of Kenneth Branagh in the past decade.

With the exception of films of unchanged stage productions, no film of Shakespeare is or can be absolutely faithful to the original, because film is different from the stage. Thus, all Shakespeare films are interpretations of the Bard, and many are adaptations. It is hard to draw a line between interpretation and adaptation or to define them precisely. Most films not only eliminate some of Shakespeare's words, but they also interpolate new dialogue to make connections or to explain omitted material. Some filmmakers place Shakespeare's story in modern settings. Recent filmmakers are increasingly inclined to concentrate on some aspects of a play and diminish others, or to add emphases not found in Shakespeare. For example, the 2004 film of *The Merchant of Venice* has Shylock dominate the film. It emphasizes the anti-Semitism of the period, diminishes the comedic aspects, and introduces a homoerotic longing of Antonio for Bassiano, who loves Portia.

In general, recent filmmatic versions of Shakespeare's plays are freer in their interpretation of Shakespeare and more inclined to emphasize contemporary, sometimes politically correct, messages than filmmakers of the past. The profusion of films of Shakespeare's plays and the freedom with which filmmakers treat Shakespeare has spawned an academic by-product, Shakespeare film criticism by scholars in universities and colleges. Unfortunately, the field is so dominated by theory that much of the writing is intelligible only to initiates.

Shakespeare's stories and some of his words are so well-known that directors may use the bones of a Shakespeare play for their own, often comedic, purposes (Table 10.2). In many cases, derivatives depend on the audience having enough familiarity with Shakespeare's work to appreciate and laugh at the cleverness of the use of the original story. More somber films, as *A Double Life* and *West Side Story*, also depend on a knowledge of the original for full understanding of the story. Occasionally the bones of the original Shakespeare story are so well buried in the flesh of the derivative film that only viewers thoroughly familiar with Shakespeare will recognize the original story.

Table 10.2 - Select List of American and British Films Freely Based on Shakespeare's Plays (in chronological order)

Men Are Not Gods (1936)
A London newspaper employee tries to save the reputation of a Shakespeare actor playing Othello badly.
Director: Walter Resich.
Cast: Miriam Hopkins,Gertrude Lawrence, Rex Harrison

The Boys from Syracuse (1940)
Musical comedy with modern setting based on *The Comedy of Errors.*
Director: A. Edward Sutherland.
Cast: Allan Jones, Joe Penner, Rosemary Lane.
Music and Lyrics by Richard Rogers and Lorenz Hart

To Be Or Not To Be (1942)
Jack Benny as Hamlet stands alone on the stage reciting "To be, or not to be." A man in the audience leaves for an assignation with Benny's wife, Ophelia,(Carole Lombard) in her dressing room. Benny is outraged and comedy develops.
Director: Ernst Lubitsch.
Cast: Jack Benny, Carole Lombard, Robert Stack

Strange Illusion (1945)
Hamlet turned into a "B" (low budget) murder mystery film. The Hamlet substitute wonders about the strange death of his father.
Director: Edgar G. Ulmer, Ben Kadish.
Cast: James Lydon, William Warren, Sally Eilers

A Double Life (1947)
An actor who plays the role of Othello on stage begins to confuse the events in the play with his off-stage life and smothers the woman he loves.
Director: George Cukor.
Cast: Ronald Colman, Signe Hasso, Edmond O'Brien, Shelley Winters

Kiss Me Kate (1953)
Musical adaptation of *The Taming of the Shrew.*
Director: George Sidney.
Cast: Howard Keel, Kathryn Grayson, Ann Miller.
Music and lyrics by Cole Porter

Table 10.2 (*continued*)

Broken Lance (1954)
Western probably inspired by *King Lear*. A rancher has disloyal and loyal sons, which produces much conflict.
Director: Edward Dmytryk, Henry Weinberger.
Cast: Spencer Tracy, Robert Wagner, Richard Widmark

Joe Macbeth (1955)
Gangster film set in Chicago. Joe Macbeth rubs out the mob boss and intends to be king of the city. His ambitious wife arranges a dinner party in order to murder other rivals.
Director: Ken Hughes, Philip Shipway.
Cast: Paul Douglas, Ruth Roman

Forbidden Planet (1956)
Science fiction loosely based on *The Tempest*.
Director: Fred McLeod Wilcox.
Cast: Walter Pidgeon, Anne Francis, Leslie Nielsen

Jubal (1956)
Western based on the *Othello* story.
Director: Dalmer Daves, Eddie Saeta.
Cast: Glenn Ford, Ernest Borgnine, Rod Steiger, Felicia Farr

West Side Story (1961)
Musical based on *Romeo and Juliet*.
Director: Robert Wise. Cast; Natalie Wood (sung by Marnie Nixon), Richard Beymer (sung by Jimmy Bryant), Rita Moreno, Russ Tamblyn. Music by Leonard Bernstein. Lyrics by Stephen Sondheim. Choreography by Jerome Robbins.

All Night Long (1962)
Othello story set in the world of jazz musicians.
Director: Basil Dearden, Stanley Hosgood.
Cast: Patrick McGoohan, Keith Mitchell, Betsy Blair, Richard Attenborough

Carry on Cleo (1964)
A farce based on *Antony and Cleopatra*.
Directors: Gerald Thomas and Peter Bolton.
Cast: Sidney James, Kenneth Williams, Amanda Barrie

Table 10.2 (*continued*)

Catch My Soul: Santa Fe Satan (1973)
A rock opera version of the *Othello* story.
Director: Patrick McGoohan, Kurt Heumann Jr.
Cast: Richie Havens, Launce LeGault, Season Hubley

Harry and Tonto (1974)
Based on *King Lear*. Retired New York teacher and his cat are evicted from his apartment. He protests his treatment and tries to live with his difficult children.
Director: Paul Mazursky.
Cast: Art Carney, Ellen Burstyn, Geraldine Fitzgerald

A Midsummer Night's Sex Comedy (1982)
Comedy about sophisticated New Yorkers exchanging partners in a summer fling.
Director: Woody Allen.
Cast: Woody Allen, Mia Farrow, Jose Ferrer. Uses music of Felix Mendelssohn

The Dresser (1985)
Story of an aging Shakespearean actor and his "dresser." Derived from *King Lear*.
Directors: Peter Yates and Andy Armstrong.
Cast: Albert Finney, Tom Courtenay

Looking for Richard (1996)
A combination of modern rehearsals for *Richard III* and scenes from the play.
Director: Al Pacino.
Cast: Al Pacino, Alec Baldwin, Kevin Spacey, Winona Ryder

10 Things I Hate About You (1999)
Taming of the Shrew story set in a modern American high school.
Director: Gil Junger.
Cast: Heath Ledger, Julia Stiles, Joseph Gordon-Levitt

Love's Labour's Lost (2000)
Shakespeare's play done as a 1930s musical.
Director: Kenneth Branagh.
Cast: Kenneth Branagh, Alessandro Nivola, Alicia Silverstone

Table 10.2 (*continued*)
O (2001) Othello story with a teen cast and set in a contemporary high school. *Director:* Tim Blake Nelson. *Cast:* Mikhi Phifer, Josh Hartnett, Julia Stiles
Source: Rothwell and Melzer, *Shakespeare on Screen*, plus other works and movie viewing.

These free adaptations indicate that the movie business knows that Shakespeare is an integral part of American culture and that Shakespeare is a source of good plots. Modern directors and writers who borrow plots from Shakespeare imitate Shakespeare, who freely adapted for his own purposes the accounts found in historical sources. An interesting aspect about Shakespeare is that he wrote no plays about his own place and time (i.e., Renaissance England). The very few plays that he wrote about England, that is, the history plays (*Richard III, Henry IV Parts 1 and 2, Henry V*) dealt with the fifteenth century and were not completely historically accurate. Many of his plays were set in the ancient world or in the Middle Ages. He also wrote plays about Italy and imaginary lands.

The Renaissance on Film

Shakespeare films demonstrate the enduring role of Shakespeare in American culture. But they are limited to the stories of Shakespeare. Many other films depict the larger Renaissance, including late sixteenth-century and early seventeenth-century England, the period in which he lived. And these give another idea of how American filmmakers look at the Renaissance.

Table 10.3 provides an unscientific listing of commercial films, excluding documentaries and films for school use, depicting the Renaissance. It is limited to films produced in the United States or Great Britain with the exception of the French film *The Return of Martin Guerre,* which had wide diffusion in the United States and Canada.

Table 10.3 - Select List of Films on the Renaissance (in chronological order)

Romola **(1924)**
Silent film of George Eliot's novel.
Director: Henry King.
Cast: Lillian Gish, William Powell, Ronald Colman.

Don Juan **(1926)**
Silent film on the legendary lover Don Juan, who did not exist, at the court of Lucrezia Borgia.
Director: Alan Crosland.
Cast: John Barrymore

The Beloved Rogue **(1927)**
Silent film on the French poet François Villon (1431–after 1463) about whom little is known.
Director: Alan Crosland.
Cast: John Barrymore

The Private Life of Henry VIII **(1933)**
Director: Alexander Korda.
Cast: Charles Laughton, Elsa Lanchester

Affairs of Cellini **(1934)**
Life of Benvenuto Cellini (1500–1571), Italian goldsmith and sculptor who wrote a colorful autobiography boasting of his deeds, not all of them true.
Director: Gregory La Cava.
Cast: Fredric March

Fire Over England **(1936)**
The English defeat the Spanish Armada in 1588.
Director: William K. Howard.
Cast: Flora Robson, Laurence Olivier, Raymond Massey

Mary of Scotland **(1936)**
Based on a Maxwell Anderson play about Mary Stuart (1542–1587).
Director: John Ford.
Cast: Katharine Hepburn

Table 10.3 (*continued*)

Tudor Rose (1936)
The life of Lady Jane Grey (1537–1554) who was Queen of England for nine days in 1553.
Director: Robert Stevenson.
Cast: Cedric Hardwicke, Nova Pilbeam, John Mills

If I Were King (1938)
Another film on François Villon.
Director: Frank Lloyd.
Cast: Ronald Colman, Basil Rathbone

Private Lives of Elizabeth and Essex (1939)
Based on a Maxwell Anderson play about Queen Elizabeth I and Robert Deverereux, Earl of Essex, who rebelled against her.
Director: Michael Curtiz.
Cast: Bette Davis, Errol Flynn

Tower of London (1939)
Richard, Duke of Gloucester, eliminates rivals for the throne. Historical drama.
Director: Rowland W. Lee.
Cast: Basil Rathbone, Boris Karloff, Vincent Price

Bride of Vengeance (1948)
Story of the Borgias.
Director: Mitchell Leisen.
Cast: Paulette Goddard

Prince of Foxes (1949)
Cesare Borgia is foiled in Italy c. 1500.
Director: Henry King.
Cast: Tyrone Power, Orson Welles, Everett Sloane, Wanda Hendrix

Young Bess (1953)
The early years of Elizabeth I.
Director: George Sidney.
Cast: Jean Simmons, Stewart Granger, Charles Laughton

The Virgin Queen (1955)
Elizabeth I as queen.
Director: Henry Koster.
Cast: Bette Davis, Richard Todd

Table 10.3 (*continued*)

Diane (1956)
About Diane de Poitiers (1499–1566), mistress of King Henry II (ruled 1547–1559) of France.
Director: David Miller.
Cast: Lana Turner

The Vagabond King (1956)
Musical about François Villon.
Director: Michael Curtiz.
Cast: Oreste, Kathryn Grayson

Tower of London (1962)
Richard III is haunted by the ghosts of those he killed.
Director: Roger Corman.
Cast: Vincent Price, Michael Pate, Joan Freeman

The Agony and the Ecstasy (1965)
Michelangelo paints the Sistine Chapel ceiling 1508–1512.
Director: Carol Reed
Cast: Charlton Heston, Rex Harrison, Diane Cilento

A Man for All Seasons (1966)
Life of Thomas More based on play of Robert Bolt.
Director: Fred Zinnemann.
Cast: Paul Scofield, Wendy Hiller, Susannah York, Robert Shaw, Orson Welles

Anne of the Thousand Days (1969)
Story of Anne Boleyn, wife of Henry VIII of England.
Director: Charles Jarrott.
Cast: Richard Burton, Geneviève Bujold

Mary Queen of Scots (1971)
Director: Charles Jarrott.
Cast: Vanessa Redgrave, Glenda Jackson

The Return of Martin Guerre (1982)
After many years' absence, man claiming to be husband returns to wife and village. Assumed identity in late sixteenth-century France.
Director: Daniel Vigne.
Cast: Gérard Depardieu, Nathalie Baye

Table 10.3 (*continued*)

***Caravaggio* (1986)**
Life of the painter (1571–1610) seen as a homosexual.
Director: Derek Jarman.
Cast: Sean Bean, Dexter Fletcher

***Lady Jane* (1986)**
Life of Lady Jane Grey.
Director: Trevor Nunn.
Cast: Helena Bonham-Carter

***Dangerous Beauty* (1998)**
Life of Venetian poetess and prostitute Veronica Franco (1546–1591).
Director: Marshall Herskovitz.
Cast: Catherine McCormack, Jacqueline Bisset, Rufus Sewell

***Elizabeth* (1998)**
Elizabeth I, who renounces marriage despite her love for Robert Dudley, in a threatening world.
Director: Shekhar Kapur.
Cast: Cate Blanchett, Richard Attenborough, Geoffrey Rush, Joseph Fiennes, John Gielgud

***Ever After* (1998)**
Cinderella is loved by the heir to the French throne in early-sixteenth-century France.
Director: Andy Tennant.
Cast: Anjelica Huston, Drew Barrymore

***Shakespeare in Love* (1998)**
The Bard suffers writer's block then falls in love during the preparation of *Romeo and Juliet.*
Director: John Madden.
Cast: Joseph Fiennes, Gwyneth Paltrow, Judi Dench, Geoffrey Rush

Source: Grendler and Wagley, "The Renaissance in the Popular Imagination," p. 275, supplemented by other works and movie viewing.

Elizabeth I of England has been the most popular subject of films about the Renaissance. Many well-known actresses beginning with Sarah Bernhardt in 1912 in *Les Amours de la reine Élisabeth* have played her. Bette Davis (in 1939 and 1955), Claudette Colbert, Glenda Jackson, Jean Simmons (as a youthful Elizabeth in *Young Bess*) through Cate Blanchett in *Elizabeth* in 1998 and Judi Dench in *Shakespeare in Love*, also in 1998, followed. And the number of female subjects (Elizabeth I, Mary Stuart, Anne Boleyn, Jane Grey, Diane de Poitiers) in older films suggests that Renaissance filmography anticipated the feminist wave of the past twenty-five years.

The Film View of the Renaissance

The film view of the Renaissance has changed over the past forty to fifty years, as can be seen by comparing popular films of the past and the present.

The Agony and the Ecstasy of 1965 had enormous diffusion and may still be the film on the Renaissance with the greatest number of viewers. It is visually sumptuous and many scenes are well done. The costumes and settings are accurate and impressive. The Vatican offered to make the Sistine Chapel available for filming, but Twentieth-Century Fox preferred to create it and the needed scaffolding on a sound stage. They had to be able to show the fresco in the process of being painted.

The film sees the Renaissance as an era of great individual achievement. Because commercial films must tell their story in about two hours, they usually concentrate on one aspect of a much bigger story, in this case, the life of Michelangelo as told by Irving Stone. The filmmakers of *The Agony and the Ecstasy* decided to concentrate on Michelangelo's frescoes on the Sistine Chapel ceiling, commissioned by Pope Julius II and executed between 1508 and 1512. In addition, it focuses on the relationship between patron and artist. Hence, the film largely becomes the story of two strong-willed and talented individuals, Michelangelo (Charlton Heston) and Pope Julius II (played by Rex Harrison, who steals many scenes from Heston). This is not historically wrong, because both were exceptionally determined men. The pope practically orders Michelangelo to paint the ceiling and badgers him to complete it, while the artist defends his vision and the time required to realize it. The pope comes into the chapel and looks up at Michelangelo and says "When will you make an end of it?" Michelangelo, paint dripping from his brow, replies between clenched teeth, "When it is finished!"

The film also emphasizes the independence and significance of the creative artist. Even more than in the book, Michelangelo defends the integrity of the artist and his art. In order to strengthen the point, the film has Raphael telling Michelangelo that artists must grovel, be courtiers, and prostitute themselves to wealthy patrons in order to have the opportunity to create art. Michelangelo disagrees. And the film argues that the artist must persevere against a philistine society to realize his or her vision. There is a hokey scene in which cardinals come into the chapel with the pope and criticize what Michelangelo is doing. One of them condemns the nude figures on the ceiling. Another cardinal objects that the figures on the ceiling do not resemble the Greeks well enough. Just to make sure that the audience realizes the meaning of the scene, the pope, with a straight face, tells Michelangelo and the movie viewers that the carping cardinals represent "piety and learning." To "cardinal piety" Michelangelo answers that God created us nude, and to "cardinal learning" he responds that he did not intend to imitate the Greeks. The pope rejects the advice of cardinals piety and learning, and tells Michelangelo to carry on. The point of the scene is to emphasize the creativity, freedom, and originality of the individual artist and, by extension, the Renaissance.

The film tries to make the viewer understand the historical reasons behind the combination of piety and worldliness that marked the Renaissance papacy. Michelangelo and Julius II serve God in different ways. Michelangelo serves God by painting. The pope serves God by trying to render his state and Italy independent and free of foreign enemies. This is why he wages war. The film does not condemn or whitewash the pope's militarism but allows the pope to explain his reasons. It is the same with corruption, such as the selling of high church offices. There is a scene in which Julius II, who desperately needs money, asks his adviser if there are any more cardinalates he can sell. He has just created three new cardinals in order to get money to pay his troops. He decides to create a fourth to get the money to buy paint (which was expensive in the Renaissance) for Michelangelo. There follows a funny scene in the pope's military camp in which the pope tries to fit a too-large cardinal's tall red hat (miter) on the head of a boy about fourteen who is squinting into the sun. (Although the information is accurate in that some teenage boys did become cardinals in exchange for money, the scene is not, because investiture was a solemn ceremony done in a church, preferably St. Peter's in Rome.) The film makes the point that Julius II sold high church offices for money for secular purposes. In other words, the film gives the reasons for some quite wrong actions of the papacy and the Catholic Church. Although the film includes individual scenes that are historically inaccurate and sometimes laughable, the overall presentation of the Renaissance and the papacy is reasonably balanced and nonjudgmental. It notes actions that were disapproved in the Renaissance and are very strongly condemned today without using the power of the film presentation to blacken them further.

Overall, the film sees the historical Renaissance as a period of remarkable individuals who accomplished great deeds sometimes against great odds. The individuals are men of integrity even when those around them are not. This view of the Renaissance is found in other films of the time, such as *A Man for All Seasons* of 1966. Based on the play of Robert Bolt, it presents the story of Thomas More who tries to be loyal to his king, Henry VIII, and his church. When he must choose, he chooses God over Henry, Rome over England, and is put to death. Thomas More in the film is another great individual figure of accomplishment and integrity.

A famous short speech in another film not about the Renaissance also expressed the common view that the Renaissance was a combination of corruption and greatness. In 1949, Orson Welles appeared in *The Third Man* (director: Carol Reed; cast Joseph Cotten, Alida Valli, Orson Welles, and Trevor Howard), a brilliant black-and-white thriller set in post–World War II Vienna. In a famous speech, Welles expressed a common view, that the Renaissance was an era of great accomplishments, and that the results more than balanced the crimes of the Renaissance. The character that he plays, a thief and trafficker in adulterated penicillin whose actions lead to the deaths of children, justifies his actions by saying, "In Italy for thirty years, under the Borgias, they had warfare, terror, murder, and bloodshed—they produced Michelangelo, Leonardo da Vinci, and the Renaissance. In Switzerland they had brotherly love. They had five hundred years of democracy and peace, and what did they produce? The cuckoo clock."[4]

These words were not in the original screenplay of Graham Greene. Welles, fresh from his role as Cesare Borgia in *The Prince of Foxes,* had the Italian Renaissance in mind and ad-libbed the speech, and the director left it in. He exaggerated the power of the Borgias; Cesare Borgia dominated only an area in central Italy inside the papal state for a few years when his father, Alexander VI, was pope (1492–1503). But the words expressed the view that the Renaissance, especially the Italian Renaissance, is remembered for its remarkable individuals, great accomplishments, and the cultural leadership of Europe. That Alexander VI was a corrupt pope, and Cesare Borgia a murderer, was less important.

The Renaissance in Recent Historical Films

The film industry view of the Renaissance has changed greatly since 1965. Three new Renaissance historical films, that is, films that claim to be historically accurate, demonstrate that the view of the Renaissance and especially of organized religion is less rosy. Two of the three see the Renaissance as a period of violence and religious persecution even more strongly than some recent novels about the Renaissance.

Dangerous Beauty (director: Marshall Herskovitz; cast: Catherine McCormack, Jacqueline Bisset, Rufus Sewell) is the story of Veronica Franco (1546–1591), a Venetian courtesan and poet.[5] Franco was a high-class prostitute, one who provided cultural and literary entertainment as well as sexual services. According to the film, Veronica, facing the prospect of an unappealing arranged marriage, leaps at the chance of an alternate career, that of courtesan. Her mother, who was a courtesan before marriage, prepares her. Not only does Veronica quickly become a sexual star, but she also soon joins a literary circle of Venetian male nobles. She engages them in poetic contests and wins. The film makes a point of comparing the closed world of upper-class Venetian wives, who cannot read and write and have no access to the larger world, with the freedom of courtesans, who socialize with the city's elite and write poetry. Because she is a courtesan, Veronica is part of the male world and able to pass on to Venetian noble wives news of the Venetian war with the Turks over Cyprus. (The film exaggerates the ignorance, isolation, and lack of freedom of noble Venetian women. Like Veronica, they were taught to read and write in Italian, but normally not Latin, at home or in convents. And while they did not participate in public life, some were well aware of events in the outside world.) An admiring noble becomes her lover but cannot marry her because of the class differences.

273

When the king of France visits Venice in 1583, he chooses Veronica as his evening playmate. After she serves his perverse (not explained or pictured) tastes, the satisfied king throws his military support to the Venetians in their war against the Turks. Veronica becomes a national hero. However, a rival denounces her to the local inquisition for witchcraft. In the climactic scene of the novel, she is tried before the doge (the ceremonial ruler of Venice) and the Venetian Senate. An evil clergyman presides over the trial, while another man in clerical garb, a vanquished poetic rival, prosecutes her. But Veronica delivers a feminist manifesto refuting the charges, and doge and senators rally to her side.

The facts are these. Veronica Franco was the daughter of a procuress and a merchant from a family of means, although not noble. Along with her brothers, she received private tutoring at home. The film does not mention that Veronica was married in the 1560s. In real life, she apparently soon separated from her husband. Why and how she became a courtesan in the middle or late 1560s is not known. The film does not mention that she bore six children by various men, of whom three survived infancy. She did write and publish poetry and letters and did participate in the literary circle organized by a noble Venetian. But the sexual encounter with the king of France is probably nonsense. Henry (Valois) III (the film has the wrong Henry) came to Venice in 1574, not 1583, and he was probably a homosexual. French support for the Venetian struggle against the Turks hardly mattered, because the war was fought much earlier (between 1569 and 1571) and settled in a peace treaty of 1573.

More facts. In 1580, the tutor of Veronica's sons denounced her for magical incantations, a minor kind of witchcraft. The Venetian Inquisition questioned Franco and dismissed the accusation. In other words, the trial scene in the film never occurred. Even if she had been questioned further, she would not have been subjected to a public trial in front of the doge and 300 senators because the Venetian Inquisition, like all inquisitions, operated in private in order to protect the confidentiality of the accused and witnesses and to prevent others from learning that they might be under suspicion. Moreover, it consisted of only six persons, three clergymen and three representatives of the Venetian government. But inserting a phoney trial scene allows Franco to enjoy a visually dramatic triumph over her detractors. Finally, Franco suffered financial losses during the plague of 1575 to 1577 and died in poverty in 1591.

The most historically accurate parts of the film are Veronica's poetry, which she recites. Franco was a good poet and some of it expressed feminist sentiment, although she was not so strong a feminist as the film argues. The interior scenes of prostitutes in their rooms, one of them copied from a famous painting, *The Courtesans* (in the Museo Civico Correr in Venice) by the Venetian artist Vittore Carpaccio (c. 1465–1526), and the costuming are well done. The scenes of Venice are as lovely and evocative as is the real city. In addition, the film deserves credit for making it clear that, in the end, the life of a courtesan, even a high-class one, is not a happy one. Despite the inaccuracies, the film tells an interesting and unusual story. Even though there were other female poets in Renaissance Italy, including a Roman courtesan, Franco really was a remarkable individual, one of many in the Italian Renaissance. The film handles the facts loosely, but it does tell the story of a talented woman in difficult circumstances. The film emphasizes a strong individual, a traditional view of the Renaissance.

The second general release historical film of 1998 is *Elizabeth* (director: Shekhar Kapur; cast: Cate Blanchett, Geoffrey Rush, Joseph Fiennes). Again the central figure is a woman. But it is a very different story and sees the Renaissance and organized religion very differently.

The film tells the story of Princess, later Queen Elizabeth I of England (b. 1533; reigned 1558–1603) during the period 1558–1563. The film begins with men roughly scraping the hair off two men and a woman, leaving blood and nicks on their bald scalps. The three are then burnt, screaming in pain, at the stake, as the camera records the gruesome details. They are Protestants executed by Mary Tudor, queen from 1553 to 1558, and this establishes a somber mood for the film and foretells a theme: bloody, fanatical Catholic Mary versus commonsensical and tolerant Protestant Elizabeth. Just to make sure that viewers get it, Elizabeth (Cate Blanchett) is young, beautiful, and as fresh as the sunny outdoors, whereas Mary is dowdy, dumpy, pallid, and pathetic. She cannot even conceive.

When Mary dies childless in 1558, Elizabeth becomes queen and immediately assumes an air of authority and shows political acumen as if born to the role. The film concentrates on two major issues she faced: the religious division and finding a husband. She tells English bishops that the people are to adhere publicly to the Church of England but may believe as they please in private. When a bishop objects that this is heresy, she retorts, "No, my lords, this is common sense." Thus, according to the film, she presents a simple and sensible solution to the religious division of England. Nevertheless, throughout the film Catholicism is the evil empire threatening her reign. The film's version of the *Star Wars* emperor wielding destructive light rays is an ugly Pope Pius V (John Gielgud) who excommunicates Elizabeth and releases English Catholics from their allegiance to her. The film makes considerable use of dark images and sounds—shadows, blackness, a heavy door clanging shut like the crack of doom—to convey melodramatically the religious and political threats that Elizabeth faced and overcame. Even the bishops from the English Church whom Elizabeth faced down—in reality not a difficult task, for they supinely followed the monarch whatever the turns in religious policy—are dressed completely in black including long black beards.

In her private life, Elizabeth and Robert Dudley (Joseph Fiennes) are lovers, shown decorously in bed in soft focus with lots of veils and bed clothing, but no bare chests or heavy breathing and moans. Dudley proposes marriage, but she is uncertain. Other suitors from royal families of Europe offer themselves, sometimes comically, in marriage. Then in 1563, at the ripe old age of thirty, Elizabeth renounces marriage. She cuts her hair, puts on white face paint, and announces that she is the Virgin Queen. Thus she symbolically becomes a nun for England. The film then jumps to the end. The "Afterword" of the film solemnly announces that at Elizabeth's death in 1603, England was the richest and most powerful nation in Europe, meaning the world. This is the result of Elizabeth's renunciation of marriage and wise policies.

The film is visual melodrama. But it is far more inaccurate historically about more important matters than *Dangerous Beauty*. There is no concrete evidence that Elizabeth and Dudley were physical lovers. In the film, Elizabeth is shocked and surprised to learn that Dudley is already married. Poppycock. Part of a monarch's job was to keep track of aristocratic marriages, even to arrange them when necessary. Elizabeth did not publicly renounce marriage in 1563, but continued to entertain proposals, usually for political purposes, through the 1570s and beyond. Pius V did not excommunicate Elizabeth until 1570, seven years after the end of the action of the film. He held off until then at the urging of King Philip II of Spain, the leading Catholic monarch who had been Mary Tudor's husband, because he hoped that England would return to the Catholic faith. And so on.

Finally, the conclusion that, thanks to Elizabeth's policies, England was the richest and most powerful nation in Europe in

1603, is not accurate. Spain, France, and the Holy Roman Empire were more powerful and richer at that time, and even the emerging United Provinces of the Netherlands was probably richer. England continued to have many unresolved differences, some of which exploded in a bloody civil war in the 1640s. Elizabeth's accomplishment was to rule, no mean achievement in itself.

Although the film makes much of the private feelings of Elizabeth and her politics, it does not pay much attention to learning, literature, and art, or Elizabeth's own accomplishments. She was intelligent, well educated (she read Latin, Italian, and other languages), and knowledgeable in many areas. Literary men found a home in her court. Indeed, her reign saw such a flowering of arts and letters that scholars created the term "Elizabethan Renaissance."

The most serious historical misrepresentation is one of mood; the contrast that the film creates between Elizabeth's tolerant religious policies and the intolerance of Catholicism and its representatives. She is portrayed as almost ecumenical and tolerant, whereas Catholic priests and popes are intolerant and evil. For example, at one point a Catholic priest comes to England, dressed in the flowing black robes of a monk; his black robes billow behind him like the wings of Satan. The reality is Catholic priests did not wear clerical clothes in England, but were forced to go about in disguise, because Elizabeth's government hunted them down, tortured them, and executed them cruelly. Elizabeth was not more tolerant of religious dissent than Mary Tudor or other rulers of the sixteenth century. One cannot find much of a view of the Renaissance in the film, because the Renaissance is hardly visible. Instead, much of the film is a condemnation of organized religion, especially Catholicism, although the bishops of the Church of England do not come off very well either. *Elizabeth* is a bad film because it lacks balance and perspective.

A third recent film also emphasizes violence and Catholic intolerance in historical depictions of the Renaissance. In February 2004, PBS Television aired a four-hour 2003 docudrama film entitled *The Medici: Godfathers of the Renaissance*. It was produced in England by Lion Television and directed by Justin Hardy. It tells the story of the Medici, the de facto rulers of Florence most of the time from 1434 through the seventeenth century. This is a film that claims to be completely historically accurate. It combines actors in costume playing Lorenzo de' Medici, Savonarola, and others, a narration done in Italian-accented English, a Web site with further historical information, and academic talking heads. But the last do not matter much, except when they make embarrassing gaffes.

The images carry the message. It has many lovely pictures of the famous art and artists of Renaissance Florence, even when the descriptions are mistaken.[6] But the docudrama also sees the Renaissance as an age of grisly violence and illustrates the point with many scenes of bloodshed. It especially emphasizes religious violence. As the film moves into the sixteenth century, it sets up a contrast between the Renaissance and the Catholic Church, with the narration reinforcing the stark choice. At one point the narrator states that "The Medici were forced to choose between the values of the Renaissance and the values of the church." Again and again the accompanying Web site makes claims about how the Catholic Church was opposed to the Renaissance and engaged in religious persecution that suppressed the Renaissance.[7] Not even inconsistencies interrupt the relentless message of religious terror. The film repeatedly describes the Catholic Church and/or the papacy as "the greatest power on earth." But if it was the greatest power on earth, why was it unable to stop Martin Luther?

The view of the Renaissance in the film is that it was a period of great accomplishment that was killed by religious oppression in the form of the Italian Catholic Church. This is an old and discredited interpretation whose roots are found in nineteenth-century Italian anticlerical intellectuals and German Protestant historians.[8] It would take several pages to correct the historical errors at the accompanying Web site of *The Medici: Godfathers of the Renaissance*. Even though they are historical films, *Elizabeth* and *The Medici* do not try to present a balanced historical perspective or to offer some explanation of the actions of churchmen and rulers that can be rightly criticized. They use images and story to condemn.

One can only speculate about the reasons why recent historical films on the Renaissance include more violence and focus on religious oppression more than those of the past. A strong possibility is that films on the Renaissance are simply following a general film trend. The majority of recent films seem to emphasize violence more than those of earlier decades. Many historical films about the past, whether ancient Rome, the Middle Ages, or the American Revolutionary War, feature graphic violence. Another possibility is that the desire for greater dramatic contrast leads to more scenes of violence to put alongside beautiful Renaissance art. The desire to heighten the drama may also explain the emphasis on religious oppression and the lack of a more balanced presentation. Or maybe filmmakers sense hostility to organized religion and churchmen in today's culture and this leads them to highlight it in films about the past. It may be that the child abuse scandals involving priests in the American Catholic Church have made the Catholic Church of the past fair game. Whatever the reasons, the emphasis on violence and religious oppression marks a change in historical films of the Renaissance compared with those of forty to fifty years ago. Some filmmakers have forgotten that the Renaissance was an immensely rich and varied period of history.

The Renaissance as Fun

Two other films of 1998 about the Renaissance are comic romps that use Renaissance historical scaffolding to support well-written and well-acted romantic comedy. *Ever After* (director: Andy Tennant) is a Cinderella story set in Renaissance France. Danielle (Drew Barrymore) is the downtrodden stepdaughter in the household of her social-climbing stepmother (Angelica Huston). In Cinderella stories, the prince usually has no name. Here he is the real Prince Henry Valois (played by Dougray Scott), who later became King Henry II of France. Prince Henry encounters Danielle in the countryside. He is smitten with this lively unknown girl but loses track of her. Alas, Henry is promised in marriage to a daughter of the king of Spain. But he persuades his father, King Francis I (reigned 1515–1547), to give him a week to find another bride before the knot is tied. He searches for the enchanting but mysterious girl. Thanks to Leonardo da Vinci, who becomes the fairy godmother figure and concocts inventions to get Danielle to a ball in the palace, the couple are united and marry. The stepmother and Danielle's two spiteful stepsisters are banished to the palace laundry, where they are condemned to scrubbing clothes in tubs of steaming water.

The film has some nice touches that remind viewers that the era witnessed a Renaissance of learning. Danielle loves knowledge and reads humanist bestsellers. She quotes from Thomas More's *Utopia* (published in Latin in 1516), which describes an imaginary land superior to Europe. She convinces Henry of the importance of learning. As a result, he announces to his father, King Francis I, that he wishes to found a university where all may study. In reality, Francis I, not Henry, established the Collège de France in 1530 with two professorships in Greek and two in Hebrew, which he filled with eminent Renaissance humanists. Additional professorships were added, and the Collège de France became an important center for Renaissance learning. And the film works in a couple of Leonardo da Vinci's inventions. In other words, the filmmaker sees the Renaissance as an era of intellectual achievement.

The film uses some real historical characters and can be dated as 1516 to 1519, because Leonardo da Vinci (c. 1450–1519) spent the last four years of his life in France. But because it is a fairy tale, accurate historical chronology does not matter. For example, the real Prince Henry Valois was born in 1519 and so was still in diapers in the time depicted by the film. Nevertheless, he did become king of France as Henry II in 1547.

Shakespeare in Love (director: John Madden) is a romantic comedy based on the English literary Renaissance. The year is 1593, the place is London, and the Rose Theatre is in trouble. The owner is broke and needs a hit, but Shakespeare (Joseph Fiennes) has writer's block. It is proposed that he write a comedy called "Romeo and Ethel, the Pirate's Daughter." Viola De Lesseps (Gwyneth Paltrow) is the stage-struck daughter of a wealthy merchant. She sneaks into the theater disguised as a man in order to audition for the role of a young man, because women did not appear on stage at that time. Shakespeare discovers that the supposed man is a beautiful young woman. In clever adaptations of scenes from the real *Romeo and Juliet* he crashes a dance in order to twirl with her, falls in love, and they consummate their love in a balcony scene. Throughout the film, both Shakespeare and Viola speak lines from *Romeo and Juliet* and Shakespeare's sonnets. Shakespeare is inspired to write the comedy but changes the name of the heroine to "Juliet."

As rehearsals continue, both Shakespeare and Viola, still dressed as a man, have parts in the play. (Shakespeare did act in some of his own plays.) Although very much in love, they cannot marry because she is betrothed to a noble. So Shakespeare changes the play into a tragedy. The film reaches its climax on opening night. The man who is to play Juliet has a cold and cannot speak in a treble voice. Viola, who has just married, sneaks away after the ceremony, comes to the theater, and plays Juliet, while Shakespeare plays Romeo. They do the play, which is a great success. Even the crusty and wise Queen Elizabeth (Judi Dench) applauds.

After the play, Viola must sail with her husband to Virginia in the New World. But before she leaves, she gives Shakespeare the idea for his next play, the comedy masterpiece *Twelfth Night*, which is the story of a woman named Viola who is shipwrecked in a far off land. In the last scene of *Shakespeare in Love*, Shakespeare is writing *Twelfth Night* while Viola De Lesseps, who has indeed been shipwrecked, walks alone on a beach. Overall, the film is a polished romantic comedy that has had great commercial success. Everybody loves Romeo and Juliet.

The film cleverly uses the fact that most viewers have some knowledge of Shakespeare and his best-loved play. It also has a number of in-jokes for those who know their Shakespeare better, such as the *Twelfth Night* conclusion. And the film cleverly alludes to the long-time controversy, did someone else, such as Christopher Marlowe (1564–1593), write Shakespeare's plays? Overall, the film's view of the Renaissance is that it was a great age for the English stage and English literature.

Iconic Renaissance Films

Two other recent films use the Renaissance or a famous icon from it without dealing with the Renaissance per se. In the comedy *Renaissance Man* (1988; director: Penny Marshall; cast: Danny De Vito, Gregory Hines), Danny DeVito is fired from his advertising position. Needing a job, he becomes a civilian instructor on an army base and is charged with improving the "basic comprehension" of eight soldiers. Unable to interest them in anything else, he latches on to Shakespeare and turns the lecture into a class on *Hamlet*. Hooked, the students turn the play into a rap musical. DeVito wins their respect, improves their comprehension, and convinces army authorities that teaching Shakespeare has positive results.

Mona Lisa Smile (2003; director: Mike Newell; cast: Julia Roberts, Kirsten Dunst, Julia Stiles) is a feminist film set in 1953. Julia Roberts, a free spirit from California, comes to teach art history at Wellesley College, a conservative (according to the film) women's college in Newton, Massachusetts. She wants to introduce her students to modern art. More importantly, she wants to broaden the horizons of young women who see college only as preparation for marriage, in which they will be contented homemakers caring for husband and children. She runs into difficulty from the college's administration and gets varied responses from the young women, who believe that they must choose between marriage and career. The enigmatic *Mona Lisa* smile symbolizes the conflict between ideal and reality. The married student who is studying the *Mona Lisa* painting gives the teacher a particularly hard time. Although she appears to enjoy a perfect marriage, she knows that her husband is having an affair. But like Mona Lisa, she continues to smile enigmatically despite her loneliness and unhappiness. Despite fine acting by the women who portray the students, the film is a feminist tract with some predictable situations and characters, including the male professor of Italian who sleeps with his students. (Is there an academic film these days that does not have a professor sleeping with students? And are professors of Italian considered to be better seducers than professors of mathematics or sociology? Surely there is a dissertation topic here.) These two films testify to the strong visibility of the Renaissance and its icons in the American cinema.

Conclusion

The scorecard on films of the Renaissance is mixed. They have the enormous virtue of bringing Shakespeare's plays to millions of viewers who do not see them on stage and have not read them since they were required to do so in high school and college English courses. This is an important positive result. Other films borrow plots and ideas from Shakespeare, which reminds viewers of his genius. But films about the Renaissance have the same tendencies and faults as historical fiction to a greater degree. They exaggerate and simplify, they emphasize individuals, and they are more historically inaccurate than novels. The films that do not claim to be faithful to history, such as *Shakespeare in Love* and *Ever After,* are more trustworthy because no one sees them as true accounts. Films such as *Elizabeth* and *The Medici: Godfathers of the Renaissance*, which pretend to be accurate, spread much wrong information and impressions.

Except for the romantic comedies, today's films value the achievements of the Renaissance less than their predecessors. Recent historical films, like novels, highlight violence, religious fanaticism, and the persecution of minorities. In particular, they indict the Renaissance Church and its clergymen for intolerance and give them little credit for cultural achievements. They have a sharper edge and are less balanced than the older films and books.

Chapter 11

HATING AND LOVING THE RENAISSANCE

Just as the Renaissance reached unprecedented heights of popularity with the general public, the academy turned against it. Beginning in the 1970s, humanities scholars in American universities began to accuse the Renaissance of heinous crimes. They brought it to trial in the court of late twentieth-century social and political values held by academics and found it guilty of being elitist, of producing high culture and great art rather than being ordinary, and of oppressing women and minorities. The sentence was exile: politically correct scholars have banished the word "Renaissance," except as the target of sneers. They substitute the bland and vague "early modern Europe."

In 1977, the historian Joan Kelly-Gadol (1928–1982) published an article with the provocative title, "Did Women Have a Renaissance?" Her answer was a resounding "No." On the basis of very limited research in a handful of literary texts, Kelly-Gadol argued that the only thing that the Italian Renaissance did for women was to make the noblewoman an aesthetic object dependent on her husband and the prince.[1] Another work of the 1970s argued that Renaissance women were "a subject sex." All was repression and subjugation.[2]

Two social and ideological movements stimulated scholars to find fault with the Renaissance for its treatment of women. The first was an awakening to the reality of discrimination against women in American society and protests against it. Many people fought for the Equal Rights Amendment and equal pay for women. Second, the increasing number of female scholars in the humanities led them to study women in the past, where they discovered that women were often oppressed.

A great deal of excellent research has shown that Kelly-Gadol's picture of women in the Renaissance is flawed and incomplete. It is true that women in the Renaissance did not have the rights that they enjoy today. But because the same is true for every other period of the past, including American society in 1970, it seems strange to single out the Renaissance for special blame. More important, many historians of women since Kelly-Gadol have documented a more nuanced historical picture than bleak oppression. Renaissance women were a force in the workplace. Women had a legal personhood, inferior to that of men, but recognized by courts. Many became authors, artists, and property holders, and a handful wielded considerable power. Wives, mothers, daughters, and nuns did not always conform to a discipline of repression in the Renaissance.[3] But even though careful investigation has disproved the stereotype, the sweeping statement that women had no Renaissance has had a major role in fostering a negative view of the Renaissance in the academy.

Scholars of literature who use literary theory to study the Renaissance are major Renaissance haters. The theory approach begins with the assumption that it is impossible to understand from the words themselves exactly what an author of the past really meant. This is because all texts are embedded in the culture of the period. The only way to understand the meaning of a Renaissance text is to apply one or more of several theoretical approaches, such as (in no particular order) deconstructionism, postmodernism, Marxism, New Historicism, notions of power and victimization borrowed from the French social theorist Michel Foucault, feminist theory, semiotics, cultural materialism, and so on, in order to bring out its true meaning. All these approaches are based on the presupposition that truth and meaning are relative, that culture determines the meaning of what is written, and that all culture is power and subjugation of others. Literary theorists reject transcendent meaning in a text, that is, meaning that is greater than the circumstances of composition, such as the universality and beauty that most readers find in Shakespeare's greatest lines. Of course, studying the culture of the times can help to understand the meaning of the text at the time. But the theory approach goes too far.

By itself, theory should not lead to a negative view of the Renaissance. But it does, because oppression is an integral part of literary theory. The notion of culture as oppression leads scholars to think that writers of the past were constantly trying to say something in opposition to the norms of society. In addition, many scholars who use theory prefer to study the works of unknown or little-known Renaissance authors, including women and people on the margins of society who, they argue, stand in opposition to a male-imposed high culture. The result is to find fault with the Renaissance, to see it as an age of white male elite dominance and repression for everyone else. Even scholars who use theoretical approaches to study major authors, such as Shakespeare, like to focus on the dark side of an author. The result is a negative view of the Renaissance.

Social historians also dismiss the Renaissance. Social history embraces study of the commonalities of life, the conditions of ordinary daily existence. Social historians want to know how men and

289

women lived. How were they born, how did they marry, reproduce, and die? How were they divided into classes, and what
kinds of associations bound them together? All of this is important, and social historians have made wonderful contributions in
these areas. However, many social historians view the Renaissance
with condescension or reject it as a fantasy.

For most social historians, Renaissance means only intellectual history and individuals. The majority of social historians do
not see ideas or ideology having significant influence in history,
nor individuals mattering very much. Real history is social data.
The dismissal of ideas and individuals is a remarkable stance at a
time when an abundance of evidence demonstrates that ideas,
such as religious beliefs and conservative political views, strongly
influence contemporary life. Moreover, "isms" based on ideas
such as Communism, Socialism, Fascism, and Nazism dominated
the twentieth century.

Probably the majority of scholars of the history of women, literary theorists, and social historians find fault with the Renaissance. They do not see the Renaissance to be a period of
considerable accomplishment by individuals in many areas of life
but an era of massive white male oppression over the rest of society. For them, the learning of the Renaissance was not a development that led to breakthroughs. Just the opposite. Renaissance
learning and education, especially humanism and its love of the
ancients, was the means by which an upper-class white male elite
exerted cultural tyranny over the rest of society. According to this
view, all Renaissance humanist education did was to train docile
and obedient upper-class servants of the state, male conformists
ready to praise murderous monarchs.[4] As for women, they were
completely barred from humanist education, the path to advancement. Consequently, many humanities scholars reject the term
"Renaissance" because it is too optimistic and upbeat. In the

words of one scholar, the term Renaissance ignores "a vast sea of human activity and misery."[5]

However, these scholars have a problem. They reject the name Renaissance and the culture of powerful white males, but they still study the ordinary people, women, and marginalized of the fifteenth, sixteenth, and early seventeenth centuries. So, they have to find a new word for the period of history that they study. They choose the name "early modern." For example, the scholarly quarterly *Journal of Medieval and Renaissance Studies*, published at Duke University, changed its name to *Journal of Medieval and Early Modern Studies* in 1996. In announcing the name change, the new editors gave no reason for substituting early modern for Renaissance. Instead, they strongly proclaimed their allegiance to theory.[6] Their message is clear: literary theory and Renaissance are incompatible. There are other examples of scholarly organizations that have discarded Renaissance in favor of early modern in their names.

Scholars who hate what they think Renaissance means prefer early modern for several reasons. Using early modern to describe the literature of sixteenth-century and early seventeenth-century England proclaims the ordinariness of the period and denies it greater significance, even though it included Shakespeare, Philip Sidney, and Edmund Spenser. Using early modern dilutes the importance of what Johann Gutenberg, Christopher Columbus, and Machiavelli accomplished.

Using early modern also means studying the oppressed and downtrodden. Just as the early twenty-first century is seen as a democratic era of popular culture, in which the marginalized and minorities should be lauded and aided, so should those of the past be uncovered and elevated. Using early modern instead of Renaissance asserts these values. It tells readers that the scholar will study "the commonplace lives of common people."[7] For the majority of scholars of women, early modern means studying women to see how they coped with the oppression of a society in which men made and enforced the rules. For literary scholars, it means studying the writing of women and others who were not hailed as great writers. In short, using the term early modern and refusing to use Renaissance, except in a negative way, is a way for scholars to state their personal values and interpretation of the past.

There are many problems with substituting early modern for Renaissance, or for Renaissance and Reformation, but space to mention only the most obvious one. Early modern has no chronological definition; no one knows what centuries it means. Scholars who use early modern do not offer a chronological definition because it is an ideological construct rather than a way of organizing the past.

The lack of chronology leads to bizarre statements by scholars. This writer has seen Pope Boniface VIII called an "early modern man."[8] Boniface VIII (b. 1235; elected pope 1294–1303) was a medieval pope who claimed papal supremacy over all men, an extreme assertion of papal power that was rejected in his own lifetime. Boniface VIII was about as far from being modern as any person could be. At the other extreme, a volume entitled *Early Modern Society Theory: Selected Interpretive Readings* features essays on Karl Marx (1818–1883), Friedrich Engels (1820–1895), and Max Weber (1864–1920).[9] Marx and Engels were the fathers of Marxism and the authors of many books about capitalism and socialist revolution. Weber was a founder of the discipline of sociology. All three were enormously influential in the twentieth century and still are. But they did not live in or have any influence on the fifteenth, sixteenth, or early seventeenth centuries, the period that one might call early modern—if the term had any chronological meaning. Applying the label early modern to figures who lived in the thirteenth, nineteenth, and twentieth centuries illustrates the problem of using historical terminology lacking clear and agreed-upon chronology.

Early modern as a substitute for Renaissance has not caught on with the general public, nor with writers for journals of opinion and major newspapers. Early modern mystifies most educated Americans outside the academy. I discovered this while serving as an associate editor in the preparation of a historical encyclopedia whose working title was "Dictionary of Early Modern Europe." When salespeople went out to inform school, public, college, and university librarians about the coming work and to take orders, they discovered that librarians did not know which centuries were to be covered. The work risked being a financial flop. So the publisher changed the title to *Europe 1450 to 1789: Encyclopedia of the Early Modern World* (6 vols, New York: Charles Scribner's Sons and Thomson-Gale, 2004). The refusal to use the name Renaissance or, worse, attacking it, is an example of the gulf separating many university-based humanities scholars from American culture and society at large.

Loving the Renaissance

Fortunately, the general public has the good sense to ignore the word games of academics. Americans love the Renaissance. They realize its importance and want to learn more. At the end of 1999, the reference book publisher Charles Scribner's Sons published *Encyclopedia of the Renaissance* in six large volumes. Despite its hefty price ($595 at publication and $790 in 2005), it has been a bestseller among encyclopedias, with sales reaching 6,850 sets at the end of 2005. It is the best-selling multivolume encyclopedia that Scribner's, a venerable publisher of reference books, has ever produced. To be sure, it is a reference work of high quality that has won prizes and commendations from critics. But the major reason for the high sales is that Americans love and identify with the Renaissance more than with any other period of the distant past.

The most important reason why Americans love and identify with the Renaissance is individualism. Because belief in the power of the individual is a very important part of the American self-identity, they look to the Renaissance for individuals to admire and emulate. That is why Raphael, Leonardo da Vinci, Michelangelo, Botticelli, Machiavelli, Christopher Columbus, Copernicus, Galileo Galilei, Shakespeare, and others, are so well-known. Americans do not see them as the products and beneficiaries of systems or organizations, even though Renaissance painters were the products of workshops with assistants who helped execute the design of the master painter. Americans see them as heroic individuals who pursued their dreams. They often went their own way against the system and triumphed. A strong belief in the power of the individual to achieve greatness against long odds is the essence of the American dream. The American belief in individualism includes the conviction that the individual can raise himself or herself by personal effort from humble origins and achieve greatness. Leonardo da Vinci is seen as an example. Although Americans realize that women and minorities were not on an equal level with men and sometimes suffered persecution, they like to emphasize how they overcame obstacles to take control of their lives, just as Artemisa Gentileschi overcame rape and male chauvinism to establish herself as a painter.

Another part of the American belief in individualism is the idea that only the individual, not the group or organization, can lead others or generate the insight needed to create something truly original. Americans believe that leadership and true originality emerge from the heart and mind of the lone individual rather than the committee or team working together in the laboratory or office. The lives of numerous Renaissance high achievers—

Columbus, Copernicus, Gutenberg, Galilei, and others—support this belief. A third element of the American belief in individualism is the notion that a true individual does not owe his success to anyone else. Americans do not like to feel beholden to others, and they do not see their heroes as owing their success to others. A man stands on his own two feet. A woman is self-reliant. Again they see exemplary models in the Renaissance.

It may be that the American belief in individualism is stronger than ever in a conservative environment in which politicians trash the largest and most important organization of all, government. Perhaps a firm faith in the power of the individual is more necessary when government fails to provide health care or a good public education for all, when family networks are weaker, and the social safety net has large rips and holes. Then Americans must rely even more on individual effort. Great individuals in the Renaissance provide assurance that this is possible; the Renaissance offers optimism that the individual can achieve greatness.

Although a belief in individualism is the fundamental reason for America's love for and identification with the Renaissance, other factors help. The Renaissance is intrinsically interesting and attractive. The combination of great individuals, great works of art and literature, and the attractive settings of Florence, Venice, Rome, and elsewhere, generate enthusiasm for the period and invite tourist visits. Americans particularly love the Italian Renaissance and the English Renaissance but do not lack interest in the rest of Europe. And the Renaissance was always colorful. The remarkable individuals of the period behaved and spoke in dramatic ways. Even the villains, such as members of the Borgia family, were colorfully evil. Henry VIII, who broke with Rome for love but also killed two of his wives, was spectacularly alive and all too human. If novelists had invented Henry VIII and Leonardo da Vinci, readers would not have believed that they could be real. But they were real. In similar fashion, fiction writers did not invent Savonarola's burning of the vanities in 1497 or the Sack of Rome in 1527. They happened.

The Renaissance has great appeal because it offers something to many different parts of society. It offers brilliant political advice to operatives and standards of political conduct and success with which to measure contemporary politicians and policies. To businessmen who aspire to lead corporations, Machiavelli and the history of Renaissance states provide a list of do's and don'ts. For civic leaders, Renaissance cities offer architectural, economic, and cultural achievements to emulate, as they try to renew American cities. A famous painting from the Renaissance provides the opportunity to churchgoers to reaffirm their religious beliefs. The colorful costumes and settings of the Renaissance are a boon to those who want to playact and have a good time at Renaissance Faires. And the abundance of fascinating story lines from the Renaissance keeps novelists and filmmakers busy. The Renaissance does all this because it was a multifaceted civilization.

A final reason for American enthusiasm for the Renaissance is that it is more historically and emotionally accessible than all other periods of history save one. Even though the Renaissance happened some 500 years ago, it seems near and easy to know. By contrast, Americans feel little identification with the men, women, and events of Europe of the seventeenth and eighteenth centuries. They see this as an age of stuffy aristocrats in powdered wigs. Nor do the French Revolution and Napoleon at the end of the eighteenth century attract Americans. The French Revolution was an age of popular uprising and the guillotine, followed by a military dictator, none of which resonates well in America. Americans find the Middle Ages attractive up to a point, especially when seen in terms of knights and ladies. But the Middle Ages lack the numerous colorful individuals of the Renaissance. Of course, Americans are fascinated by Hitler and World War II. They read countless novels, see numerous films, and view much newsreel footage on The History Channel about the war and the Nazi era. But they certainly do not admire Nazi Germany, and they realize the terrible cost of World War II. By contrast, Americans really love the American West of the second half of the nineteenth century, portrayed in novels and countless films as an age of cowboys, Indians, the calvary, dashing train robbers, gunmen, and mysterious lone riders who avenge evil. Like the Renaissance, it is viewed as an age of individual achievement. Nothing compares with the importance of the American West in the American imagination. But the Renaissance comes next.

The Renaissance has a secure place in American life. It will continue to be admired, cited, relived, and reenacted for a long time to come.

NOTES

Chapter 1

1. Matteo Palmieri, *Della vita civile*, as quoted and translated in *The Renaissance Debate*, ed. Denys Hay (Huntington, NY: Robert E. Krieger Publishing, 1976), 9.

2. Paul Oskar Kristeller, *Renaissance Thought: The Classic, Scholastic, and Humanistic Strains* (New York: Harper and Row, 1961), 9–10. It is reprinted in Kristeller, *Renaissance Thought and Its Sources*, ed. Michael Mooney (New York: Columbia University Press, 1979), 22.

3. The expression appears in Erasmus' famous colloquy, "The Godly Feast," a wide-ranging irenic discussion of religious belief. See Desiderius Erasmus, *Colloquies*, trans. and annot. Craig R. Thompson. *Collected Works of Erasmus*, vol. 39 (Toronto and Buffalo: University of Toronto Press, 1997), 194 and 233–235, note 215.

4. For expansion of some of the points made here and further reading, see three related articles, Ingrid D. Rowland, "Renaissance Art," Andrea Bolland, "Education and Training," and

Frederika H. Jacobs, "Women Artists," in *Encyclopedia of the Renaissance*, ed. Paul F. Grendler, et al., 6 vols (New York: Charles Scribner's Sons, 1999), vol. 1, 123–141.

5. This was equally true in Canada, even though it had a large French-speaking Catholic population in Quebec.

6. Felix Gilbert, *A European Past: Memoirs 1905–1945* (New York and London: W. W. Norton, 1988), 172.

Chapter 2

1. See the Web site for Heart of the Renaissance Renaissance Faire, now operated by Kevin and Leslie Patterson. It claims that Phyllis and Ron Patterson created the first Renaissance Faire in 1963 (http://www.forestfaire.com/origins/origins1 .html). Kevin and Leslie Patterson of As You Like It Productions are the current owners of Heart of the Forest Renaissance Faires. In addition, the Renaissance Pleasure Faire of Southern California claims that it is the continuation of the "original Renaissance event in the U.S. . . . started by Ron and Phyllis Patterson in North Hollywood." The most recent Renaissance Pleasure Faire of Southern California was held at Glen Helen Park in Devore in the foothills of the San Bernardino Mountains over seven consecutive weekends between April 17 and May 31, 2004. It claimed attendance of 200,000 (http://www .renaissancefestival.com/viewEvent.asp?eventID=233).

2. See http://www.renaissancefestival.com/viewEvent.asp?event ID=232.

3. Because there is no scholarly study or print journalism account of faires, one must use the online information, which is quite comprehensive. For the following discussion of faires (description, location, dates, advertising statements, admission, foundation dates, themes, estimated attendance, management, etc.)

there are two important directories. The first is the Faire Directory at http://www.renaissancefestival.com/rendir/asp. It is organized according to states. Click on a state to get a list of faires in that state, then click on individual faires for more information, including URLs. If further information on a particular faire is desired, the URL brings up its Web site. This directory is particularly useful because it gives brief promotional material, themes, and often foundation dates. It lists 134 Renaissance and medieval faires. (Most faires do not make a clear chronological distinction between the two periods and mix the two together.) Slightly more comprehensive, because it lists 157 faires and estimated attendance for 144 of them, is http://www.renaissancemagazine.com/fairelist.html. But it gives less additional information about individual faires. Both directories list some other faires with no connection to the Renaissance or Middle Ages. These have been excluded. Unless otherwise indicated, this footnote serves for all information presented about individual faires, including the quotations given below, which reproduce the spelling, capitalization, and punctuation at the Web sites. It would be tedious and take up considerable space to list the URL for each bit of information.

4. See http://www.renfaire.com/Sites/index.html. Of course, the figure is unofficial and cannot be verified.

5. The count is based on http://renaissancemagazine.com/faire list/html. It gives estimated attendance figures for 144 faires for a total of 5,773,900, an average of 40,097. The thirteen fairs lacking attendance figures included five new faires in 2004. Because the faires lacking attendance estimates are new, or only open for a day or two, or are little known, or are located in less populated part of the United States, it is estimated that they were small and attracted only about 130,000. That brings the total attendance to 5,900,000.

6. The information in this paragraph comes from an online discussion entitled "Buying and Selling of Merchant Booths." The Web site is http://www.renaissancefestival.com/community/discussion/topic.asp?TOPIC_ID=1053.

7. The information in this paragraph comes from the results of a survey of the readers of *Renaissance* of May 27, 1998, as found at http://www.renaissancemagazine.com/img/press-release.html. Ms. Kim Guarnaccia, founder and editor of *Renaissance,* estimated that the number of respondents was 300 to 500 (e-mail message Kim Guarnaccia to Paul F. Grendler, November 10, 2004). It is a very useful survey for Renaissance fairegoers because 98 percent of the respondents attend at least one Renaissance faire every year.

8. This information comes from a posting of June 3, 2003, by "Calith" in the discussion forum Squires Tavern, topic "Ren/medievalists unite," at http://www.renaissancefestival.com/community/discussion/topic.asp?TOPIC_ID=226. All participants in the online discussions use pseudonyms based on their Renaissance faire personae.

9. "The first Faires partook of the rich lore and age-old customs of English springtime markets and 'Maying' customs" (http://www.forestfaire.com/origins/origins1.html).

10. See http://www.geocities.com/alaric667/Hopeless-Romantics.html.

11. See http://www.italianrenaissancefestival.com/courtesans_page.html.

12. See http://www.renaissancefestival.com/viewEvent.asp?eventID=232.

13. See http://www.renaissancefestival.com/viewEvent.asp?event ID=206. The online material on Renaissance faires sometimes has grammatical, capitalization, and punctuation errors, most of which I have silently corrected.

14. See http://www.renaissancefestival.com/viewEvent.asp?event ID=131.

15. See http://www.pgh-renfest.com/firsttime.html.

16. See http://www.renaissance-man.com. There are many similar individuals and groups who perform at faires. Often the Web sites of individual faires provide links to the Web sites of performers.

17. See http://www.bobdavinci.com.

18. See http://trianglesings.org/NCRenaissanceFaireMadrigal Singers/call.html.

19. The information on Renaissance costumes for sale comes from visiting faire booths and especially the Web sites of the many costume houses with links to http://www.renaissancefestival .com and other Renaissance faire Web sites.

20. The following is based on reading through pattern catalogues in a fabric store in Durham, North Carolina. Every catalogue has a costume section.

21. See http://www.renaissancefestival.com/viewEvent.asp?event ID=206.

22. The following is primarily based on an online discussion entitled "How did you become interested in ren faires?" found at http://renaissancefestival.com/Community/Discussion/topic .asp?TOPIC-ID=1181. This Web site has dozens of topics and thousands of archived responses.

23. See, for example, Paul F. Grendler, "Chivalric Romances in the Italian Renaissance," in *Books and Schools in the Italian Renaissance* (Aldershot, UK: Variorum, 1995), chapter II.

24. What follows is based on Janna Casstevens, "The Player's Handbook of Basics for the Serious Renaissance Faire Playtron," found at http://www.renaissancefestival.com/columns/playtrons/playershandbook.asp. The author is the director of a Renaissance performing company and presents the point of view of the professional. However, her views and terminology echo throughout online discussions of Renaissance faires, especially on the behavior of participants.

25. For two of the winning essays, see http://www.renaissancefestival.com/columns/essay_contest/furniture.asp and http://www.renaissancefestival.com/columns/essay_contest/ren essay.asp.

26. For more information, see http://www.sca.org.

27. What follows is based on http://www.renaissancemagazine.com/kimisa.html, entitled "How the Magazine Got Started."

28. Unless otherwise indicated, the following is based on the last nine issues, through no. 40, of *Renaissance*, supplemented by the Web site http://www.renaissancemagazine.com.

29. Gunnar Johnson (The Court Jester), "Medieval TV Guide," *Renaissance* 9, no. 5, issue 39 (2004), 38–39.

30. *Renaissance* 9, no. 2, issue 36 (2004), 93, 95, for the wedding and "Olde Soles" ads.

31. Dave Barry, "76 trombones and a varlet," *The News & Observer* (Raleigh, NC), March 12, 1999, 2E.

Chapter 3

1. There are several English translations and many editions. I use Baldesare Castiglione, *The Book of the Courtier*, trans. Charles S. Singleton (Garden City, NY: Doubleday, 1959), with many reprints.

2. Based on the biography of Philip Lader in *Who's Who in America* and the biographies of both at http://www .renaissanceweekend.org/Founders.htm.

3. What follows is based on the material found at http:// renaissanceweekend.org and the printed invitation material of 2004.

4. For 1982 and 1989, see the news stories at http://www .renaissanceweekend.org/Media.htm, plus Jill Dougherty/ CNN, "Clinton Gets New Year Advice at Renaissance Weekend," December 31, 1996, at http://www.cnn.com/ALL POLITICS/1997/9612/31/1/1dougherty.ip/, and *The News & Observer* (Raleigh, NC), January 1, 1999, B1.

5. Again, this material including the quotes comes from the invitation literature and http://renaissanceweekend.org.

6. *The News & Observer* (Raleigh, NC), January 1, 1999, B1.

7. This paragraph is based on the lists of past participants found at http://www.renaissanceweekend.org/Past_Parts/Past_Parts .htm.

8. The information on participants and program is based on the list of participants and schedule of activities for the February 17–21, 2000, Renaissance Weekend.

9. See http://www.renaissanceweekend.org/Past_Parts/Politics .htm.

10. Jay Nordlinger, "The Joy of Tokenism," *National Review* 56, no. 15 (August 9, 2004): 26–27.

11. An Internet search for "Living Last Supper" yielded a number of churches that staged Living Last Supper dramas in 2003 and 2004 and posted pictures to their Web sites. Much of the information in this and the following paragraphs comes from the Web sites.

12. See http://japanupdate.com/en/?id=425: Koza Baptist men present "Living Lord's Supper," Posted: April 11, 2003.

13. See http://www.palletmastersworkshop.com/supper.html.

14. Giorgio Vasari, *The Lives of the Artists*, Selected and trans. by George Bull (Harmondsworth, Middlesex: Penguin, 1972), 262–263.

15. The poster is reproduced in *The Power of Feminist Art: The American Movement of the 1970s, History and Impact*, eds. Norma Broude and Mary D. Garrard (New York: Harry N. Abrams, Inc., 1994), 17.

16. See http://www.guildhall.org/shopping.ihtml?id=41.

Chapter 4

1. This is a shortened version of an ad appearing in *The Washingtonian* 33, no. 5 (February 1998): 166.

2. Jacob Burckhardt, *The Civilization of the Renaissance in Italy*, trans. S. G. C. Middlemore, ed. Irene Gordon (New York: New American Library, 1960), 124–28.

3. *The News & Observer* (Raleigh, NC), May 11, 2001, B7.

4. Chris O'Brien, "Archie Davis, cornerstone of RTP, dies at 87," *The News & Observer* (Raleigh, NC), March 14, 1998, B1, B7.

5. Hillel Italie, "A true Renaissance Man," *The News & Observer* (Raleigh, NC), March 2, 2004, E8.

6. As quoted by James Brady, "In Step With Lauren Bacall," *Parade Magazine*, November 21, 1999, 30.

7. Miller Williams, as quoted by Patrick Healy, "Bowing to Critics, Clinton Declines Invitation to Give Prestigious Humanities Lecture," *The Chronicle of Higher Education*, October 1, 1999, A44.

8. No author, *The News & Observer* (Raleigh, NC), May 3, 2004, B3.

9. For what follows, including lists of the Renaissance Scholar Prize winners, see http://www.usc.edu/programs/ugprograms/renaissance/index.shtml.

10. Michael Bradley, "Smothered with Affection," *Sporting News*, February 14, 2000, 13.

11. *The News & Observer* (Raleigh, NC), Tuesday, April 3, 2001, CC4. This was a special section of the paper issued the day after Duke won the championship, and the player was Shane Battier.

12. No author, *Sporting News*, February 14, 2000, 27.

13. Welch Suggs, "Athletes and Colleges May Be Losing 'The Game of Life,'" *The Chronicle of Higher Education*, February 2, 2001, A41.

14. The ad appeared in *The Washingtonian* 33, no. 5 (February 1998): 166; the follow-up story appeared in 33, no. 10 (July 1998), 14.

15. *San Jose Mercury News*, March 30, 1999, D7.

16. *The Washingtonian* 36, no. 4 (January 2001): 219; 35, no. 5 (February 2000): 187; 35, no. 4 (January 2000): 219; and 36, no. 5 (February 2001): 188.

17. *The News & Observer* (Raleigh, NC), What's Up 26, March 20, 1998; *The Washingtonian* 35, no. 4 (January 2000): 220.

18. *The Washingtonian* 34, no. 12 (September 1999): 187.

19. Two examples of a Renaissance woman seeking another woman are found in *Independent Weekly* (Durham, NC) 21, no. 10 (March 10, 2004): 92; and 21, no. 12 (March 24, 2004): 92.

20. *The Washingtonian* 35, no. 4 (January 2000), p. 221.

21. *The News & Observer* (Raleigh, NC), December 22, 2000. Dilbert is nationally syndicated.

22. *The News & Observer* (Raleigh, NC), February 10, 2004, E3.

23. Michael J. Gelb, *How to Think like Leonardo da Vinci: Seven Steps to Genius Every Day* (New York: Dell Publishing, 2000) (paperback reprint). The author's Web site and e-mail address are www.michaelgelb.com and daVincian@aol.com.

24. Ibid., 15, 19, 80.

25. Ibid., 65.

Chapter 5

1. See http://www.dynamicchocolates.com.

2. Unless otherwise indicated, what follows in the next few pages is based on telephone directories for various American cities and on Web site searches.

3. See http://www.timesreview.com/sun10–25–02/stories/dinner.htm.

4. See http://www.libbey.com/Libbey/LibbeyGlass.

5. See http://www.michelangelos.com.

6. I have no intention of listing a Web site for cheaters.

7. "'Da Vinci Diet' Digs Carbs," available at http://www.cbsnews .com/stories/2004/06/15/health/printable623260.shtml.

8. See http://www.golfcoursehome.net/doc/communities/ Community-Rena.htm.

9. Fall 1998 catalogue of *Isabella Bird by The Territory Ahead*.

10. The head of *David* appears in the summer 1999 catalogue of Design Toscano of Elk Grove Village, Illinois. The title of their catalogue is *Design Toscano: Historical European Reproductions for Home and Garden*. The smaller David and stand are found in the autumn 1998 catalogue of Langenbach, Galesburg, Illinois, whose catalogue is entitled *Langenbach: A Collection of the World's Finest Garden Tools*.

11. See http://www.renaissancegreenhouses.com.

12. The advertisement appears regularly in the sports section of the Sunday *News & Observer* of Raleigh, North Carolina.

13. These are found at http://www.cafepress.com/shop/science/ browse/Ntt-venus_nr-1–N-20769061_Ntk-A and http://www .neckties.com/item.jsp?id=RM133370.

14. See http://www.rencenter.org.

15. E-mail message of Agnes Chan, program coordinator, reporting the views of former director Claudia Viek, to Paul F. Grendler, March 8, 2005.

16. See http://www.renaissancelawyer.com.

17. Douglas S. Robertson, *The New Renaissance: Computers and the Next Level of Civilization* (New York: Oxford University Press, 1998), 28.

18. Paul Graham, "The Word 'Hacker,'" available at http://www.paulgraham.com/gba.html. This is a chapter in his book, *Hackers & Painters* (Sebastopol, CA: O'Reilly, 2004). Incidentally, Graham studied art in Florence.

19. Andrea L. Foster, "High-Tech Renaissance," *The Chronicle of Higher Education* 51, no. 25 (February 25, 2005): A33–A35; and http://www.renci.org.

20. E-mail message from Daniel A. Reed to Paul F. Grendler, March 10, 2005.

21. "Mona Lisa" was published by Famous Music Corporation, New York, in 1949.

22. I am grateful to Professor Kenneth Gouwens of the University of Connecticut for telling me about Money Lisa and providing me with a lottery ticket.

23. David Remnick, "Our woman of secrets," *The New Yorker*, February 8, 1999, 23–24. For many other uses of Mona Lisa, see Donald Sassoon, *Becoming Mona Lisa: The Making of a Global Icon* (New York: Harcourt, 2001).

24. Frank Rich, "The Year of Living Indecently," *The New York Times*, February 6, 2005. See http://www.nytimes.com/2005/02/06/arts/06rich.html?pagewanted=print&position=.

25. Maureen Dowd, "Wherefore Art Though, Clint?" *The New York Times*, February 6, 2005. See http://www.nytimes.com/2005/02/06/opinion/6dowd.html?pagewanted=print&position=.

26. Nicholas D. Kristoff, "Crowning Prince George," *The New York Times*, September 1, 2004. See http://www.nytimes.com/2004/09/01/opinion/01kristof.html?hp-&pagewanted=print&pos.

27. Ibid.

28. "Patron Sweethearts," photographs by Tina Barney, text by Maura Egan. *The New York Times Magazine*, October 3, 2004, sec. 6, pp. 84–91.

29. Jason DeParle, "Goals Reached, Donor on Right Closes Up Shop," *The* New York Times, May 29, 2005. See http://www.nytimes.com/2005/05/29/politics/29olin.html?ei=5094&en=768283340a3637b6.

30. Paul Attner, "Driven to Win," *Sporting News* 228, no. 29 (July 19, 2004): 26.

31. *The Atlantic* 293, no. 3 (April 2004). The cover story is Michael J. Sandel, "The Case Against Perfection," 50–62.

32. Hue Q. Ha, "Divine Touch," *The News & Observer* (Raleigh, NC), December 20, 1998, E1, E3.

33. *Rhymes with Orange*, May 30, 1999; *Funky Winkerbean*, April 11, 2004; and *Non Sequitur*, November 18, 1999.

Chapter 6

1. Robert C. Alberts, *The Shaping of the Point: Pittsburgh's Renaissance Park* (Pittsburgh: University of Pittsburgh Press, 1980), 58.

2. Unless otherwise indicated, the following account of the Pittsburgh Renaissance (later called Renaissance I) is based on Michael P. Weber, *Don't call me boss: David L. Lawrence, Pittsburgh's Renaissance Mayor* (Pittsburgh: University of Pittsburgh Press, 1988); Weber, "Rebuilding A City: The Pittsburgh Model," in *Snowbelt Cities: Metropolitan Politics in the Northeast and Midwest since World War II*, ed. Richard M. Bernard (Bloomington and Indianapolis: Indiana University Press, 1990), 227–246; Jeanne Lowe, *A Race With Time: Progress and Poverty in America's Renewing Cities* (New York:

Random House, 1967), 110–163; and Roy Lubove, *Twentieth-Century Pittsburgh: Government, Business, and Environmental Change* (Pittsburgh: John Wiley & Sons, 1969), 106–176.

3. See its Web site: http://fdncenter.org/grantmaker/rkmellon/history.html.

4. Weber, *Don't call me boss.*

5. Ibid., 215.

6. Ibid., 256–266.

7. No author, "Pittsburgh Renascent," *Architectural Forum* 91 (November 1949): 59–73, 112.

8. Karl Schriftsgiesser, "The Pittsburgh Story," *Atlantic Monthly* 187, no. 5 (May 1951): 66–70, quote at 69.

9. Sherie R. Mershon, "Corporate Social Responsibility and Urban Revitalization: The Allegheny Conference on Community Development, 1943-1968" (Unpublished PhD dissertation, Carnegie Mellon University, 2000), 633–635; and e-mail message from Sherie R. Mershon to Paul F. Grendler, September 17, 2004. I am grateful to Dr. Mershon for answering my questions and to Professor Joel Tarr of Carnegie Mellon University, who supervised the dissertation, for putting me in touch with Dr. Mershon.

10. Remarks of Arthur B. Van Buskirk at the Junior Chamber of Commerce of Pittsburgh Man-of-the-Year Dinner, February 1, 1954, in "Speeches" file, ACCD Archives, Historical Society of Western Pennsylvania, as quoted in e-mail message of Sherie R. Mershon to Paul F. Grendler, September 17, 2004.

11. Lawrence's speech is found at the Carnegie Library of Pittsburgh Web site at http://www.clpgh.org/exhibit/neighborhoods/point/point_n102.html.

12. Weber, *Don't call me boss*, 155.

13. Herbert Kubly, "Pittsburgh: The City that Quick-changed from Unbelievable Ugliness to Shining Beauty in Less than Half a Generation," *Holiday* 25, no. 3 (March 1959): 155 (whole article 80–87, 152–156).

14. Weber, *Don't call me boss*, 275, 395–396.

15. Alberts, *The Shaping of the Point*, 202.

16. Mershon, "Corporate Social Responsibility," 657.

17. Although all accounts date the beginning of Renaissance I to 1945, and most conclude it about 1960, some extend it to 1970, to include the completion of some projects begun earlier. See Weber, "Rebuilding a City," 234. All accounts agree that there was no Renaissance during Peter Flaherty's mayoral administration, 1970 to 1977.

18. Weber, "Rebuilding a City," 234–235; Roy Lubove, *Twentieth-Century Pittsburgh*. Vol. 2: *The Post-Steel Era* (Pittsburgh and London: University of Pittsburgh Press, 1996), 59–60.

19. Lubove, *The Post-Steel Era*, 24.

20. The best guide to Renaissance II is Lubove, *The Post-Steel Era*, beginning with chapter 2: "A Second Renaissance," followed by the rest of the book. Weber, "Rebuilding a City," offers a good summary of Renaissance I and II.

21. Weber, "Rebuilding a City," 237.

22. Jon C. Teaford, *The Rough Road to Renaissance: Urban Revitalization in America, 1940–1985* (Baltimore and London: The Johns Hopkins University Press, 1990), 9.

23. For what follows, see William J. V. Neill, "Promoting the city: Image, reality and racism in Detroit," in *Reimaging the Pariah City: Urban Development in Belfast & Detroit*, eds. William J. V. Neill, Diana S. Fitzsimons, and Brendan Murtah (Aldershot, U.K.: Ashgate Publishing, 1995), 113–161; Arthur M.

Woodford, *This is Detroit 1701–2001* (Detroit: Wayne State University Press, 2001), esp. 180–236, with its excellent photographs; and Woodford, "How the Renaissance Center changed the landscape of Detroit," an undated (but about 1996) summary of the Renaissance Center, at the *Detroit News* Web site, http://info.detnews.com/history/story/index.cfm?id =122&category=locations. For stunning color photographs of Detroit, see *Detroit: The Renaissance City*. Photography by Balthazar Korab; Introduction by Elmore Leonard (Charlottesville, VA: Thomasson-Grant, 1986).

24. Neill, "Promoting the city," table on 121.

25. Ibid., tables on 117 and 123.

26. On Young, see Coleman Young and Lonnie Wheeler, *Hard Stuff: The Autobiography of Coleman Young* (New York: Viking, 1994); and Wilbur C. Rich, *Coleman Young and Detroit Politics: From Social Activist to Power Broker* (Detroit: Wayne State University Press, 1989).

27. See its Web site, http://www.detroitrenaissance.com.

28. For what follows, see Woodford, *This is Detroit 1701–2001*, 237–254.

29. See the Web site, http://www.gold.ky.gov/renmain/.

30. For a thoughtful overview of urban Renaissances, see Teaford, *Rough Road to Renaissance.*

31. For the importance of building in fifteenth-century Florence, see Richard A. Goldthwaite, *The Building of Renaissance Florence: An Economic and Social History* (Baltimore and London: The Johns Hopkins University Press, 1980).

32. See Richard A. Goldthwaite, *Wealth and the Demand for Art in Italy 1300–1600* (Baltimore and London: The Johns Hopkins University Press, 1993).

Chapter 7

1. For biographical information and an assessment of Burnham's other works, see Francis P. Sempa, "The First Cold Warrior," *American Diplomacy* 5, no. 4 (Fall 2000), an electronic serial published by the University of North Carolina at Chapel Hill Curriculum in Peace, War, and Defense and the Triangle Institute for Security Studies. It can be accessed at http://www .AmericanDiplomacy.org or http://www.unc.edu/depts/ diplomat/archives.

2. There is a large literature on Strauss, including published proceedings of conferences devoted to understanding his thought. The authors in such volumes are usually followers and supporters. A typical example is *The Crisis of Liberal Democracy: A Straussian Perspective*, eds. Kenneth L. Deutsch and Walter Soffer, Foreword by Joseph Cropsey (Albany, NY: State University of New York Press, 1987). A comprehensive, largely sympathetic study is Ted V. McAllister, *Revolt Against Modernity: Leo Strauss, Eric Voegelin, and the Search for a Postliberal Order* (Lawrence: University Press of Kansas, 1996). For a critical perspective, see Shadia B. Drury, *The Political Ideas of Leo Strauss* (Houndmills, Basingstoke, Hampshire, and London: The MacMillan Press, 1988); and *Leo Strauss and the American Right* (New York: St. Martin's Press, 1997).

3. Leo Strauss, *Thoughts on Machiavelli* (Glencoe, IL: The Free Press, 1958; repr., Seattle and London: University of Washington Press, 1969). Two useful analyses of the book are Drury, *Political Ideas*, 114–132; and McAllister, 85–109. For the reactions of reviewers, see Drury, *Political Ideas*, 115, 231.

4. Pietro Pomponazzi, *On the Immortality of the Soul*, trans. William Henry Hay II, rev. by John Herman Randall, Jr., annot. by Paul Oskar Kristeller, in *The Renaissance Philosophy*

of Man, eds. Ernst Cassirer, Paul Oskar Kristeller, and John Herman Randall, Jr. (Chicago and London: University of Chicago Press, 1969), 280–381, 363–365.

5. This is the argument of James Mann, *Rise of the Vulcans: The History of Bush's War Cabinet* (New York: Viking, 2004), esp. 24–29.

6. The biographical sketch is based on Ledeen's biography found at the American Enterprise Institute Web site (www.aei.org/scholarsID) plus two other biographical sketches: Jim Lobe, "Veteran neo-con advisor moves on Iran," June 26, 2003, from the Asia Times Online (www.atimes.com); and William O. Beeman, "Who is Michael Ledeen?" May 8, 2003, from Alter-Net.org (www.alternet.org).

7. Ledeen, *Machiavelli*, 76–77.

8. Ibid., 81.

9. Quotes in this paragraph from Ledeen, *Machiavelli*, 112, 100, 174.

10. Quotes in this paragraph from Ledeen, *Machiavelli*, xvii, 15–16.

11. Ledeen, *Machiavelli*, 108.

12. Alfred G. Cuzán, *Is Fidel Castro a Machiavellian Prince?* (Miami: The Endowment for Cuban American Studies, 1999). The Endowment for Cuban American Studies is the publishing arm of the Jorge Mas Canosa Freedom Foundation, which is "an independent, non-profit organization dedicated to the re-establishment of freedom and democracy in Cuba." It supports "the right to private property; free enterprise; and economic prosperity with social justice." Cuzán has been a fellow of the Heritage Foundation, a conservative think-tank in Washington, DC.

13. Cuzán, *Is Fidel Castro a Machiavellian Prince?*, 55.

14. Howard Zinn, *Declarations of Independence: Cross-Examining American Ideology* (New York: HarperCollins, 1990), 9–31, quote on 27.

15. Nelson A. Blue, *Machiavelli's The Republican: The best possible America and how to achieve it* (Chapel Hill, NC: Chapel Hill Press, 2000) 96–97.

16. James Moore and Wayne Slater, *Bush's Brain: How Karl Rove Made George W. Bush Presidential* (Hoboken, NJ: John Wiley & Sons, 2003), 138.

17. For a copy of the letter, see http://www.esquire.com.features/articles/2002/021202_mfe_diulio_1.html. See also Suskind's article in *Esquire*, January 2003, at http://www.gregsopinion.com/archives/002687.php.

18. Kevin Phillips, *American Dynasty: Aristocracy, Fortune, and the Politics of Deceit in the House of Bush* (New York: Viking, 2004), 320–331 for the conclusion, and 320–321, 328 for the quotes. Other references to Machiavelli are on 94 and 147–148.

19. Richard Reeves, "In war, strangers to the truth," *The News & Observer* (Raleigh, NC), October 9, 2004, A20.

20. Robert Wright, "What Would Machiavelli Do?" *The New York Times*, August 2, 2004, A17.

21. See a series of stories on McGreevey in *The New York Times* from July 14 through August 13, 2004.

22. E. J. Dionne Jr., "Tests for an Unbending Pope," *The Washington Post National Weekly Edition* 22, no. 27 (April 25–May 1, 2005): 26.

23. Niccolò Machiavelli, *The Prince and the Discourses*, trans. Luigi Ricci. Introduction Max Lerner (New York: The Modern Library, 1950); *The Prince*, chapter 18, p. 64.

24. James MacGregor Burns, *Roosevelt: The Lion and the Fox* (New York: Harcourt, Brace & World, Inc., 1956), 472–477, quote at 477.

25. Machiavelli, *The Prince and Selected Discourses*, 87.

26. All quotes from Guiccardini's *Considerations* in these two paragraphs come from *Francesco Guicciardini: Selected Writings*, ed. Cecil Grayson, trans. Margaret Grayson (London: Oxford University Press, 1965), 66–67, 77, 92.

Chapter 8

1. I cite the revised and enlarged edition: Antony Jay, *Management and Machiavelli: Discovering a New Science of Management in the Timeless Princes of Statecraft* (Amsterdam: Pfeiffer & Company, 1994).

2. Ibid., 3.

3. Ibid., 5.

4. Alistair McAlpine, *The New Machiavelli* (London: Aurum Press, 1997); "V," *The Mafia Manager: A Guide to the Corporate Machiavelli* (New York: St. Martin's Press, 1997); Richard W. Hill, *The Boss: Machiavelli on Managerial Leadership* (New York: Pyramid Media Group, 2000); Ian Demack, *The Modern Machiavelli: The Seven Principles of Power in Business* (London: Allen & Unwin, 2002); Richard H. Buskirk, *Modern Management and Machiavelli* (London: Business Books, 1974); and Gerald R. Griffin, *Machiavelli on Management: Playing and Winning the Corporate Power Game* (New York: Praeger-Greenwood, 1991).

5. Niccolò Machiavelli, *The Prince and Selected Discourses*, trans. Daniel Donno (New York: Bantam Books, 1966), ch. 17, p. 60.

6. Alan F. Bartlett, *Profile of the Entrepreneur or Machiavellian Management* (London: Keats Web Offset, 1981), quote from the preface.

7. Stanley Bing, *What Would Machiavelli Do? The Ends Justify the Meanness* (New York: HarperBusiness, 2002), table of contents, vii–ix.

8. The biography is James B. Stewart, *DisneyWar* (New York: Simon & Schuster, 2005). The review is by Bob Woodward in *The Washington Post National Weekly Edition*, March 14–20, 2005, 32–33, quotes on 32.

9. Rinus van Schendelen, *Machiavelli in Brussels: The Art of Lobbying the EU* (Amsterdam: Amsterdam University Press, 2002), 11–12, 105 (quote), 132, and 165, for the references in this and the following paragraph.

10. Daniel Burstein, *Turning the Tables: A Machiavellian Strategy for Dealing with Japan* (New York: Simon & Schuster, 1993), 15–16.

11. Stuart Crainer, *The Ultimate Book of Business Gurus: 110 Thinkers Who Really Made a Difference* (New York: Amacom, 1998), 136.

12. Alan Axelrod, *Elizabeth I CEO. Strategic Lessons from the Leader Who Built an Empire* (Paramus, NJ: Prentice Hall Press, 2000), quote on xiii, Machiavelli section on 235–237.

13. What follows is based on *Machiavellian Intelligence: Social Expertise and the Evolution of Intellect in Monkeys, Apes, and Humans*, eds. Richard W. Byrne and Andrew Whiten (Oxford: Clarendon Press, 1988); and *Machiavellian Intelligence II: Extensions and Evaluations*, eds. Andrew Whiten and Richard W. Byrne (Cambridge: Cambridge University Press, 1997). The two books contain thirty-nine studies by forty-one scholars

from the United Kingdom, the United States, Austria, Canada, Germany, The Netherlands, and Switzerland.

14. This and the case described in the next paragraph come from Richard W. Byrne and Andrew White, "Tactical deception of familiar individuals in baboons," in *Machiavellian Intelligence*, 205, 208 (whole article 205–210).

15. Richard W. Byrne and Andrew Whiten, "Machiavellian intelligence," in *Machiavellian Intelligence II,* 1, 12 (whole article, 1–23).

16. Richard Elliott, "Contra postmodernism. Machiavelli on limits to the malleability of consciousness," in *Machiavelli, Marketing and Management*, eds. Phil Harris, Andrew Lock, and Patricia Rees (London and New York: Routledge, 2000), 55–65.

17. Machiavelli, *Discourses*, book 1, ch. 14, in Niccolò Machiavelli, *The Portable Machiavelli*, trans. and eds. Peter Bondanella and Mark Musa (Harmondsworth, England: Penguin Books, 1979), 216–218.

Chapter 9

1. The words of Irving Stone in 1986 as quoted in Sharon Malinowski, "Stone, Irving," in *Contemporary Authors*, ed. Deborah A. Straug. *New Revision Series*, vol. 23. (Detroit: Gale Research Company, 1988), 394 (whole article, 392–400). This article with its interview and several quotes from Stone is the most useful summary of his career. See also the entry in *Who Was Who in America with World Notables*. Vol. 10: 1989–1993 (New Providence, NJ: Reed Reference Company, 1993), 350.

2. Interview with Stone in 1964 as quoted in Malinowski, "Stone, Irving," 395.

3. In addition to Malinowski, "Stone, Irving," see *Irving Stone: A Bibliography*. Compiled by Lewis F. Stieg (Los Angeles: Friends of the Library, University of Southern California, 1973), 35–39.

4. Stone explaining his preparation for the book at the conclusion of Irving Stone, *The Agony and the Ecstasy. A Biographical Novel of Michelangelo* (New York: New American Library, n.d.), 759. Although this paperback edition lacks a date, it is the fiftieth paperback edition after the original publication of 1961. For the full explanation of his preparation and his bibliography, see 759–776. The next quotation in this paragraph also comes from p. 759.

5. Ibid., 121.

6. Contessina de' Medici first appears in *The Agony and the Ecstasy* on pp. 73–74, makes further appearances in Michelangelo's life, and dies on pp. 570–571.

7. Stone, *The Agony and the Ecstasy*, 252–257, 265–266.

8. Ibid., 202–215.

9. Giorgio Vasari, *The Lives of the Artists*. A Selection Translated by George Bull (Harmondsworth, Middlesex, 1972), 333.

10. Stone, *The Agony and the Ecstasy*, 691.

11. Stone's words as quoted in Malinowski, "Stone, Irving," 396.

12. I use the critical edition: George Eliot, *Romola*, ed. Andrew Brown (Oxford: Clarendon Press, 1993).

13. Eliot, *Romola*, 677–679, "George Eliot's Preparatory Reading for *Romola*." Noticeably missing are Georg Voigt's *Die Wiederbelebung des classischen Alterthums oder das erste Jahrhundert des Humanismus* (1859) and Jacob Burckhardt's *Die Cultur der*

Renaissance in Italien: Ein Versuch (1860). These were the two most important books on the Italian Renaissance written in the nineteenth century. Burckhardt was not yet available in English, and only a few pages of Voigt were finally translated into English in 1965.

14. Samuel Shellabarger, *The Prince of Foxes* (Boston: Little, Brown, 1947), 363–379.

15. In addition to the novel, see the interview with the author conducted by Stephanie Smith and dated October 13, 2004, at http://www.yorkshiretoday.co.uk/ViewArticle2.aspx?Section ID=1298&ArticleID=869723.

16. For information on the author, see http://www.svreeland.com.

17. The most important studies of Artemisia Gentileschi are Mary D. Garrard, *Artemisia Gentileschi: The Image of the Female Hero in Italian Baroque Art* (Princeton, NJ: Princeton University Press, 1989), which includes English translations of the trial and letters; Garrard, *Artemisa Gentileschi around 1622: The Shaping and Reshaping of an Artistic Identity* (Berkeley, CA: University of California Press, 2001), both strong feminist accounts; and R. Ward Bissell, *Artemisia Gentileschi and the Authority of Art: Critical Reading and Catalogue Raisonné* (University Park, PA: Pennsylvania State University Press, 1999), which is skeptical of some aspects of the feminist interpretation. For short accounts, see Ann Sutherland Harris, "Gentileschi, Orazio" and "Gentileschi, Artemisia" in *The Dictionary of Art*, ed. Jane Turner (London: Grove, 1996), vol. 12, 304–309; and Mary D. Garrard, "Gentileschi, Artemisia," in *Encyclopedia of the Renaissance*, eds. Paul F. Grendler, et al., vol. 3 (New York: Charles Scribner's Sons, 1999), 29–31.

18. Alexandra Lapierre, *Artemisia: The Story of a Battle for Greatness*, trans. Liz Heron (London: Chatto & Windus, 2000),

especially x, 279–304, 429–431. This was originally published in French in 1998. Lapierre did a great deal of archival research on Artemisia and uncovered new information but decided to tell Artemisia's story in fictionalized form, very much like Stone's *The Agony and the Ecstasy*. However, she provides a full bibliography of archival and other sources and explanations for her conclusions.

19. For the fact sheet under the heading "New Film Distorts History to Create a Fictionalized and Sensationalized 'Truth,'" and "Now that you've seen the film, meet the real Artemisia Gentileschi," see http://songweaver.com/art/artemisia.html.

20. The novel relies heavily on the biography based on detailed archival research of Julia Cartwright, *Beatrice d'Este, Duchess of Milan, 1475–1497: A Study of the Renaissance* (London: J. M. Dent & Sons, 1899), reprinted seven times through 1920.

21. See any recent edition of *Who's Who in America* for a brief biography.

22. George Herman, *Carnival of Saints* (New York: Ballantine Books, 1994), 62. For a succinct account of *commedia dell'arte*, see Louis George Clubb, "Commedia dell'arte," in *Encyclopedia of the Renaissance*, vol. 2, 50–52.

23. Erick Ives, *The Life and Death of Anne Boleyn 'The Most Happy'* (Oxford: Blackwell Publishing, 2004), 14–17.

24. Ibid., 16–17 and 369, note 75.

25. For the malformed fetus, incest, and witchcraft interpretation, see Retha M. Warnicke, *The Rise and Fall of Anne Boleyn: Family Politics at the Court of Henry VIII* (Cambridge: Cambridge University Press, 1989), 191–242. Incidentally, there are reproductions of contemporary paintings of Mary Boleyn, her husband William Carey, and her son Henry Carey,

between pages 180 and 181. For the counter argument, see Ives, *The Life and Death of Anne Boleyn,* 296–305.

26. I am grateful to Professor Norman Jones of Utah State University for his advice on this matter.

27. Francesco Colonna, *Hypnerotomachia Poliphili: The Strife of Love in a Dream,* trans. with introduction by Joscelyn Godwin (London: Thames & Hudson, 1999). There are also several earlier partial English translations. For a reproduction of the original 1499 edition with an Italian translation, see Colonna, *Hypnerotomachia Poliphili,* eds. Marco Ariani and Mino Gabriele, 2 vols. (Milan: Adelphi, 1998).

28. Ian Caldwell and Dustin Thomason, *The Rule of Four* (New York: The Dial Press, 2004), 282, 283, for the quotes.

29. See Edward Wyatt, "For 'Code' Author, 24 Months in a Circus," *The New York Times,* March 21, 2005, as found at http://www.nytimes.com/2005/03/21/books/21code.html ?pagewanted=print&position=; and Edward Wyatt, "A Mystery: When Will 'Da Vinci' Go Into Paperback?," *The New York Times,* May 30, 2005, as found at http://www.nytimes .com/2005/05/30/business/media/30book.html?pagewanted =print.

30. For example, see Bart D. Ehrman. *Truth and Fiction in The Da Vinci Code: A Historian Reveals What We Really Know about Jesus, Mary Magdalene, and Constantine* (New York: Oxford University Press, 2004); and *Secrets of the Code: The Unauthorized Guide to the Mysteries Behind the Da Vinci Code,* ed. Dan Burstein (New York: CDS Books, 2004). Although the latter book has some interesting speculation about the attraction of the book and prints some scholarly criticism, it gives too much space to the pseudoscholarship on which *The Da Vinci Code* is based. See also Michael and Veronica Haag, *The Rough Guide to the Da Vinci Code. An Unauthorized Code.* With Jane

McConnachie (London: Rough Guides Ltd., 2004). One Renaissance scholar finds *The Da Vinci Code* silly; see Ingrid D. Rowland, "Pop Esoterica! Leonardo da Vinci at the beach," *New Republic*, Issues 4,674 and 4,675, August 16 and 23, 2004, pp. 21–26. In January 2005, The History Channel aired two hours of pictures and interviews in which scholars politely pointed out the historical errors in the book.

31. See Carl Olson and Sandra Miesel, *The Da Vinci Hoax. Exposing the Errors in the Da Vinci Code* (San Francisco: Ignatius Press, 2004).

32. I thank Professor Marcia Hall for telling me about this book.

33. Iain Pears, *The Raphael Affair* (New York: Berkley Books, 1998), 16.

Chapter 10

1. For a list of the prizes won by *Shakespeare in Love*, see http://www.imdb.com/title/tt0138097/awards.

2. Kenneth S. Rothwell and Annabelle Henkin Melzer, *Shakespeare on Screen: An International Filmography and Videography* (New York and London: Neal-Schuman, 1990), 127, film number 238.

3. Ibid.

4. Graham Greene, *The Third Man. A Film by Graham Greene and Carol Reed* (New York: Simon & Schuster, 1968), 114, note 78.

5. The film is loosely based on a scholarly study, Margaret F. Rosenthal, *The Honest Courtesan: Veronica Franco, Citizen and Writer in Sixteenth-Century Venice* (Chicago: University of Chicago Press, 1992). There are other works on Franco, especially in Italian, and a bilingual (Italian-English) edition of her poems and some of her letters: Veronica Franco, *Poems*

and Selected Letters, trans. and eds. Ann R. Jones and Margaret F. Rosenthal (Chicago: University of Chicago Press, 1998).

6. For example, the film states that Michelangelo's Medici tombs in Florence were sculpted for the famous Lorenzo "the Magnificent" de' Medici (1449–1492) and his brother Giuliano. Wrong. They were sculpted for two later and lesser Medici princelings.

7. See the various pages of the Web site for *The Medici*, especially http://www.pbs.org/empires/medici/renaissance/index.html, http://www.pbs.org/empires/medici/renssiance/counter.html, and http://www.pbs.org/empires/medici/renaissance/heresy .html.

8. See John W. O'Malley, *Trent and All That. Renaming Catholicism in the Early Modern Era* (Cambridge, MA, and London: Harvard University Press, 2000), 22–35, 39, 78–85, 107–08.

Chapter 11

1. Joan Kelly-Gadol, "Did Women Have a Renaissance?" in *Becoming Visible. Women in European History,* eds. Renate Bridenthal and Claudia Koonz (Boston: Houghton Mifflin Company, 1977), 137–164.

2. *Not in God's Image. Women in History from the Greeks to the Victorians*, eds. Julia O'Faolain and Lauro Martines (New York: Harper & Row, 1973), xiii–xxi, 127–217.

3. For an excellent and balanced study, see Margaret L. King, *Women of the Renaissance* (Chicago and London: The University of Chicago Press, 1991).

4. Anthony Grafton and Lisa Jardine, *From Humanism to the Humanities. Edcuation and the Liberal Arts in Fifteenth- and*

Sixteenth-Century Europe (Cambridge, MA: Harvard University Press, 1986).

5. Leah S. Marcus, "Renaissance/Early Modern Studies," in *Redrawing the Boundaries. The Transformation of English and American Literary Studies,* eds. Stephen Greenblatt and Giles Gunn (New York: The Modern Language Association of America, 1992), 41–63, quote at 43. This is a strong statement of Renaissance bashing and preference for "early modern." No serious historian of the period would recognize the picture of the Renaissance given here. It is a straw man to be demolished.

6. See the statement on the reverse side of the title page in *The Journal of Medieval and Early Modern Studies* 26, no. 1 (Winter 1996), no pagination. The half-page announcement mentions "theory" and "theoretical" six times, along with "poststructuralism," "postmodernity," and other buzz words from the theory world. The mission statement of the journal under its previous name simply stated that it published "scholarly articles on any aspect of late medieval and Renaissance culture and society" and listed various disciplines (art, philosophy, history, theology, etc.) in which it would entertain articles.

7. Marcus, "Renaissance/Early Modern," 44.

8. This comes from an article submitted for publication to *Renaissance Quarterly*, the leading journal in the world for Renaissance studies in all fields, when I was articles editor from 2000 to 2003. The article was rejected because of its poor quality.

9. *Early Modern Social Theory. Selected Interpretative Readings*, ed. Murray E. G. Smith (Toronto: Canadian Scholars' Press, 1998).

INDEX

ABOUT THE AUTHOR

Paul F. Grendler is a distinguished scholar of the Italian Renaissance. The author of numerous books and editor in chief of *Encyclopedia of the Renaissance* and *Renaissance: An Encyclopedia for Students*, he has been president of three scholarly organizations including The Renaissance Society of America. He is currently a Fellow of the American Philosophical Society. Grendler taught at the University of Toronto for thirty-four years.